BEST BET INTERNET

Reference and Research When You Don't Have Time to Mess Around

Shirley Duglin Kennedy

BEST BET INTERNET

Reference and Research When You Don't Have Time to Mess Around

Shirley Duglin Kennedy

AMERICAN LIBRARY ASSOCIATION
CHICAGO AND LONDON
1998

Project manager: Susan Betz

Cover design by Richmond Jones

Composition by the dotted i in Times and Helvetica using QuarkXpress 3.32

Printed on 50-pound Victor Offset, a pH-neutral stock, and bound in 10-point coated cover stock by Victor Graphics

The paper used in this publication meets the minimum requirements of American National Standard for Information Sciences—Permanence of Paper for Printed Library Materials, ANSI Z39.48-1992.∞

Library of Congress Cataloging-in-Publication Data

Kennedy, Shirley Duglin.
    Best bet Internet : reference and research when you don't have time to mess around / Shirley Duglin Kennedy.
        p.   cm.
    Includes bibliographical references and index.
    ISBN 0-8389-0712-1 (alk. paper)
    1. Computer network resources.   I. Title.
  ZA4201.K46   1997
  025.04—dc21   97-22091

Printed in the United States of America.

02 01 00 99   5 4 3

Contents

Preface

Reports frequently arise of wasted afternoons spent plowing through the Web trying to find that one morsel of useful information amidst the vast reservoirs of gossip, rumor, and political propaganda. Hope springs eternal; with all this horse manure, there's just got to be a pony in there somewhere.

—Langdon Winner, *Technology Review,* Nov./Dec. 1995, 66

Okay. You be cool. You be wired! You can point and click your way around the Web with the best of the cybernauts. And you know how to get to all those popular search tools—AltaVista, Lycos, Infoseek, Yahoo! et al. You can do a keyword search and get *lots* of results, right? Thousands, in fact. And isn't it fun sorting through them? You have hours and hours to kill, right? If you're a librarian . . . the patron isn't standing there looking over your shoulder, right? If you're a businessperson . . . your boss doesn't mind if you spend the bulk of your working hours cruising the Web.

Yeah, right.

Anybody can surf the Net—including my six-year-old son, once you dial him in and crank up Netscape. Attempting to use the Net as a practical information-gathering tool is another kettle of fish entirely. I've been doing Internet training and consulting for about six years now, and I've watched the frustration building—especially among librarians and other trained information professionals.

Traditional, tried-and-true information-gathering skills are invaluable in using the Internet as a research tool, but it's far from a "business as usual" situation. Due to the decentralized, disorganized nature of the Internet, it's necessary to learn how to use traditional skills in new—and nontraditional—ways. And to acquire new, nontraditional skills.

Did most trained information professionals dream, when they attended library school, that they would end up having to be computer geeks to function effectively in the workplace? Every new electronic tool—proprietary database, CD-ROM product, public-access PC—adds more complexity and technostress to our days. The Internet is rapidly turning into the straw that breaks the virtual camel's back for too many of us.

I've watched the initial excitement of "being wired" fade—especially among librarians, teachers, and school media specialists—after repeated frustrating attempts to extract useful information from the Net in a timely and efficient manner. The idea for this book actually came out of a lively online discussion in CARR-L (Computer Assisted Research and Reporting), an Internet mailing list for "wired" journalists. This mailing list—and many others, in my experience—suffers the ongoing "phenomenon" of students posting questions to the group in an effort to get someone else to do their research for them. Many CARR-L members have grown increasingly rude and nasty to these wide-eyed innocents, subjecting them to "colorful" electronic abuse, bemoaning their lack of basic research skills. (UTFL is an amusing acronym I picked up here. Obviously derived from the venerable RTFM, it stands for *Use the "Fine" Library.* The point, of course, is to do your own basic research rather than expecting your fellow list members to do it for you.)

After yet-another one of these online melodramas threatened to render the group unreadable and useless for the better part of the week, a few participants raised the questions of how research skills were being taught in the so-called Age of the Internet and why traditional methods were increasingly inadequate. Which prompted me to share a story relayed to me by my older son, who, in a middle-school gifted class, was learning to use e-mail and the World Wide Web.

His teacher, who had worked for a high-tech company prior to becoming an educator, was very enthusiastic about the Internet—a Good Thing. Then came the day she demonstrated search engines for the kids. She headed straight for AltaVista, touted for superiority due to its speed and the enormous size of its database. She typed the word *iguana* into the simple search form and ran the search. Of course, said my son, "Eighty zillion hits came back." The teacher started clicking on the results one by one. "The first eight or so," according to my son, "were all IguanaCams"— Web sites where individuals with too much time on their hands, typically college students, trained a video camera on a poor, unsuspecting reptile and wired the camera to a computer connected to the Internet, allowing anyone with Net access and a graphical Web browser to spy on the critter (**http://iguana.images.com/dupree/**).

Everyone in the class thought these were "cool," said my son, "but there really wasn't anything there you could use in a report." The teacher ended up having to go through several screens of results before finding actual, *usable* information about iguanas—by which time the class period had ended, and the point of the whole exercise had withered away.

When I shared this story with CARR-L, I appended to it the obvious (to me) conclusion— learning to use the Internet and learning to *do research* on the Internet are two completely different things. I was quite unprepared for the dramatic "Amen, sister" responses generated by my message. Half a dozen folks e-mailed me for permission to use my remarks in speeches they were giving or columns they were writing. And I heard from people on a variety of other mailing lists, indicating to me that people had forwarded my message around the Net.

I was intrigued by this. It appears that the initial thrill of getting wired has worn off for just about everyone who needs to use the Internet for work or study. Yes, there are nifty search tools and indexes popping up nearly every day. But who has the time to keep track of them—let alone scrounge through the mounting pile of digital manure? It's no exaggeration to say that everybody and his brother have a Web page now. When I made the mistake recently of telling an airport rental-car shuttle-bus driver what I do for a living, he asked me how he could register his home page URL with the major search engines.

Visit the Internet section of your local bookstore. Is there room for yet-another tome on the joys of getting wired? No, although publishers seem to be churning them out by the score anyway. And, in too many cases, publishers seem to equate quantity with quality. Throw away your free weights and pick up a couple Internet books to pump up your biceps. Who has the time to read these things? My *job* involves reading these things, and I'm overwhelmed.

You don't have to be. Because I wrote *this* book for you.

Acknowledgments

It would be impossible to list here all of the professional colleagues whose knowledge, support, and guidance ultimately contributed to this book. Identifying them by group is somewhat easier— and less embarrassing, should I inadvertently miss someone. Even a sincere "thanks" is probably inadequate, alas. But I've been luckier than most in my professional life to be associated with:

- The folks in the reference department at the Clearwater (Florida) Public Library. You are *the Best!*
- My colleagues in Suncoast Information Specialists—diverse, interesting, always stimulating
- My virtual colleagues on the NETTRAIN, Web4Lib, and CARR-L mailing lists

And then, of course, my mom, Eleanore Duglin, who always said, "I know you have a book in you," even if I'm not entirely sure this was the one she had in mind; my best friend, Janice Redington Ballo, drinking buddy, shoulder to cry on, perpetual source of inspiration and encouragement; my guys:

- Sean, for making me laugh and still thinking I'm cool in spite of the fact that I'm a computer geek, a librarian, *and* a birdwatcher
- Patrick, for being so generous with the hugs and kisses
- Tom, for . . . pretty much everything. And that's the truth!

1

Why Is It So Hard to Find Things on the Internet?

It Ain't Just You!

ME (discussing the Internet with a sixth-grade class during the Great American Teach-In, November 1996): Who puts information on the World Wide Web?

BOY (raising hand and shrugging simultaneously): Everybody!

What's Here?

That Was Then, This Is Now

The Issues

Lack of Authority Control
Lack of Quality Control
Ephemeral Nature of Internet Resources
Technical Instability and Limitations

That Was Then, This Is Now

Tim Berners-Lee, working at the European Particle Physics Lab (CERN) in Switzerland back in 1989, came up with a nifty new way for researchers to share their results. Called the World Wide Web, it involved a method of linking documents electronically via hypertext. While perusing a research report on a computer, a physicist who wanted to check out another research paper mentioned in a footnote or bibliography could merely tab down to the highlighted title of that document, press Enter, and instantly it would appear on the screen, a copy having been retrieved from the computer on which it was stored. The physical location of the host machine was irrelevant; it could be a computer in an office down the hall or a workstation in a lab at a research center halfway around the world.

Amazing stuff. It sure made life a lot easier for the physicists. It eliminated, in many cases, the need to walk over to the library, locate the physical copy of the report, and make a copy. Or to try to track down the author of the paper and ask him or her to mail a copy.

Since the advancement of science as a whole is a collaborative effort, it's easy to see how this hypertext system could facilitate the sharing of research results in a timely manner. When Berners-Lee originally applied his creative efforts to this project, he could never have foreseen the evolution—some would say mutation—of the World Wide Web.

You can track down virtually any book in print, purchase it online, and have it delivered to your door within two or three days (**http://www.amazon.com/**).

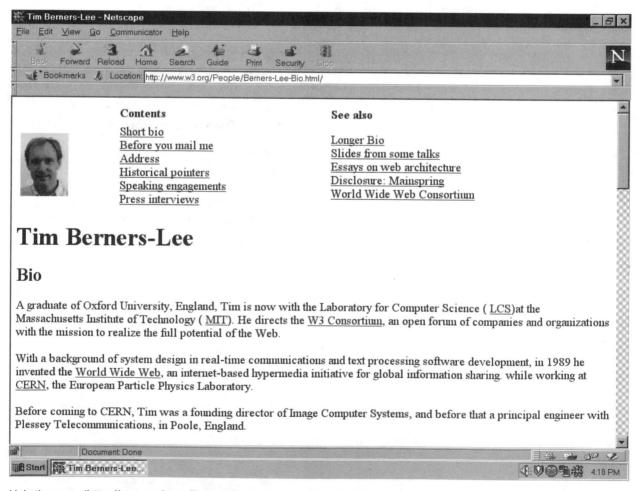

He's the man (**http://www.w3.org/People/Berners-Lee-Bio.html/**)!

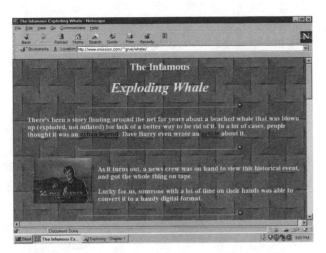

On the Web, you can watch a video of an exploding whale (**http://www.xmission.com/~grue/whale/**).

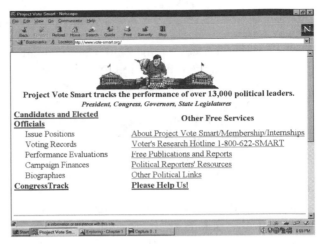

You can keep tabs on your elected officials (**http://www.vote-smart.org/**).

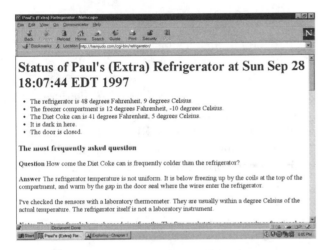

You can check the Status of Paul's (Extra) Refrigerator (**http://hamjudo.com/cgi-bin/refrigerator/**).

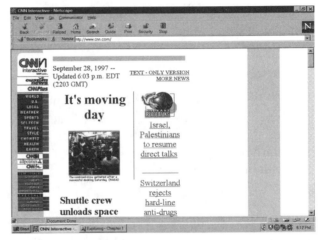

You can obtain up-to-the-minute breaking news (**http://www.cnn.com/**).

The Issues

The World Wide Web was never designed to be a mass information storage and retrieval system, but that's exactly what it's become. Except it's not a very straightforward or convenient one. If you're used to searching online public access library catalogs (OPACs) or proprietary databases offered by vendors like Dialog, OCLC, and SilverPlatter, searching the Internet can be a time-consuming and frustrating experience. Why?

- Lack of authority control
- Lack of quality control
- Ephemeral nature of Internet resources
- Technical instability and limitations

Lack of Authority Control

Authority control attempts to provide a uniform vocabulary to facilitate comprehensive and efficient search access to a database. Libraries rely on such tools as the *Sears List of Subject Headings* or the *Library of Congress Subject Headings* (**gopher://marvel.loc.gov/11/services/ cataloging/weekly/**) to provide a standard subject vocabulary for their collection databases. MeSH is the National Library of Medicine's controlled vocabulary thesaurus for searching its databases (**http://www.nlm.nih.gov/databases/databases. html**), such as MEDLINE. The Education Resources Information Center (ERIC) makes available a Thesaurus of ERIC Descriptors (**http://ericir.syr.edu/Eric/**) to assist in searching its databases.

Well, on the Internet, there ain't no such animal. Documents are indexed in the various search tools and directories by the cornucopia of imaginative names given to them by their individual creators. Which leads to unusual subject headings such as Yahoo!'s Body Art (**http://www.yahoo. com/Arts/Visual_Arts/Body_Art/**).

What this means to you, the intrepid Internet researcher, is that you have to be equally creative when using these search engines and indexes. Although the tools keep improving—and at a remarkable pace—you still need to try lots of synonyms. Some search tools allow you to enter a whole bunch of terms at one time. Another tried-and-true option is to make liberal use of the Boolean operator OR.

Lack of Quality Control

This is a biggie! In fact, after talking to a number of librarians about this book, I was motivated to include this particular issue. So if you really can't wait, turn to chapter 12 immediately. Otherwise, keep reading and see how the current mess evolved.

Before the advent of the Web, it wasn't easy to publish on the Internet. You maybe had to cozy up to a systems administrator somewhere to gain access to a gopher or an FTP server, and you may have also needed to know a bit of Unix. Personal Internet accounts were not all that common; usually, you had to work for a university or other research institution in order to get access.

Gradually, the Internet became privatized and commercialized. Personal accounts with online services and Internet providers became available. And along came the World Wide Web and HyperText Markup Language (HTML), its lingua franca. HTML is not rocket science. It's just plain vanilla ASCII text, gussied up with a series of tags that describe to a Web browser like Netscape how to display a document.

These days, many personal Internet accounts include a bit of Web server disk space on which a user may store personal Web pages. Many providers even make HTML editing tools available free for the downloading.

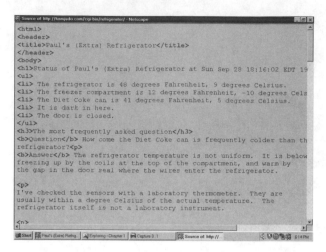

This HTML code tells the browser how to display the text for the Status of Paul's (Extra) Refrigerator.

The end result of all this? Any fool can publish on the Internet, a shocking number have already done so, and each passing day brings an alarming increase in the amount of net.garbage. It's no longer enough to have an e-mail address on your business card. These days, in order to be cool, you need your own URL as well, no matter how awful your Web site may be (**http://www. webpagesthatsuck.com/**) or how inaccurate its information is.

One scandal that surfaces in the library reference community from time to time is the existence on the Internet of numerous versions of the periodic table of the elements. How many elements does it contain right now, at this moment in time? Uh-huh . . .

Caveat emptor!

The degree of scientific literacy among information professionals is probably no higher than it is among the general public, except for those who actually work in sci-tech subject areas. If I weren't already aware of this particular problem and I located one of these online periodic tables, how would I know to verify the number of elements? At least the person responsible for the version at **http://www.universe.digex.net/~kkhan/periodic. html** had the moxie to post a disclaimer.

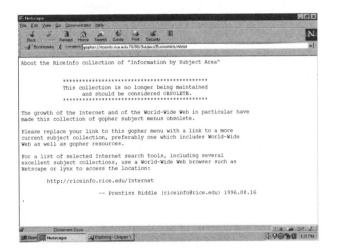

At least sometimes, a user is warned that the resource is no longer being maintained (**gopher://riceinfo.rice. edu:70/00/Subject/Economics/About**).

Ephemeral Nature of Internet Resources

You've done the search engine thing. You've waded through several screens of "results." Finally, you see a URL title and summary that look extremely promising. You click on the link: 404. Not found. Bummer.

Oh where, oh where did the resource go? Well, maybe the student maintaining it graduated, and his or her university-provided Internet account vanished. Maybe the resource became a victim of its own success; the number of people hammering on the server from all over the world caused a meltdown, and an irate systems administrator removed the offending files. (Porn sites are especially ephemeral for this reason.)

Maybe the resource migrated to another server and left no forwarding address. Maybe the Internet provider maintaining the server could no

longer ante up for the T-1 connection, and so the plug was pulled. Maybe the resource violated some sort of copyright restriction, and a threatening letter from an attorney caused it to disappear. Maybe the person maintaining the resource got another job, and the new boss wouldn't allow the resource to be stored on the company server.

Or, as happens quite often, the creator of the resource got sick and tired of maintaining it and, late one night in a fit of pique, nuked all the files. Which, in most cases, is preferable to just abandoning the resource online, allowing it to die a slow, lingering death.

The Internet is full of ghost towns. The sites are still there, but no one lives there anymore. This is a common phenomenon in gopherspace. (See chapter 9.) Those of us who have been on the Net since pre-Web days remember when gopher servers were hot, hot, hot! Now, in most cases, they are cold and stiff. And rather than being dismantled and given an honorable burial, they have been left moldering online, to wither away from neglect. You'll want to tread carefully before relying on information found on gopher servers these days.

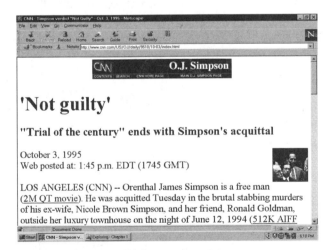

Caused yet-another Web server meltdown.

This is not just a gopherspace phenomenon. As the number of Web servers grows exponentially, the number of Web ghost towns does likewise. These are often a result of someone's boss deciding that "we need a home page," hiring some skinny young kid with a ponytail to throw one together, and giving no further thought to how the thing would be updated and maintained. As even a freshly minted library science graduate knows, old information can be much worse than no information at all.

Technical Instability and Limitations

The patron is standing at the desk waiting, watching as you hunch over your Internet terminal. It's two o'clock in the afternoon. It takes you three tries to get into AltaVista (**http://www.altavista. digital.com/**) and six tries to get into Yahoo! (**http://www.yahoo.com/**). You type your search terms. You click on the Submit button. And you wait. . . .

And the patron waits . . . and begins to shift from one foot to the other . . . deep sigh . . . rolling eyes. "Never mind. I really didn't need it that badly anyhow."

Even the casual Internet user is aware, on some level, that rush hour does indeed exist on the fabled information highway. On the East Coast of the United States, we have a slight advantage. We can hop online first thing in the A.M. and get our Internet work done while the bitstream is still moving at a decent clip. Let's face it—once all those propellerheads in California get out of bed and down that first cuppa joe, the whole darn grid is going to slow to a crawl.

Afternoons on the Net especially can be the pits. "Desirable" servers that offer truly useful information or services are often slow or completely unreachable. And special circumstances frequently cause severe traffic jams.

Ever try to get into one of Netscape's machines on the day a new browser beta is released? Lots of luck! Is there a killer storm approaching? Don't go knocking on the National Hurricane Center's virtual door. Has the jury finished deliberating on the fate of some whacked-out celebrity who ran afoul of the law? You'll suffer repetitive stress injury trying to get into one of the breaking news sites as the verdict is handed down (**http://www.cnn.com/US/OJ/daily/9510/ 10-03/index.html**).

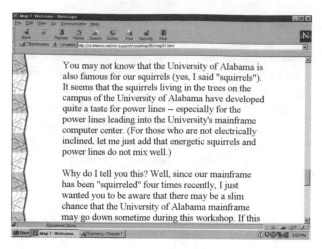

Yes, it really does happen. And more frequently than you might think.

Various techno-pundits are predicting the impending collapse of the Net—notably, Bob Metcalfe, the "father" of Ethernet (**http://www. infoworld.com/cgi-bin/displayArchives. pl?dt_iwe47-96_24.htm**)—and the universities are talking about stringing their own cable. The whole network keeps wheezing and limping along, amazing many of us that it works as well as it does much of the time.

Alas, this is small comfort in the middle of the afternoon as a patron hovers over you, watching and waiting for a key document to appear on your screen. A router in Atlanta is down, there's been a hard disk crash in Cleveland, some knuckle-headed dictator in yet another ravaged third world nation has yanked the cord, the carpet guys unplug the server to facilitate installation (happened to me once), cybervandals have their way with yet another federal government server. A hungry squirrel on some campus decides to chomp down on the power lines (**http://rs.internic.net/ nic-support/roadmap96/map01.html**).

Sometimes, *the system is down*. Period. This book won't help you. You may as well head over to the closest decent bookstore and browse the Zen section. But if the system is up, even if it's crawling, keep reading—and learn how to get to the good stuff as fast as possible.

2

Starting Points

Indexes, Resource Catalogs, and Subject Trees

As librarians, we believe that for the most part, language and ideas are simply too ambiguous for automated retrieval systems to properly identify and evaluate. It appears that artificial intelligence technologies will not meet this challenge in the near future, so intellectual labor is necessary to provide qualitative assessment of the Internet's information.

—Argus Clearinghouse, Mission and Philosophy statement
(http://www.clearinghouse.net/mission.html)

What's Here?

Subject Trees
BUBL
CyberDewey
Tradewave Galaxy
Yahoo!

**Distributed Subject Trees
(and Meta-Pages)**

Argus Clearinghouse
WWW Virtual Library
About Meta-Pages

Hard as it might be to imagine, there are scads of folks out there being paid to surf the Net, find worthwhile sites, write reviews of them, and organize them as a comprehensive resource for others. The number of people doing the same thing as a labor of love—or as part of their regular job duties somewhere—is infinitely higher. Since it's a strong belief of mine that effective research on the Internet is predicated on not reinventing the wheel, it pays to take a close look at some of the major subject trees and directories, which can save you an awful lot of time and frustration.

It's basic to understand that there are two major ways of locating information—browsing and searching. On the Internet, there has come to be a fairly incestuous relationship among the various information-finding tools, to the extent that you'll find, at most major sites now, both a search engine and a subject tree. This chapter discusses the browsing tools—subject trees, directories, resource catalogs. The search engines are discussed in chapter 5.

What is a subject tree? Personally, I like the definition in Bryan Pfaffenberger's *Web Search Strategies* (**http://watt.seas.virginia.edu/~bp/searchme/welcome.htm**), published by MIS/Henry Holt:

> A subject tree is a Web site that attempts to categorize Web documents using subject classifications. Resembling the subject catalog in a library, subject trees contain active links to the documents they index. Unlike starting points pages, subject trees try to be comprehensive, although even the biggest of them indexes only a small fraction of the documents available on the Web.

Pfaffenberger also offers an excellent definition of *distributed subject trees:*

> A distributed subject tree does not rely on a centralized system for discovering and classifying Web sites, but instead distributes this responsibility to dozens or hundreds of volunteers, each of whom is responsible for maintaining a page in his or her subject area of expertise.

I've used my understanding of these definitions to start subdividing this chapter. If you're doing research or reference work on the Web reg-

ularly, it pays to visit all of these sites and explore their features. Likely, you'll find a few that you prefer, for whatever reason, and these are the ones upon which you'll end up relying as "starting points" when you're looking to explore a subject broadly (as opposed to seeking a quick answer).

Subject Trees

BUBL

Great Britain's BUBL Information Service (**http://bubl.ac.uk/**) originated as a resource for the academic library community in Great Britain, and its original subject tree was gopher based. It now features a sophisticated Web-based subject tree called BUBL Link (BUBL being an acronym for *Bulletin Board for Libraries*), which can be searched or browsed from its home page at **http://bubl.ac.uk/link/**. If you wish to browse, you have three choices: the traditional subject arrangement, alphabetized (**http://bubl.ac.uk/link/subjects/**); a Dewey decimal–based arrangement, divided into the ten main classes (**http://link.bubl.ac.uk/isc2/**); and Random, which features sort of a weird graphical interface punctuated by ten main topic areas (**http://bubl.ac.uk/link/random/**).

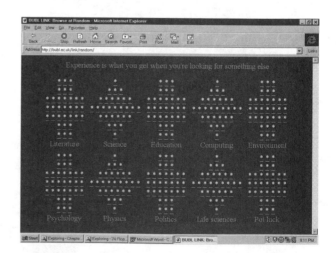

"Experience is what you get when you're looking for something else" is the theme of BUBL Link's graphical random-browsing option.

Although BUBL appears to be a much smaller resource than Yahoo! it's well worth exploring. Every resource included here is handpicked and evaluated by real, live librarians, so there's an assured measure of quality control. According to BUBL's FAQ (frequently asked questions document, at **http://bubl.ac.uk/admin/faq.htm**), the BUBL staff gathers resources by subscribing to numerous Internet mailing lists that "announce new resources and services." They also solicit submissions from individuals, who may nominate resources to be evaluated for inclusion. The Library and Information Science (LIS) collection (**http://www.bubl.bath.ac.uk/BUBL/Library.html**) is particularly strong; there's an extensive collection of LIS journals—mostly tables of contents and abstracts— that are browsable and searchable (**http://bubl.ac.uk/journals/lis/**).

You can keep current on additions and updates to BUBL by subscribing to the lis-link e-mail list. Details are available at **http://www.mailbase.ac.uk/lists/lis-link/**.

CyberDewey

David A. Mundie, the creator of this resource (**http://ivory.lm.com/~mundie/CyberDewey/CyberDewey.html**), appears to be a computer person rather than a librarian. Indeed, he says, "I am sure that professional librarians would be shocked at some of my assignments, but who cares?"

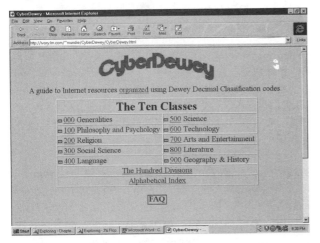

Dewey or don't we care that the creator of this resource is *not* a librarian?

Actually, Mundie seems to have developed a profound appreciation of the principles of the Dewey decimal classification bordering on unbridled enthusiasm. To wit:

I have gone on to use the DDC to categorize my personal files, my computer manuals, my books, my road maps, my hand tools, my mail-order catalogues, my medicine cabinet, and my record collection. Even my son's toys are labeled: the box with his car collection is "388.3 Automobiles," his coin collection "737 Numismatics," and his stuffed animals "591.074 Zoological Collection." I have not yet labeled my spice rack "633.8" nor my vegetable bin "635," but it may come to that.

This is not a bad collection, and if you understand Dewey, it's fun to browse. Note that some of the classifications, particularly the more obscure ones, may not include any resource links. On the other hand, 004 (Systems) is loaded with computer-oriented links. For the non-Dewey user, there's also an alphabetical index.

You'll find a comprehensive overview of the Dewey decimal classification here if you click on the Hundred Divisions link (**http://ivory.lm.com/~mundie/CyberDewey/DivisionSummary.html**). There's no search engine, but it's an intriguing attempt at a subject tree and, for that reason alone, is worth a look.

Tradewave Galaxy

Galaxy (**http://galaxy.einet.net/**) has been around since the summer of 1993, which makes it downright ancient in Internet terms. Several features differentiate this resource from other subject tree sites. For one thing, it's always included searchable/browseable directories for both telnet and gopher sites; this unique item makes Galaxy well worth bookmarking and exploring.

What else is notable about Galaxy? The folks behind it (Tradewave, a purveyor of "industrial strength" security solutions for the Internet) apparently have a deep respect for information professionals. From About the Galaxy (**http://galaxy.einet.net/about.html**):

We employ professional information specialists to organize Galaxy and oversee the classification process. We also offer an internship program to students of several top ten Library and Information Science programs across the United States. Web pages are actually *much*

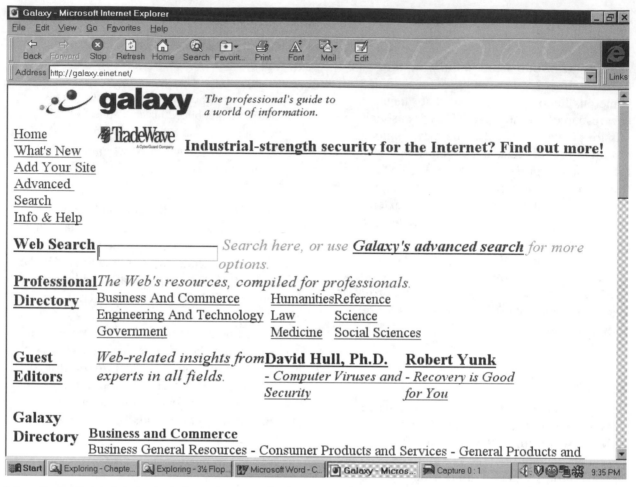

Interestingly, Galaxy's index includes only pages that have actually been submitted to it. Apparently, it does not employ professional surfers like some of the other resources discussed in this chapter. This would have to limit the size of the database, although documentation at the site claims that it contains more than 450,000 links.

harder to classify than other media; people frequently lump unrelated information together or leave out important details like contact information or geographical location.

Search options are numerous here. Search the Galaxy—which includes only the links in its database—offers three choices: All Text (searches full text of indexed pages), Title Text (searches page titles only), and Link Text (searches text of indexed pages for links).

Easy gopher and telnet searching are available here, too. Galaxy incorporates two key directories for these non-Web resources: Gopher Jewels (**http://galaxy.einet.net/GJ/**) and Hytelnet (**http://galaxy.einet.net/hytelnet/START.TXT.html**). These are both searchable from the advanced search menu (where you go to use Boolean operators, etc.), which allows you to search the Web

and Galaxy pages, as well as gopher titles and telnet resources, by checking the appropriate boxes.

Alternately, you can go directly to the front pages of either Gopher Jewels or Hytelnet and browse or search there, although it's not easy to find the direct links to them.

Gopher Jewels in its heyday (1993–94) was a catalog of primo gopher sites unearthed by members of the now-defunct Gopher Jewels Internet mailing list and organized categorically by the list owner, David Riggins, of the Texas Department of Commerce. Since so many gophers have been left to wither on the vine, or else have been supplanted by Web sites, this resource isn't as useful as it once was. (More detail about gophers can be found in chapter 9.) But it can still be relied upon to point to almost any gopher housing useful information, and if you're doing a comprehensive search in any subject area, you may want to browse here or toss a quick keyword or two into the search box at the bottom of the page.

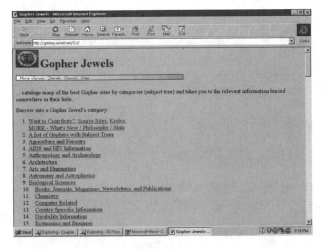

All the gophers you will ever need.

If you have much occasion to go searching in online public access library catalogs, you'll definitely want to get cozy with Hytelnet (**http:// galaxy.einet.net/hytelnet/START.TXT.html**). Hytelnet originated as a stand-alone client program that, when loaded on your own computer or workstation, offered a comprehensive directory of instant links to library catalogs and other telnet-accessible sites (e.g., Free-Nets, online BBSs, etc.).

One-stop shopping for telnet sites.

But most users found a site where the Hytelnet interface was available. The primary site is at the University of Saskatchewan (**http://library.usask. ca/hytelnet/**), where Peter Scott, the "father" of

this resource, is employed. (Scott has stopped updating and is merging Hytelnet's files with a new resource, but check out Scott's newer directory, WebCATS [**http://library.usask.ca/hywebcat/**], a comprehensive collection of library catalogs accessible from the World Wide Web.) Rodent enthusiasts will find a gopher-based Hytelnet at Washington and Lee University (**gopher:// liberty.uc.wlu.edu/11/internet/hytelnet/**). Note that Hytelnet offers a lot of online help, both for the telnet protocol itself and for navigating the sometimes-arcane OPAC interfaces.

By the way, Galaxy hosts a number of volunteer guest editors, who share their subject-area expertise with visitors (**http://galaxy.einet.net/ editors.html**). Here you might find in-depth information about a topic in which you need to do research.

Yahoo!

Yahoo! (**http://www.yahoo.com/**) is user-friendly in the extreme. You can sit even the most computer-phobic person down in front of a screen where Netscape is open to Yahoo! and show him or her how to use a mouse, and he or she will almost always be able to find something useful or interesting in less than two minutes.

Yahoo! is one of those net.cinderella stories. According to its history page (**http://www.yahoo. com/docs/pr/history.html**):

> The two developers of Yahoo!, David Filo and Jerry Yang, Ph.D. candidates in Electrical Engineering at Stanford University, started their guide in April 1994 as a way to keep track of their personal interests on the Internet. Before long they found that their home-brewed lists were becoming too long and unwieldy. Gradually they began to spend more and more time on Yahoo!

> And it paid off. Handsomely. Yahoo! is now a publicly traded company, Filo and Yang are millionaires, and mothers like me are repeating this saga to teenage sons and daughters everywhere.

Having evolved into much more than a simple Web directory, Yahoo! is now heavily laden with features of various kinds. Indeed, new stuff is being added so frequently that writing about Yahoo! is like trying to change the tires on a moving car. Some of the coolest stuff?

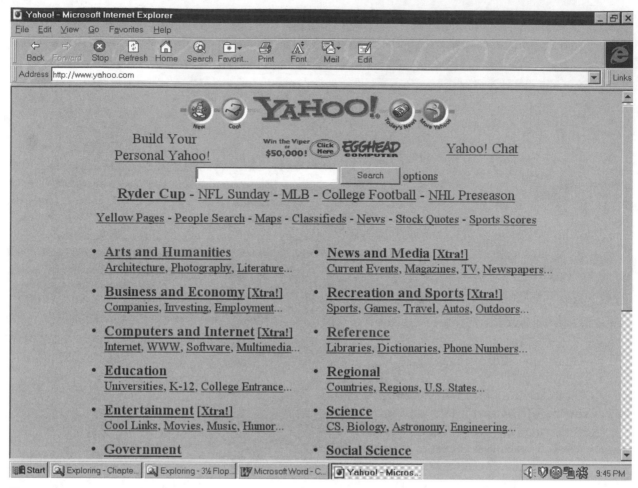

The source!

YAHOOLIGANS

This full-service Web guide (**http://www. yahooligans.com/**), aimed at kids between the ages of eight and fourteen, focuses on both fun and educational links that are screened for "appropriateness."

MY YAHOO!

A personal version of the Yahoo! home page, My Yahoo! (**http://my.yahoo.com/**) lets you customize the directory and get up-to-the-minute news, weather, and sports in categories of your choosing. After you "build" your page, you bookmark it, and then you can use it as your browser's default home page.

YAHOO! GET LOCAL

Geographically oriented versions of the Yahoo! directory are available for several foreign countries and a number of U.S. metropolitan areas. Or you can generate your own version at **http://local. yahoo.com/local/**.

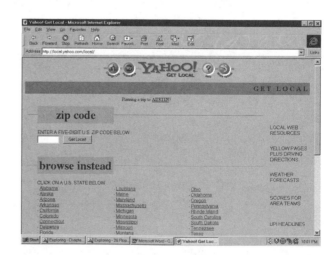

Input your five-digit zip code and get a customized Yahoo! page of local news, weather, sports, and various links to government, business, entertainment, education, and other local resources. Or you can browse by state and then city to get to the same information.

YAHOO! WHAT'S NEW

There are daily (**http://www.yahoo.com/new/**) and weekly (**http://www.yahoo.com/picks/**) versions of What's New. The weekly page lets you sign up online to receive it via e-mail. Picks tend to be a mix of the whimsical and the informational; if you're looking for pure scholarly current awareness, this is probably not it.

RANDOM YAHOO! LINK

Serendipitous surfers might like to click on this from the main page and be taken at random to a remote site. (Warning: These are not all captivat-

ing. Last time I tried it, I ended up at some boring online brochure for an employee benefits company.)

You can also generate street maps on the fly here (**http://maps.yahoo.com/yahoo/**); search white or yellow pages directories; browse Beatrice's Web Guide, a Yahoo! Women's Wire Collaboration (**http://www.bguide.com/**); and get current news, sports scores, weather reports, and stock prices.

Oh yeah—in case you've forgotten, Yahoo! is also a subject tree. You can start with the broad categories on the main page and work your way down, browsing in any area of interest. An extensive FAQ is available at **http://www.yahoo.com/docs/info/faq.html**.

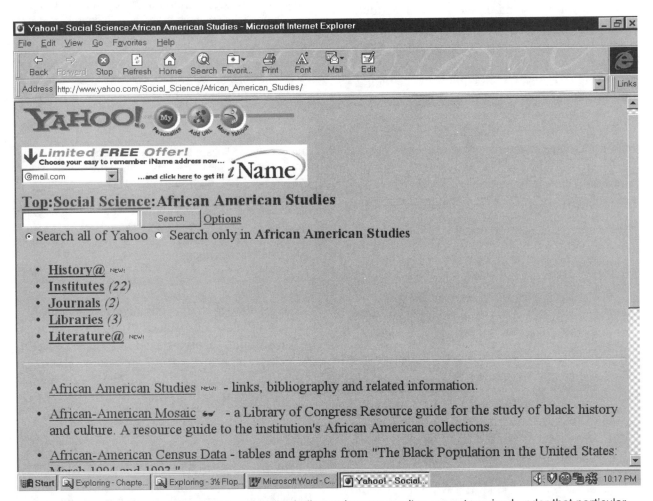

The number in parentheses after a subject heading indicates how many sites are categorized under that particular heading. The @ symbol that appears at the end of a category means this heading is listed in multiple places within Yahoo!'s hierarchy. Clicking on the heading will take you to the primary location. If you see an [Xtra!] tag next to a Yahoo! category, it links to a Reuters newsfeed for that subject. Headlines, summaries, and full-text stories are updated hourly. Sites that have a little sunglasses symbol after them are ones Yahoo! employees (professional surfers and catalogers) think have good presentation and content for their respective topic area. It's a good idea to check these first. A "new" tag indicates that the entry was added within the last week. If it appears next to a directory, it means that entries in that directory's hierarchy were modified within the last three days.

As if that weren't enough, the line between what is a search engine and what is a directory has gotten extremely blurry on the Web. Yahoo! started out purely as a directory, and now it incorporates a search engine that offers some fairly sophisticated features (just as most of the major search engines now offer some type of directory).

While there's good documentation available at the site (**http://search.yahoo.com/search/help?**), read on for a few hints and tips to get you started.

The simple search, available from the main page and at each category page throughout the hierarchy, is not a bad place to begin. Type your keyword(s) into the little query box, click on the Search button, and Yahoo! will search through the four areas of its database (categories, individual sites, Net events and chat, and the most recent seven days' worth of news articles). What you'll get back is a page or pages of links, ranked according to relevancy: documents containing more of the keywords are ranked higher than those containing fewer; documents where key-words are found in a page's title are ranked higher than documents where the keywords are found in the body or URL; and categories matching higher up in the Yahoo! subject tree (i.e., more general) are ranked higher than those farther down (more narrowly focused). For better searching:

- Use double quotes around words that are part of a phrase: *"George Washington Bridge."*
- Use a plus sign (+) in front of words that must appear in the results: *Hamlet + Branagh.*
- Use the minus sign (−) in front of words that must not appear in the results: *rockets − basketball.*

Some advanced search tips:

- Using *t:* restricts a search to the document titles only: *t:Internet Movie Database.*
- Using *u:* restricts a search to the document's URL only: *u:microsoft.*
- An asterisk (*) can be used as a wild-card character (at the right side of a word only): *child*.*
- The different syntax options may be combined in a single query: *t:RICO − Puerto.*

Don't forget that Yahoo! allows you to limit your search to a specific category, at every level of the hierarchy. Click the radio button that says Search Only In . . . rather than the default, which says Search All of Yahoo!

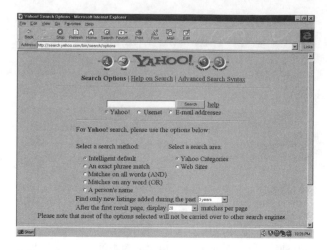

Still not getting what you want? Visit the Search Options page (**http://search.yahoo.com/bin/search/options/**—click the options link next to the simple search box), and also take advantage of the advanced search syntax that's available. Here you can choose a search method, including Boolean options, exact phrase matching, per-sonal names, or Intelligent Default, which is the obvious choice for single-keyword queries. You may also select one of the four areas of Yahoo!'s database that you want searched. And a drop-down box allows you to nar-row your search by time—specifying that you want to see only those links added in the last day, week, month, etc., on up to three years back. Yahoo! by default will carry your search on over to AltaVista and, by individual choice, to most of the other major search engines. Many of the options Yahoo! allows, however, won't work on other search engines (and most of them have unique options that can't be utilized unless you start searching from their respective pages).

Even though there's human effort behind Yahoo! not just a computerized *robot* or *spider*, you'll still find plenty of dead links in the data-base. You can provide a real service by reporting these via an online form (**http://www.yahoo.com/docs/writeus/deadlink.html**).

In January 1997, Yahoo! added a live chat component to its site (**http://chat.yahoo.com/**). If you're curious to see what you're missing by not having access to chat rooms on America Online (AOL) and other online services, check this out. Register on-site and pick a log-in name and a password. (Once you're registered, you can pick alternate identities and flesh them out with demo-graphic variables of your choice. So the usual caveats apply—beware of thirteen-year-old boys masquerading as "hot chicks" and the occasional philandering spouse pretending to be your per-sonal love goddess or Prince Charming.)

If you're a Windows or Mac user with a recent version of Netscape or Microsoft Internet Explorer, Yahoo!'s chat software comes in the form of a downloadable browser plug-in. Users of other platforms or browsers may choose between a Java or HTML interface. The plug-in offers frames-based navigation. Choose to join one of Yahoo!'s preestablished rooms, or create one of your own.

The level of discourse is about what you'd expect. When I stopped by one Friday afternoon in January 1997, about fifty people were in the Romance room, but no one was in Business and News or Science and Technology.

Finally, if you still haven't had enough, click on the Other Chats menu option to get to Yahoo!'s Net Events, a roundup of online events and real-time chats, including Internet Relay Chat channels.

Distributed Subject Trees (and Meta-Pages)

If you intend to use the Internet for research on a regular basis—which I assume is true, since you're reading this book—you owe it to yourself to become intimate with both of the resources discussed in this section. You'll find them especially appealing if you're a network nostalgia buff, who reminisces longingly about the good old days when folks created resources for the collective good of the Internet community, rather than to make a quick buck or attract attention to themselves.

Whereas the other sites discussed in this chapter are centralized resources—maintained by a particular organization, institution, or individual—distributed subject trees parcel out that responsibility to a wide range of individuals who have

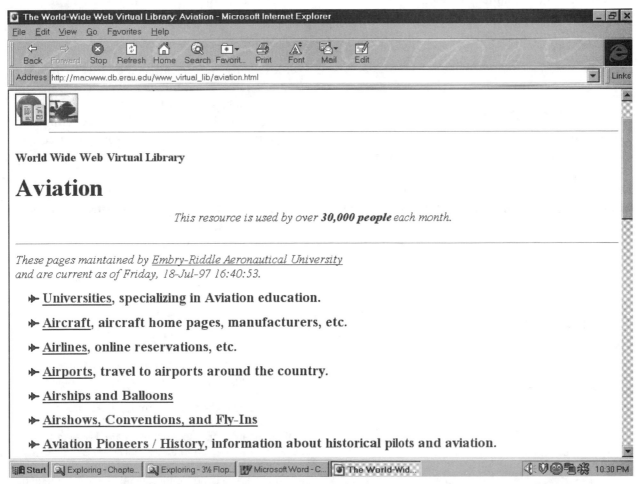

I'll often start a comprehensive Internet research project by turning to one or both distributed subject trees—especially if I'm dealing with a topic about which I have little or no personal knowledge. I doubt, for instance, that I'd do a better job of tracking down quality Net-based resources about aviation than the folks at Embry-Riddle Aeronautical University (**http://macwww.db.erau.edu/www_virtual_lib/aviation.html**).

subject-area expertise. Thus, the main pages of both resources in this section are essentially tables of contents to remote sites housing handpicked catalogs of relevant Internet sites.

The odds are that when it comes to subject-specific collections of Internet resources, someone has almost always been there first—and you can save yourself a lot of time and aggravation by taking advantage of these efforts. Some very bright and knowledgeable people are involved in the creation and maintenance of these resources. The Argus Clearinghouse has a very stringent set of submission guidelines (**http://www.clearinghouse.net/submit.html**) for any resource it includes in its collection, and the WWW Virtual Library lays out specific instructions (**http://www.w3.org/pub/DataSources/bySubject/Administration.html**) for the maintainers of the various subject areas there.

Spend some time browsing at both of these sites so you'll have an idea of what's there when you need it. And perhaps you'll even find a subject-area niche that you or your institution can fill!

Argus Clearinghouse

Long-term internauts may remember the Clearinghouse's somewhat-humble beginnings in 1993 as a gopher server run by the University of Michigan School of Information and Library Studies. Louis Rosenfeld, a doctoral student and an instructor there, set his students to work on a series of subject-specific Internet guides, back when there was no Yahoo!, no AltaVista, no sophisticated finding tools. Rosenfeld came to

realize that it made sense to also include similar guides that had already been produced by subject-area specialists at other institutions. The resource quickly became so useful that thousands of Internet researchers were finding their way to it, despite a total lack of publicity.

Well, the Clearinghouse has gone through numerous permutations since its early text-based days, but Rosenfeld's original concept, as quoted earlier, remains the same. Argus Associates (**http://argus-inc.com/**), the Web consulting and design firm behind today's Clearinghouse (**http://www.clearinghouse.net/**), was cofounded by Rosenfeld, who is its president.

The Clearinghouse is arranged in classic subject tree format, with a main menu of broad categories—Arts and Entertainment, Business and Employment, Education, Engineering and Technology, Environment, Government and Law, Health and Medicine, Humanities, News and Publishing, Regional Information, Science, Social Sciences and Social Issues—on the top-level page. The next layer down offers the actual subtopical guides themselves, each listed by title with the author's name. Each title is a hyperlink to the Clearinghouse's descriptive entry for that particular guide, which includes a qualitative rating and a link to the actual guide itself, usually housed on a remote server where its creator or maintainer keeps it.

The Clearinghouse's rating system (**http://www.clearinghouse.net/ratings.html**) is a complex beast, based on five criteria: (1) level of resource description, (2) level of resource evaluation, (3) guide design, (4) guide organizational schemes, and (5) guide meta-information.

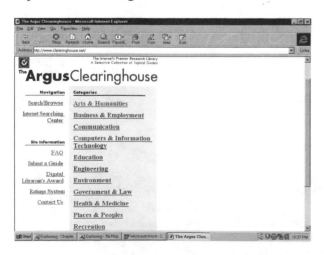

"The Internet is as much about collaboration and cooperation as anything else, and the Argus Clearinghouse symbolizes that kind of group effort. Individuals and organizations make their information resources available, usually free of charge, via the Internet. Guide authors search for, describe, evaluate, repackage, and essentially add value to these individual resources by including them in their guides. The Clearinghouse does much the same thing for the guides—we find, describe, evaluate, and make available these guides via a single central location" (Argus Clearinghouse FAQ, **http://www.clearinghouse.net/faq.html/#staff**).

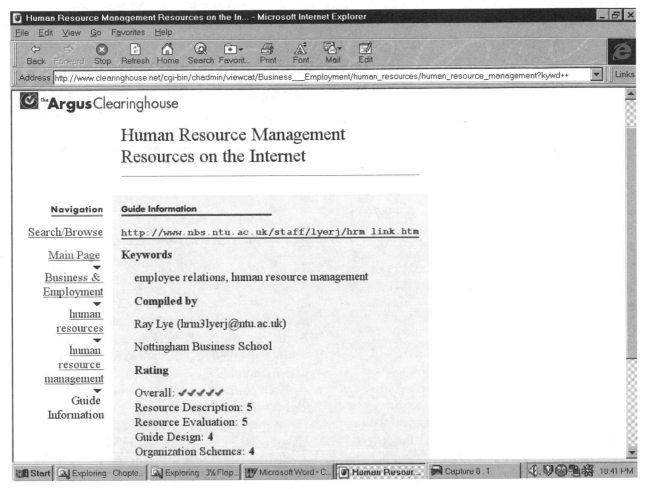

See the Clearinghouse rating before you jump to the actual guide.

LEVEL OF RESOURCE DESCRIPTION

Descriptive information provides users with an objective sense of what the Internet resources cover, including:

- Description of the resources' content (ranging from keywords to abstracts)
- Description of the traffic levels, level of moderation, features (e.g., digests) for mailing lists and Usenet newsgroups
- Intended audience for the resources
- Description of the update frequencies for resources
- Access instructions for the resources
- Technical performance levels of the resources (i.e, a server is frequently down)

LEVEL OF RESOURCE EVALUATION

Evaluative information provides users with a subjective sense of the quality of the Internet resources, including:

- Quality of the content of resources (e.g., discussion in mailing lists and Usenet newsgroups, information in a Web site)
- Assessment of the resources' usability (e.g., document layout, readability, appropriate use of graphics, organization)
- Authority (e.g., reliability) of resource authors

GUIDE DESIGN

Quality guides balance aesthetics with usability:

- Images (are images attractive, do they support ease of navigation, do they load quickly)
- Layout (does the author make appropriate use of headers, mixed font sizes, and white space)
- Navigational aids (is it easy to find your way around, do you have a consistent sense of context or understanding of where you are in the guide at any given time)

GUIDE ORGANIZATIONAL SCHEMES

Guides can be organized in one or more ways, including:

- By subject (i.e., sports can be broken up into soccer, racquetball, etc.)
- By format (e.g., mailing lists, Web sites, etc.)
- By audience (e.g., academic vs. general users)
- By chronology (for a history guide)
- By geography (for a guide to a region)
- By authors (for a literature guide)

Additional points will be assigned to guides with multiple organizational schemes.

GUIDE META-INFORMATION

Meta-information is information about other information. In this case, meta-information describes the guide itself and may include:

- Mission of the guide: why it was created, what it contains and what it leaves out
- How the guide was researched and constructed
- Information about the authors, their professional or institutional affiliations, and their knowledge of or experience with the subject
- Information on how to contact the author and submit feedback and suggestions
- Update frequency

The Clearinghouse staff (**http://www. clearinghouse.net/staff.html**) comprises mainly seasoned information professionals with a variety of subject-specific expertise. Some additional features that you'll find at the Clearinghouse include the following:

- The Digital Librarian's Award (**http://www. clearinghouse.net/dla.html**) is chosen by the staff each month as a particularly exemplary resource. (There's a link to past winners from this page.)
- A limited search feature allows users to search the Clearinghouse's information pages for the guides (rather than the full text of the guides themselves, since they are housed on a multitude of remote servers). The Boolean operators AND and OR are supported, as is truncation with the wild-card character (*). Search results contain guide title, author name, keywords, ratings, and a link to the guide's information page.

Finally, if you can't find what you want within the Clearinghouse (which is kind of difficult to imagine, given the depth and breadth of the collection that is here), the Internet Searching Center link (**http://www.clearinghouse.net/searching/ find.html**) offers you the opportunity to try other indexes and search tools.

WWW Virtual Library

The top page of the Virtual Library (VL) offers two choices to browsers: a standard alphabetical subject list or one that's arranged according to the Library of Congress classification scheme (**http://vlib.stanford.edu/LibraryofCongress. html**). It is noted that the latter arrangement is "experimental."

Each category (and, where they exist, subcategories) of the VL is maintained by a volunteer with subject-area expertise. If you would like to volunteer to create a new area or help maintain an existing one, see **http://vlib.stanford.edu/ AboutVL.html** for details.

Unlike the Clearinghouse, the VL does not incorporate a rating system per se. There are style and structure guidelines for section maintainers, however, and at the very least, you should find a contact e-mail address. The different sections of the VL appear to vary in overall quality; some maintainers do an extremely thorough job, while others don't appear to update their resources as often, etc. Since there is no rating system here, caveat emptor is a much larger factor at VL than at the Clearinghouse.

You won't find any sort of search engine here either, although browsing is pretty straightforward. At the end of the subject listings is a link to some other virtual libraries, at **http://vlib. stanford.edu/Virtual_libraries.html**. Except several of the links on this page were dead, which gave me kind of a bad feeling about this resource as a whole.

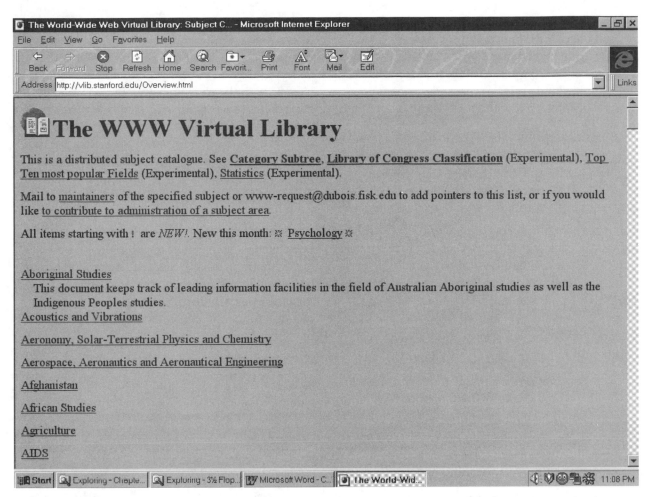

The WWW Virtual Library project (**http://vlib.stanford.edu/Overview.html**) predates the Clearinghouse. It was started in 1991 by Tim Berners-Lee, creator of the World Wide Web, as a way to keep track of the Web's development. Arthur Secret has maintained the project since then, although the Virtual Library became a *distributed* subject tree in 1993, when Lou Montulli (creator of Lynx, the text-based Web browser, now employed by Netscape) suggested that the VL's history section be maintained at the University of Kansas, which had already produced an extensive guide to history-oriented Internet resources (**http://history.cc.ukans.edu/history/WWW_history_main.html**).

About Meta-Pages

Another way of thinking about both the Argus Clearinghouse and the WWW Virtual Library is that they are collections of individual *meta-pages*. What are meta-pages? Well, I've also heard them referred to as *pathfinder pages*, *trailblazer pages*, *centers of excellence*, *subject hubs*, *guru pages*, *treasure pages*. These are Internet sites where an individual—or a group of individuals or maybe an institution—has used subject-area expertise to select the best and most useful Internet resources in a specific category.

The glitzy subject trees like Yahoo! and the powerful search engines like AltaVista are mentioned everywhere as research tools and hyped ad nauseam in the popular media. Learning to use these resources effectively will, of course, turn you into a decent Internet searcher. But learning to locate and utilize subject-specific meta-pages—ah, *then* you'll have earned the right to call yourself an Info-god or Info-goddess!

Where do you find these crown jewels of the Internet? The two distributed subject trees described above are a good place to start looking. If you read Usenet newsgroups or join Internet mailing lists that are specific to your area of interest (see chapter 8), new and relevant meta-pages are often announced there, where a natural audience exists. Mailing lists for librarians, journalists, and others who do a lot of research are also good sources of information about key subject-oriented resources.

And you can mine Yahoo! Under most of the main headings and larger subheadings, you'll often find a menu item called Indices. Click on this, and you're likely to be rewarded with a selection of meta-pages in that particular subject area. Remember that the items tagged with the little sunglasses icon are the sites Yahoo!'s indexers and catalogers feel are the "best of the best."

Then there's the people connection. If you've got Web-surfing friends or colleagues with specific professional or avocational expertise, ask them if they know any quality sites. Nobody can be an expert in everything and keep track of the best Internet-based information in every subject area. For example, I don't know very much about genealogy, but my friend and colleague Doug Cornwell, bibliographic instruction librarian at Palm Beach Community College (**http://www. pbcc.cc.fl.us/llrc/about.htm**), is an expert. He was only too happy to provide me with a list of the best genealogy resources on the Net and recommend an article in a professional journal as a starting place. (If you're interested, it's "Searching for Generations Past" by Kathryn Lively, in the September/October 1996 issue of *Link-Up* magazine.)

Something basic in human nature makes most folks happy to share their special knowledge—and this is particularly true for those of us in the information profession. The Internet, at its best, is a monument to that.

3

Selective Subject Trees and Resource Catalogs

More Starting Points

What's Here?

Subject Catalogs Integrated with Major Search Engines

Excite Web Guide
Infoseek Directory
Lycos and Point Top 5% Reviews
WebCrawler Select

Stand-Alone Catalogs

LookSmart
Magellan (by Excite)
Yanoff's Internet Services List

Other General Resource Collections

The Awesome Lists
Nerd World Media
PC Magazine's Top 100 Web Sites
WebDictionary

Subject-Specific Meta-Sites

Business and Finance
Government

Subject Catalogs Integrated with Major Search Engines

Most professional and other serious Internet searchers take the time to learn the ins and outs of the various major search engines (see chapter 5). But to the amorphous mass that comprises the Web-surfing general public, these tools are all pretty much the same. The average user may develop a preference for one search tool over another—based, perhaps, on speed or on the user-friendliness of its interface. In actuality, most casual users simply click on Netscape's Net Search directory button, whereupon they are taken to Netscape's search page (**http://home.netscape. com/home/internet-search.html**), which features one or another of the major search engines on a rotating basis, while providing quick links to the others. (Experienced users quickly discover that

bookmarking their favorite search engines is a better strategy. Think about the vast number of people all over the world who are clicking, simultaneously, on Netscape's Net Search button, and you'll no longer wonder why this route is the slow-boat-to-China way of getting to a particular search tool.)

At any rate, each individual search engine is desirous of being your best friend. Why? For sure it's not a matter of virtual love. Each site wants you to visit as often as possible because high Internet traffic is what attracts advertisers—and their wallets. (Ka-ching!)

Since the vast majority of surfers don't really differentiate among these tools, the search engines make themselves unique in ways they hope are attractive to users. They've begun offering a plethora of special directories, maps-on-the-fly generators, etc. And most of the major search

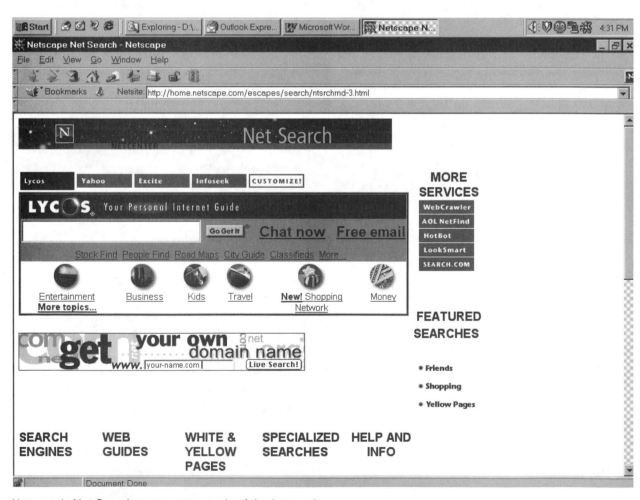

Netscape's Net Search page—crossroads of the Internet!

engines now offer some sort of "selective" catalog that professes to include "best of the Net" sites in a range of subject categories. Often, professional editors and reviewers are involved in writing up descriptions of the individual sites. As you might expect, some do a better job than others. Still, these are not bad places to start research on a broad topic.

Excite Web Guide

Excite says that its Web Guide includes about 140,000 "sites that matter." Roughly 25,000 of these sites have been reviewed by Excite's "experts," a small cadre of writers and editors with various degrees of expertise in one or another subject area.

Click on one of Excite's fourteen topical "channels" on the home page (**http://www. excite.com/**). A subject tree–like branch of sub-topics appears on one side of the next page. Click on a subtopic and up comes a list of the related sites in the Web Guide. An editor's review link is available for each site that has been reviewed. The reviews include a brief description of what the site has to offer. The language can get a bit cutesy sometimes. The sites are rated pictorially on a descending scale of 4 ("must see") to 1 ("if you're desperate") of Excite's little "leaping man" logos.

Infoseek Directory

Infoseek (**http://www.infoseek.com/**) no longer boasts about the size of its Web directory. Rather,

it highlights its "award-winning search and spider-ing technology" and its ease of use. A press release archived at the Web site claims that the directory is organized with the assistance of a text analysis software program called Convectis:

> "Infoseek's team of *expert librarians* [author's emphasis] uses Convectis to dynamically build and maintain its directory to offer the most current, comprehensive ontology of Web sites in the world," said Daniella Russo, Vice President of Product Management at Infoseek. "Convectis allows us to scale directly to the explosive growth of the Web, and helps us automate the overwhelming task of reading, understanding and making decisions about the content of millions of Web pages."

The descriptions of the cataloged sites are extremely brief—only a line or two. You can't search the directory sites separately from the entire Web, although if your search retrieves any of Infoseek's directory sites, these "select" items are indicated by red check marks.

Like Excite, Infoseek is loaded with lots of extras now, too, including a News Center, an e-mail address directory, a business directory, a cal-endar of live Net events, etc.

Lycos and Point Top 5% Reviews

The Lycos search engine offers the Top 5% Sites (**http://point.lycos.com/categories/**), which fea-tures more than ten thousand sites reviewed by the most authoritative experienced Web watchers in

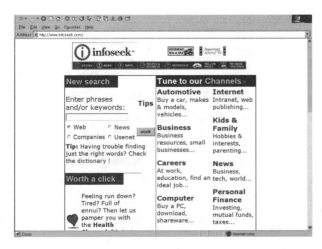

Puffery? Infoseek claims its directory contains more than "500,000 of the best pages on the Web."

three categories: content, presentation, and overall experience. If you've been around the Web for a while, you should know this is a reincarnation of the Point stand-alone directory.

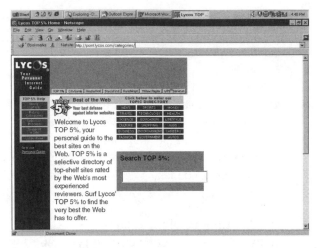

For each of the eighteen main categories (the "usual suspects") in the Top 5% Sites, you can choose a display of reviewed sites by date reviewed (although I couldn't find a specific date anywhere on the actual reviews I browsed) or descending rating scores by content, presentation, or experience. (Top score is fifty points.) You can restrict a Lycos search to the Top 5% Sites via a drop-down box on the search form.

WebCrawler Select

Okay—see if you can follow this: WebCrawler Select (accessible from **http://www.webcrawler. com/**) used to be GNN Select. GNN, which stands for *Global Network Navigator,* used to be America Online's flat-fee Internet service provider subsidiary and, before that, a component of O'Reilly and Associates, the geeky-turned-trendy computer book publisher. GNN "went away" after AOL started offering flat-fee pricing in late 1996.

O'Reilly's best-selling *Whole Internet User's Guide and Catalog,* by Ed Krol (**http://www.ora. com/catalog/twi2/**), included a "Resources on the Internet" catalog section that was originally augmented and updated via O'Reilly's Web site—before this *Whole Internet Catalog* (not O'Reilly itself) became part of GNN. (WebCrawler, by the way, was a stand-alone resource before it got sucked up by AOL.)

Is your head spinning yet? Take several deep breaths.

Actually, the paragraph-length reviews (written by WebCrawler's editors) provide helpful, pithy information. There's no numerical rating system here, as in the Lycos Top 5%, but it's no great loss. Located by each review is a clickable WebCrawler logo that you can use to "Search the Web for more like this."

Navigation is easy via a standard subject tree format. You could do a lot worse than to invest some time browsing here, especially if you're involved in Internet training or researching the Net on behalf of others.

Stand-Alone Catalogs

The search engines haven't sucked up all the larger Web catalogs yet. Alas, who knows what the future will bring? As a matter of fact, Magellan was bought out by Excite in early 1997, although it was still a stand-alone service six months later.

LookSmart

LookSmart (**http://www.looksmart.com/**), a project of the Australian subsidiary of Reader's Digest, is basically a directory of about 160,000

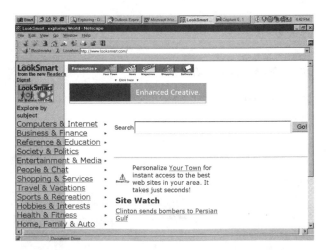

LookSmart's search engine will only match reviews that contain all of the terms entered in the search field (the Boolean AND, not the OR). Truncation is fully supported; LookSmart will search for the "streams" of many words (e.g., *climb* as well as *climbing, movie* as well as *movies*). All searches are case insensitive. (Documentation available at the site indicates that LookSmart's editors "attempt to exclude listings for pornographic or violent sites.")

Web sites reviewed by an editorial staff of twenty-three and organized into thirteen thousand(!) categories. The database is updated daily.

Its initially cumbersome interface has been refined to the point that it is now the site's best feature. It uses cascading menus to show you where you're coming from in the subject tree and what your next options are. You can choose to "Explore" the database by category, search the sites in the database, or search the entire Web via AltaVista. A Personalize option allows you to select and retain your favorite sites in five categories—Your Town, News, Magazines, Shopping, and Software.

If you opt to query the database of LookSmart reviews, Search will look for your keyword or phrase in both the titles and the full text of the Web site reviews. LookSmart will display a list of up to thirty hits at a time that match your search terms. Click on any title that interests you, and you'll be directly connected to the selected Web site.

Magellan (by Excite)

Magellan (**http://www.mckinley.com/**) has always been a nifty resource. It includes original editorial content, a directory of rated and reviewed Internet sites, a vast database of yet-to-be-reviewed sites, and a fairly powerful search engine. In addition to the reviews, a numerical rating system is used here—awarding one to ten points in each of three areas:

1. **Depth.** Is it comprehensive and up-to-date?

2. **Ease of exploration.** Is it well organized and easy to navigate?

3. **Net appeal.** Is it innovative? Does it appeal to the eye or the ear? Is it funny? Is it hot, hip, or cool? Is it thought provoking? Does it offer new technology or a new way of using technology?

This results in an overall rating of one to four stars:

> 28 to 30 points = 4 stars
> 22 to 27 points = 3 stars
> 13 to 21 points = 2 stars
> 1 to 12 points = 1 star

You can browse or search here, and you can restrict your search to rated and reviewed sites only. You can also opt to search for Green Light Sites Only—Magellan marks with a green dot those sites that are free of adult content—a useful feature for those who work with children.

There's good documentation here, and navigation is simple and elegant. Coolest thing about Magellan? Search Voyeur (**http://voyeur.mckinley. com/cgi-bin/voyeur.cgi**), which allows you to

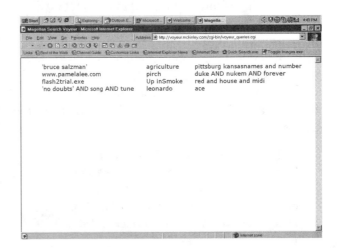

Magellan is a project of the McKinley Group, an international team of publishers, technologists, and information specialists, and it does seem to have some real brain power behind it.

If you've ever pondered the notion that Web search tools may eventually obviate the need for trained information professions, a look at Search Voyeur will quickly disabuse you of that notion.

peek at twelve randomly selected real-time searches actually being performed in the Magellan database. (Warning: This is not for the easily offended or faint of heart, given the questionable taste of the masses.)

Yanoff's Internet Services List

If it's really true that Internet years are like dog years—i.e., one "Internet" year equals seven "real" years—then Scott Yanoff's Internet Services List (**http://www.spectracom.com/islist/index.html**) is downright ancient! Yanoff—once with the University of Wisconsin–Milwaukee and now a systems administrator and Web developer for SpectraCom (**http://www.spectracom.com/home.html**)—started his list back in 1991, with his personal collection of *six* Internet resources!

While Yanoff's list is certainly not the most glitzy or comprehensive subject directory on the Internet by a long shot, it's still an amazing resource when you figure he's been updating it on a regular basis since its inception. You won't find tons and tons of links in each subject category here. But the sites included in the list, heavily weighted toward academic resources, all have something tangible to offer—beyond being eye candy.

You won't find a search engine here. The list is meant to be browsed. The topics are presented in alphabetical order in three parts, on three separate pages. Interestingly, Yanoff has not forgotten that valuable resources are available in those sometimes-forgotten parts of the Internet outside the realm of the World Wide Web. So you'll also find pointers here to gopher, telnet, and FTP sites, as well as to mail servers.

An online form is available for anyone who would like to submit a site. Yanoff's guidelines are simple:

> The Internet SERVICES List is for FREE services. Please do not submit any site that is a company, advertisement/promotion, adult-oriented, or is SELLING/PROMOTING products or services. You will NOT be added to the list!

So in spite of the fact that the Internet Services List is now housed on a commercial server—that of Yanoff's employer—it may well be the *only* strictly noncommercial subject directory on the Internet these days. And if only for that reason, it's worth a visit and a bookmark.

Other General Resource Collections

By no means have we looked at all the subject catalogs available on the Web. I've tried to hit the major ones, but I've probably left out someone's favorite. Sorry. Here's what I consider to be the best of the rest. If you're feeling a need to break out of your usual surfing routine and would like to try exploring the Web from a new jump station—which may increase your chances of stumbling onto one of those serendipitous finds that keep us coming back for more—any of the following sites are worth a try.

The Awesome Lists

John Makulowich, a journalist and Internet trainer, maintains his own small collection of resources he thinks are Truly Awesome or just plain Awesome (**http://www.clark.net/pub/journalism/awesome.html**). Both sections are simple, alphabetically organized lists of links. The emphasis is on quality rather than quantity. Makulowich updates the site regularly, and I check periodically

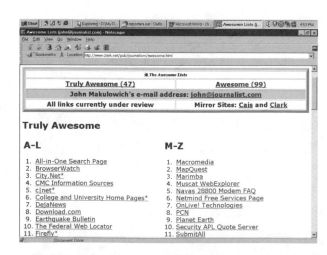

If you do Internet presentations for public groups, Truly Awesome is not a bad choice as a jump station.

to make sure there isn't some awesome new resource I somehow managed to miss.

Nerd World Media

At Nerd World Media's top page (**http://www. nerdworld.com/**), you can browse either of two subject trees: Leisure Categories or Knowledge Categories. Or you can start with an Easy Access Category Tree, in table form (**http://www. nerdworld.com/cattree.html**). Either way, it's easy to navigate here, among approximately 275,000 links. The collection is an eclectic mixture—educational, commercial, and recreational—with links to Usenet newsgroups and FTP archives as well as Web sites.

If you like what you see here, the folks at Nerd World will assist you in creating your own Internet subject index. It's actually a link to a personalized version of Nerd World Media. Interesting concept. You fill out an online form, and they send you a few lines of HTML code that you place on your own home page to create a link to a personalized version of the Nerd World subject index on their server.

Don't have your own home page? Not a problem. Fill out the form, and "You will be sent a link to place in your browser's preferences that will let you view your personalized index every time you logon to the Internet."

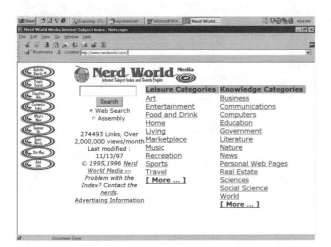

Links may be submitted by users, but Nerd World sends out a "Web robot" several times a week to bring in fresh material in bulk.

PC Magazine's Top 100 Web Sites

PC Magazine's Top 100 Web Sites (**http://www. zdnet.com/pcmag/special/web100/_open.html**), which appears in the publication from time to time, is updated periodically on its Web site. The list of subject headings isn't huge: Commerce, Computing, News, Entertainment, and Reference. The reference section is worth checking for links to add to your own virtual reference desk. You can view the entire collection of links at once, as an alphabetical list, if you so desire.

WebDictionary

Here's an interesting concept in Web directories. WebDictionary (**http://pantheon.cis.yale.edu/ ~jharris/webdict/webdict.html**) is arranged, like the traditional dead tree versions, in alphabetical order. Click on a letter of the alphabet and you see a list of words. Click on a word, and you're taken to an actual site somewhere on the Web that defines that word. The sites range from serious to silly, and the collection of words under every letter of the alphabet is quite extensive, although there's no search engine.

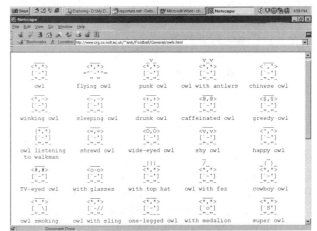

When you browse WebDictionary, you're absolutely guaranteed to run across something you probably wouldn't have found otherwise—like this wonderful collection of ASCII art owls, at **http://www.crg.cs. nott.ac.uk/~anb/Football/General/owls.html**, that popped up when I clicked on Owl.

Subject-Specific Meta-Sites

When it comes to using the Internet for research, less is usually more. A couple of really comprehensive, well-organized sites may be all you need. In this section, I'll describe a few especially well-regarded sites in two of the most popular research categories: business (including finance) and government (federal, state, and local).

Business and Finance

Business information that people are seeking on the Internet comes in several flavors—facts about individual businesses themselves (i.e., to prepare for a job interview); financial information (i.e., to research and manage investments); and information about business generally (i.e., research material in specific subject areas or industries).

For information about a specific company, first track down its Web site. Either try one of the major search engines (which may also lead you to things that have been written *about* that company) or make a guess as to the URL by trying the standard format *http://www.companyname.com*. Alternately, search in the NetPartners Company Site Locator (**http://www.netpart.com/company/search.html**), which makes use of the InterNIC's list of registered domain names. The advantage to using this tool, besides the simple interface, is that it will provide you with a list of all a company's registered domains.

If you had your heart set on owning the underarms.com domain name, you're already too late. Procter and Gamble has beaten you to it. (It grabbed up badbreath.com as well. Bummer . . .)

If it's a U.S. publicly owned company, snag its financial statements from the Securities and Exchange Commission's EDGAR database. WhoWhere? EDGAR (**http://edgar.whowhere.com/**) has a particularly user-friendly interface. (See chapter 7 for more information about this site.)

For individuals, the Syndicate (**http://www.itlnet.com/moneypages/syndicate/**) offers consumer information and a large collection of (annotated) personal finance links.

Researchers may want to bookmark the Reference Desk at CNN's Financial Network

(**http://www.cnnfn.com/resources/referencedesk/**); you can search Hoover's MasterList corporate directory, look for company Web sites, browse a glossary of business and finance terms, and link to a variety of ready reference resources and business-oriented government information sites.

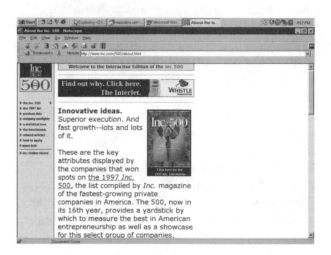

Be aware that it can be difficult to locate information about small companies, especially those that are privately held. One place to try is *Inc.* magazine's *Inc.* 500 (**http://www.inc.com/500/about.html**), which is an annual listing of America's fastest-growing private companies.

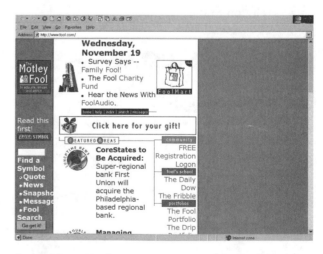

A good first stop for the individual investor is the Motley Fool (**http://www.fool.com/**). This is the Web incarnation of America Online's popular online financial forum. Besides current news, statistics, and analysis, you'll also find a model portfolio . . . and, in spite of the name, plenty of common sense.

More about Business and Finance

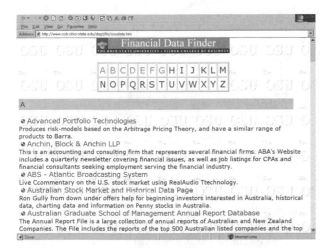

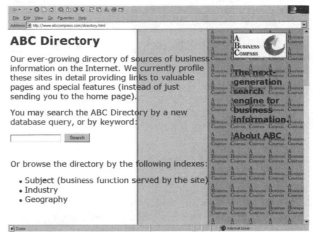

Those with a hankering for the hard stuff will want to visit the Financial Data Finder at Ohio State University's Department of Finance (**http://www.cob.ohio-state.edu/dept/fin/osudata.htm**). If it's a financial statistic and it's on the Internet (or lots of other places, for that matter), you'll find a link to it here. There's also a collection of pointers to large business libraries and some advice on Couch Potato Investing.

A Business Compass Directory (**http://www.abcompass.com/directory.html**) is a nicely organized collection of sites that are indexed in four ways: by business function, industry type, location, and language. The scope is international, and it attempts to be selective in the sites it includes.

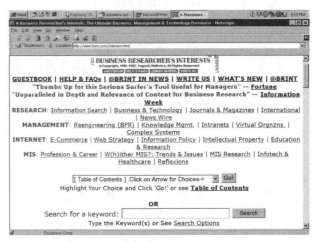

Don't miss the Investment FAQ home page (**http://www.invest-faq.com/**), a collection of frequently asked questions and answers about investments and personal finance, including stocks, bonds, options, discount brokers, information sources, retirement plans, life insurance, etc.—the collective wisdom of one of the oldest Usenet discussion groups, misc.invest. Here you'll find the entire multipart FAQ document that you can search online or print out, plus a large (annotated) collection of investment-related links.

A Business Researcher's Interests (**http://www.brint.com/interest.html**) has pretty much everything, according to Yoghesh Malhotra, its developer and maintainer: "The focal theme of this site is issues that are contemporary and have relevance to the future of the organizations and the business world."

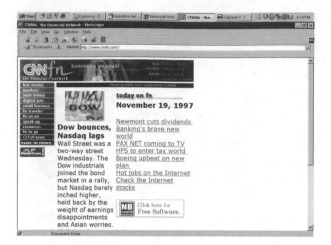

CNN Financial Network (**http://www.cnnfn.com/**) is a constantly updated repository of just about any type of business or financial news and information you could want or need.

Madalyn (**http://www.udel.edu/alex/mba/main/netdir2.html**) is a "business research tool" maintained by the University of Delaware's MBA program, featuring an annotated collection of resource links categorized by major business disciplines and information type.

Government

I have another secret to confess. When I worked in a public library, I was one of those reference librarians who—at the site of a patron approaching with a drawerful of *Federal Register* microfiche—suddenly remembered something that had to be done in the staff office. Working with government documents has long been a specialized niche of librarianship due to the unique knowledge and skill set required to locate government information and help people use it.

But now that so much government information is making its way onto the Internet, it's much easier for end users—and docu-phobes like me— to get to it. Alas, there's a downside. The sheer volume of information that's become available is overwhelming. How can you keep up with it? Where do you even start to look? How do you know which agency collects and disseminates the information you need? The smart thing to do is to rely on experts.

The most outstanding jump station for government information is the Federal Web Locator (**http://www.law.vill.edu/Fed-Agency/fedwebloc.html**), developed and maintained by Kenneth P. Mortensen, teaching fellow and director of operations at Villanova University Law School's Center for Information Law and Policy. This site is organized in the manner of that venerable ready-

reference item *The United States Government Manual* (searchable online, by the way, via the National Archives and Records Administration at **http://www.access.gpo.gov/nara/nara001.html**). The Locator is broken down into six main sections: Legislative Branch, Judicial Branch, Executive Branch (with Departments), Independent Agencies, Quasi Official Agencies, and Non-Governmental Federally Related Sites. The last two sections in particular make it easy to find less-well-known agencies and organizations that may prove useful for specific types of information— e.g., FinanceNet (the Federal Financial Information Network), the National Technology Transfer Center, and an assortment of international organizations, private-sector publishers of government information, and think tanks.

A solution to the "keeping up with" problem is available here, in the Latest Links section, which lists pointers to new government servers recently added to the Locator. And, mirabile dictu, there's a search engine available, and it supports the AND/OR Boolean operators. I was able to find a link to the Catalog of Federal Domestic Assistance (**http://www.gsa.gov/fdac/**) in one quick shot. Not too shabby for someone who used to break out in a cold sweat at the very thought of confronting a government document!

The U.S. Government Printing Office's GPO Access System, implemented in 1994, provides online access (free since December 1995) to a variety of key federal government databases—the Congressional Record, the Federal Register (1994 through the present), Economic Indicators, etc. (A complete list, with information and search tips, is available at **http://www.access.gpo.gov/su_docs/aces/aaces003.html**.) You can get to these through the GPO itself or via a number of Federal Depository Library Gateways (**http://www.access.gpo.gov/su_docs/aces/aaces004.html**), some of which are linked directly from the Federal Web Locator.

One commodity the government churns out in staggering quantity is statistics. And we all tend to ignore them as meaningless until we happen to have a specific need. It's sometimes extremely difficult to determine which agency is likely to have what you want. The University of Michigan Library Documents Center (**http://www.lib.umich.edu/libhome/Documents.center/stats.htm**) has taken the user-friendly approach of categorizing statistical sources by subject rather than agency. Select any topic—from agriculture to weather—and find links (annotated) to relevant government sources.

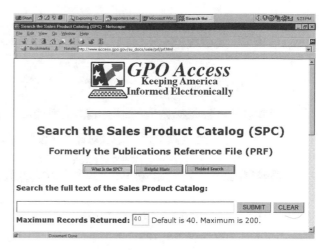

If you want to purchase a U.S. government publication, or if you want to check to see what's available in a given subject area, the GPO Access Sales Product Catalog (**http://www.access.gpo.gov/su_docs/sale/prf/prf.html**) is a choice fishing hole. Most government information products available for sale by the GPO are in this database. Fielded searching is supported here, as are the standard Boolean operators. Extensive online help is available.

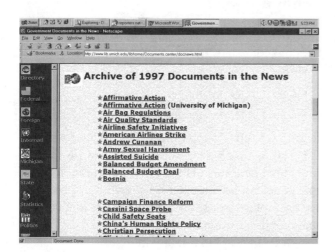

Another excellent starting point for government information is the University of Michigan Libraries Documents Center. The Documents in the News section provides annotated pointers to documents related to hot topics—from 1995 to the present. Do yourself a big favor and check here before scrounging around all over the Net for topical government information.

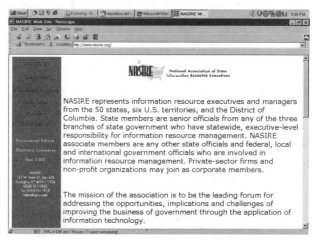

For state government information, the best one-stop-shopping site is StateSearch (**http://www.nasire.org/**), maintained by the National Association of State Information Resources Executives (NASIRE).

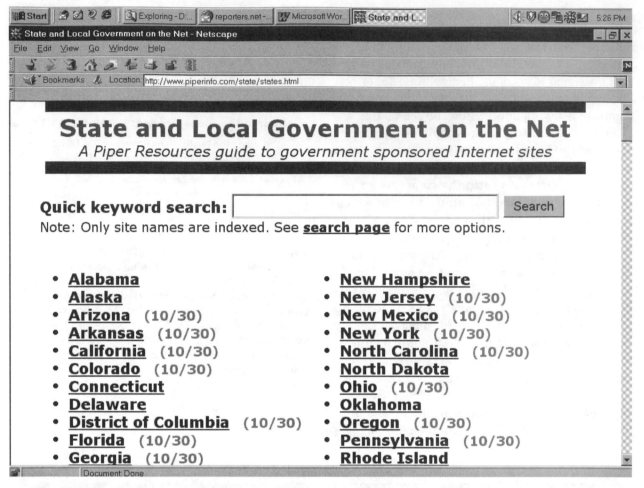

Piper Resources, publisher of a newsletter for government administrators, offers an excellent collection of pages called State and Local Government on the Net (**http://www.piperinfo.com/state/states.html**). It includes pointers to state and local government agencies and to a directory of U.S. chambers of commerce.

Full-Text State Statutes and Legislation on the Internet (**http://www.prairienet.org/~scruffy/f. htm**) is a collection of state laws, constitutions, etc., available online, with brief annotations by "Scruffy," the creator of this page. I have no idea who Scruffy is, but the list of links is useful.

If you enjoy this sort of thing, more of the same is served up by the Municipal Code Corporation (MCC) at **http://www.municode.com/**, which boasts "MCC is the nation's leading publisher of local government Codes of Ordinances. The company has published Codes for more than 2,500 cities and counties in 48 states." You won't find all 2,500 codes full text online here; the col-lection is kind of spotty. Probably because MCC is based in Tallahassee, there are lots of Florida municipal codes available. Each individual munic-ipal code can be searched by keyword or phrase— for example, you can look for all the ordinances that mention swimming pools.

Keep in mind that many individual counties and cities are now putting the full text of their ordinances on their own Web sites. Piper's State and Local Government on the Net provides a lot of direct links to city and county home pages. Alternately, try Yahoo! Get Local (**http://local. yahoo.com/local/**), where you can search by zip code or browse by individual state, city, or county.

4

Virtual Libraries and Newsrooms

What Librarians and Journalists Know

What's Here?

Why Librarians and Journalists?

What Librarians Know

Librarians' Index to the Internet
Edinburgh Engineering Virtual Library
INFOMINE
Internet Public Library

Reference Help for Students . . . and Teachers

Ready Reference Using the Internet
RiceInfo: Internet Navigation
School Librarian Links: Cruise Control for the Information Superhighway

The Art of Electronic Collection Development

Where the Wild Things Are: A Librarian's Guide to the Best Information on the Net
IMHO . . .

What Journalists (and News Researchers) Know

Barbara's News Researcher's Page
The Poynter Institute for Media Studies
The Beat Page et Al.
Finding Data on the Internet: A Journalist's Guide
David Milliron's Links to Searchable Databases
KSG One-Stop Journalist Shop
MediaSource
The *New York Times* Navigator
Wired Cybrarian

Why Librarians and Journalists?

I know a little something about both of these professions. I was a journalist for several years before I became a librarian. And now I move easily back and forth between these two occupations. It's no great mystery what they have in common: *information* and *people*.

By and large, the library profession "hit" on the Internet before the journalists did. Since Internet access was available earlier in (noncommercial) places where librarians worked—e.g., academic and research institutions—this is understandable. As more and more librarians piled onto the Internet to take advantage of its resources, something interesting happened. Librarians actually began creating resources for the Internet community to use. And since librarians know—by training and disposition—how to organize information to make it useful to those who need it, it's not surprising that so many of the most helpful and effective resources on the Internet are the work of library professionals.

The journalists came along later. In many ways, the Internet is a natural environment for them, since it's such a great ocean of people and information, journalism's stock and trade. The speed with which the profession as a whole has integrated Internet use into its skill set is quite remarkable. The number of highly useful Internet resources by and for journalists has grown astronomically, and a number of them hold treasured positions on my personal bookmark list.

One key fact to keep in mind: both librarians and journalists are dyed-in-the-wool skeptics when it comes to information—its quality and veracity. This alone should convince you to take a look at the Internet resources they find useful.

What Librarians Know

Virtual Reference Desks have been around at least since gopher was in its heyday. Intrepid librarians were tracking down useful Internet resources and arranging the links into user-friendly menu structures.

It's fairly obvious that the number of useful Internet resources has exploded right along with the so-called Internet Boom. At the same time, the amount of Net-based garbage has soared as well. But who's still out there pursuing quality, performing electronic collection development, organizing information to make it accessible? That's right.

Although this book is being published by the American Library Association, I have no way of knowing right now how diverse its readership will be. The public has an interesting perception of librarians, beyond the bun-and-glasses-on-a-chain stereotype. When I worked behind a public library reference desk, it was not at all uncommon to hear a satisfied patron say something like "You gals [ignoring the fact that we did have several male staff members] know everything." Wrong. (Just ask my teenage son.)

But we do know how to go about *finding* everything. While we're taught the basics in library school, on-the-job experience develops the intuition that tells us where to begin looking, where not to bother looking, whether a particular source is credible, etc. Although we receive our master's degree in library and information *science*, a large element of what we do is *art*, which is probably true to a greater or lesser extent for almost any profession.

So if you're a librarian reading this book, by all means take advantage of the wonderful resources your peers have already made available on the Internet—which extend well beyond the selection I'll describe here. If you're a nonlibrarian, please explore what our profession has to offer. Librarians have enriched the Internet in immeasurable ways—which can save you precious time and reduce your frustration level.

Librarians' Index to the Internet

Originally developed by the Berkeley (California) Public Library, the comprehensive Librarians' Index to the Internet (**http://sunsite.berkeley.edu/ InternetIndex/**) may well be the Mother of All Virtual Reference Desks. You'll find this very easy to navigate. Browsable by topic and searchable, it's a comprehensive collection of pointers to useful Internet resources in a broad range of subject areas, purposefully selected by professional librarians. Great starting point.

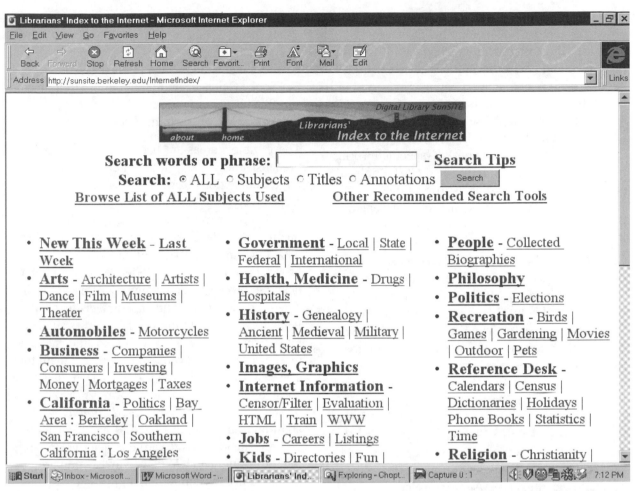

Unique feature here? Check the New This Week link for a selection of "The most informative and interesting new sites found on the Internet this past week." True enough.

Edinburgh Engineering Virtual Library

At the time I was working on this book, I was also working part-time in a science and engineering library, where I had been for less than six months. I needed to get up to speed quickly on worthwhile Internet resources for my clientele. As a strong proponent of the "don't reinvent the wheel" school of Internet research, I began hunting down existing engineering-oriented virtual libraries.

Edinburgh Engineering Virtual Library (**http://www.eevl.ac.uk/welcome.html**) is definitely one of the most comprehensive of such resources. EEVL (great acronym) is a British-based project of eLib (Electronic Library Programme), JISC (Joint Information Systems Committee), and the University Library and Institute for Computer Based Learning of Heriot-Watt University (Edinburgh). You'll find more than

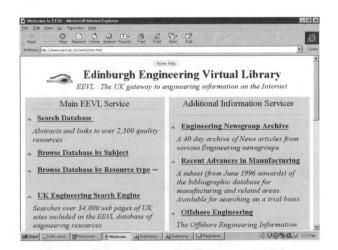

EEVL is more than simply a large collection of links. Each listing provides a general description of the resource, a link to a more detailed description, and a connection to the actual site.

2,300 browsable and searchable links here. For browsing, choose one of nine major categories—chemical, civil, electrical, mechanical, petroleum, materials, and environmental engineering, engineering design, and general engineering—and drill down through the subdivisions.

Fairly sophisticated searching options allow users to specify both resource type and whether they wish to see UK- or non-UK-specific information. The standard AND, OR, and NOT Boolean operators are supported, as is truncation.

If you do much research in science and engineering, you may also want to bookmark the University of Virginia Science and Engineering Libraries site (**http://www.lib.virginia.edu/science/SELhome.html**). There's a little jewel here called Brief Guide to Engineering Information on the WWW, which I found helpful, and a link to Frank Potter's Science Gems (**http://www-sci.lib.uci.edu/SEP/SEP.html**), a remarkable collection of more than two thousand science-related Internet links sorted by category, subcategory, and grade level. ("Frank Potter is my name. Physics is my profession.")

Yet another specialized virtual library that will knock your socks off is the one for Maps and References at the University of Iowa Center for Global and Regional Environmental Research (**http://www.cgrer.uiowa.edu/servers/servers_references.html**). If it's on the Internet and it's remotely related to maps, you'll find a link to it here. (Which is why I included it, even if it wasn't created by librarians.)

- Maps and GIS
- Physical Sciences, Engineering, Computing, and Math
- Regional and General Interest
- Social Sciences and Humanities (Reference, Business, Literature . . .)
- Visual and Performing Arts

These subject areas are listed in order of comprehensiveness; the first two areas contain the largest collections of resources—1,500 and 1,300, respectively.

This is far from just a huge list of links. For one thing, all the links are annotated and indexed, which facilitates a variety of access points for both browsers and searchers. Under each major subject heading, browsers may prowl by date (e.g., What's New), title, table of contents (subjects listed alphabetically), subject (Library of Congress subject terms), and keyword. Searching by title, subject, or keyword is also available under each main topic. The search engine is quite sophisticated. It supports "nested" Boolean options—*(proteins or sequences or DNA or RNA or genetic) and databases*—in addition to the simple AND/OR and truncation with the standard wild-card character (*). Searching, browsing, and a What's New section are available under each major subject heading.

You'll find additional "one-stop" links to ready-reference information (such as acronyms, time zones, dictionaries, currency converters, etc.); Internet search tools (emphasizing those the

INFOMINE

INFOMINE (**http://lib-www.ucr.edu/**) could well be the premier academic virtual library. It got its start in 1994 as a project of the Library of the University of California, Riverside, and contains somewhere around 10,000 links to substantive databases, guides to the Internet for most academic disciplines, textbooks, conference proceedings, journals, and other resources. The broad subject classifications included here are:

- Biological, Agricultural, and Medical Sciences
- Government Information
- Instructional Resources—K–12
- Instructional Resources—University
- Internet Enabling Tools (Help, HTML, Finding Tools . . .)

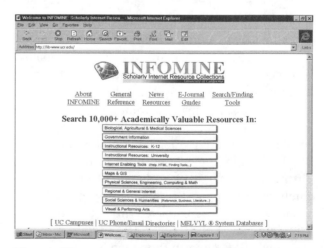

There is almost too much information here, except the documentation available at the site is extensive and well written, and the resources are logically organized for easy navigation.

INFOMINE development team has relied upon to build and maintain this resource); news resources; and a collection of guides to scholarly e-journals.

For each individual item in INFOMINE, there's a search button that says Click for Terms Leading to Related Resources. The resulting display shows all related subject and keywords (all clickable links to more related resources) and an annotation describing the resource.

Not every resource described and indexed in INFOMINE is Internet accessible. Some are "local resources" that are available only on CD-ROM in University of California System libraries (or possibly in a large public or academic library near you; something to keep in mind). For these non-Internet resources, you'll find just a description without a live link to an actual URL.

Serious information junkies could get lost for months rummaging around in INFOMINE. ("Just slide the pizza under the door, thanks. . . .") I find it extremely useful as a starting point for specialized government information; a subject or keyword search will turn up some likely resources, with a paragraph or so of descriptive material to tell you exactly what a particular directory, database, etc., contains. This assistance is invaluable if you don't work with government documents on a regular basis. Similarly, INFOMINE is a good launchpad for research in scholarly subject areas where your personal knowledge is not strong. Each resource here is handpicked and described by a subject-area expert, which is a major indicator of quality.

books, and magazines; a classroom, with links to Internet tutorials; a section with resources of interest to librarians and other information professionals; a directory and tour; and pointers to Web search engines, with descriptions of each. Personally, I enjoy the Exhibit Hall, which features a changing collection of both locally mounted and remotely linked art and museum exhibitions.

A number of "special collections" and features are real jewels:

- Associations on the Net (**http://www.ipl.org/ref/AON/**) contains more than five hundred Internet links to a wide variety of professional and trade associations, cultural and art organizations, political parties and advocacy groups, labor unions, academic societies, and research institutions. Descriptive information about each association and its site is provided.
- POTUS (**http://www.ipl.org/ref/POTUS/**), an acronym for *Presidents of the United States,* offers background information, election results, cabinet members, presidency highlights, and some odd facts on each of the presidents. You'll also find links to biographies, historical documents, audio and video files, and other presidential sites.
- If you're not savvy about Internet acronyms, you might assume the Internet Public Library MOO (**http://www.ipl.org/moo/**) has something to do with cows. Wrong. MOO stands for *Multi-User Object Oriented* environment, an interactive system accessible by telnet,

Internet Public Library

The Internet Public Library, IPL (**http://www.ipl.org/**), which bills itself as "the first public library of and for the Internet community," originated in a graduate seminar at the University of Michigan's School of Information and Library Studies in the winter 1995 semester. Since that time, it's gone from a student project to a thriving freestanding entity, supported by grant funding and employing a full-time staff.

The IPL utilizes a generally familiar public library metaphor for navigation (users can choose a graphical or a text-based interface). There's a reference department; sections for teens and kids; a reading room, with links to online newspapers,

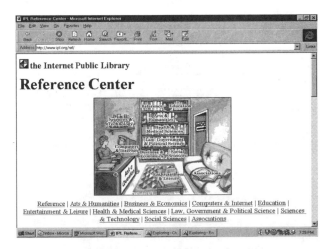

Click on the librarian's desk and type out a reference question to a real, live librarian!

where information seekers and librarians can interact in real time. Regular reference service on the MOO (a pilot project) has been discontinued, although librarians are periodically available at erratic times to answer questions. The service may resume again in the future.

- The Youth Division offers an ever-changing online story hour and a Science Fair Project Resource Guide (**http://www.ipl.org/youth/ projectguide/**). The Teen Division includes an Issues and Conflicts section with annotated links to resources about such topics as abuse, cultural diversity, disabilities, driver education, gangs, and sexuality.

- The IPL Reference Center (**http://www.ipl. org/ref/**) graphical front end features a "sensitive map," where users may click on the appropriate part of a reference room image in order to access different resource areas.

Reference Help for Students . . . and Teachers

Ready Reference Using the Internet

While this resource may not look exciting from a visual standpoint, it's an incredible collection of full-text resources and databases suitable for ready reference. Developed and maintained by Ellen

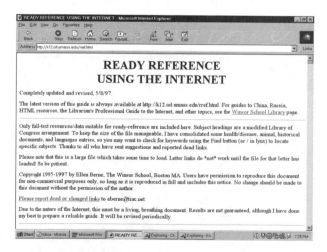

If your library serves a research paper–writing student population, you'll probably want to bookmark Ellen Berne's collection of Internet ready-reference links.

Berne, library director at the Winsor School in Boston, Ready Reference Using the Internet (**http://k12.oit.umass.edu/rref.html**) can be a bit tough to navigate; it's essentially a long listing of links arranged in alphabetical order, according to modified Library of Congress subject terms. There is no search engine. An alphabet navigation aid at the top contains live links to take you to the appropriate parts of the list; however, Berne does warn, "Please note that this is a large file which takes some time to load. Letter links do *not* work until the file for that letter has loaded! So be patient." Berne has added brief annotations to each link, which are always helpful, and the majority of the pointers are to resources appropriate for different areas of the K–12 curriculum, especially for middle and high school.

A related resource, new and fairly promising, is Researchpaper.com (**http://www.researchpaper. com/**), which claims to be "the Web's largest collection of topics, ideas, and assistance for school related research projects." Old Dominion University Library's Start Your Research Here site (**http://www.lib.odu.edu/start/index.html**) is an academic library's noncommercial take on the same thing. It consists of a variety of keywords and phrases under nine subject headings: Arts and Humanities; Business and Public Administration; Education; Engineering and Technology; Health Sciences; Physical and Biological Sciences; Psychology; Social Sciences; and Sports, Recreation, and Leisure. The Idea Generator (**http://www.lib. odu.edu/idea/ideagenerator.html**) is a help for someone who is really stuck for a topic.

There's an Idea Directory, with more than two thousand suggested topics; a Writing Center, with a growing collection of help for planning and executing research papers; and a Discussion Area, with bulletin boards where you can post questions, discuss your project with others who are working on something similar, and share useful Web resources.

Researchpaper.com is a free offering of Infonautics Corporation (**http://www.infonautics. com/**), a purveyor of various online information and research services, including the subscription-based Electric Library (**http://www.elibrary. com/**), designed for home and family use. For a monthly fee, this offers online access to hundreds of full-text magazines, newspapers and newswires, maps, pictures, TV and radio transcripts. Libraries and schools can purchase site licenses. (You can search here for free; citations include article title, author, publication title, date, and reading level.)

RiceInfo: Internet Navigation

RiceInfo (**http://riceinfo.rice.edu/Internet/**) began its virtual life as a gopher—indeed, a subject tree gopher that was one of the most useful resources of its day. The Web version is pretty cool, too, and the librarians here have not forgotten that plenty of valuable Internet resources are not Web based. The hidden gem? Rice's Subject Guides to Internet Resources (**http://www.rice.edu/Fondren/Netguides/netguides.html**). Each guide is tagged with a color-coded dot to indicate whether it was created by a member of the library staff, a university department, or an individual at the university. These vary in quality, from simple lists of links to annotated pathfinders.

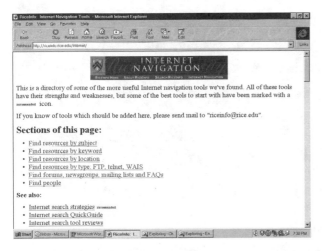

RiceInfo's navigation scheme is simple, geared toward the type of resource a user wants to find.

School Librarian Links: Cruise Control for the Information Superhighway

Although designed as "an all-in-one reference site for school librarians and teachers new to locating resources on the Internet," School Librarian Links (**http://www.yab.com/~cyberian/**) is a nicely organized, easy-to-navigate collection of links that are useful for everything from doing online research to learning about the Internet and integrating it into school curriculums. Most of the links include brief annotations. Folks who are involved in bringing Internet access to any kind of public institution for the first time will want to take a look at the section of pointers to information about acceptable-use policies and censorship. This site was developed by Kathleen Gentili, Peoria Unified School District librarian, Glendale, Arizona.

Another site geared primarily toward the K–12 community and offering a nicely maintained collection of pointers to a variety of quality Internet resources is Kathy Schrock's Guide for Educators (**http://www.capecod.net/Wixon/wixon.htm**). Schrock—a library media specialist at N. H. Wixon Middle School in Dennis, Massachusetts—claims that she updates this site daily. Most of the links are briefly annotated, and Schrock has included online versions of Internet-related workshops and tutorials she's developed. Grant seekers should be sure to check out her Grant Sources for Educators page (**http://www.capecod.net/Wixon/business/grants.htm**).

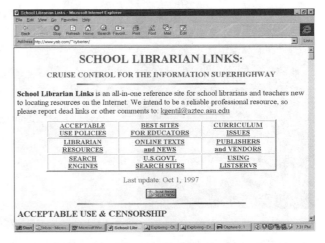

If you work with the K–12 community, you'll want to bookmark School Librarian Links.

The Art of Electronic Collection Development

Where the Wild Things Are: A Librarian's Guide to the Best Information on the Net

Another resource that emphasizes quality over quantity, Where the Wild Things Are (**http://www.sau.edu/CWIS/Internet/Wild/index.htm**) is maintained by Marylaine Block, a librarian at St. Ambrose University in Davenport, Iowa. Her subject categories tend to be more user-friendly than formal librarian-like, but her eye for excellent Internet resources is unparalleled. (I got lost for a while—definite occupational hazard—browsing one of her picks under Neat New Stuff I Found This Week.) Check out Unaccustomed As I Am

(**http://speeches.com/index.shtml**), a repository of speeches by well-known people, plus resources and tutorials for speechwriters, pointers to quotation sites, etc. Block has a very nice index to archives of images from art, nature, medicine, and science, and her Hot Paper Topics page is full of useful links for student researchers.

Another resource worth bookmarking is WebGEMS: A Guide to Substantive Web Resources (**http://www.fpsol.com/gems/webgems.html**), by Nancy O'Hanlon, a professional librarian turned Web publisher and consultant. The site features easy frames-based navigation and annotations for each of its nine-hundred-and-growing resources.

And, finally, don't miss Jenny's Cybrary to the Stars (**http://sashimi.wwa.com/~jayhawk/index.html**), home of the Librarians' Site du Jour.

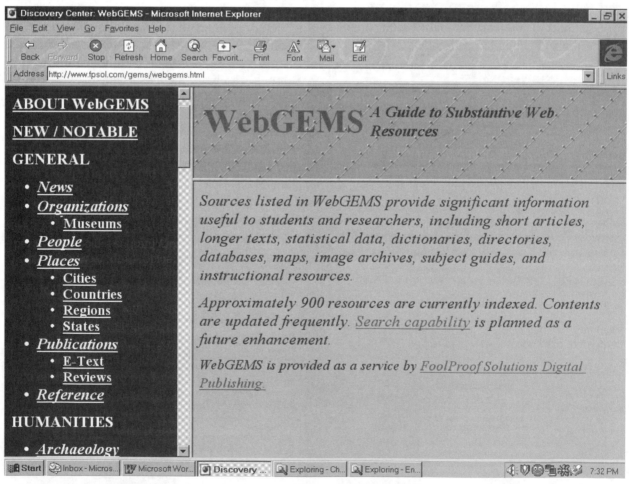

Nancy O'Hanlon, professional librarian turned Web consultant, plans to add searching capability to her WebGEMS collection.

("Always a site with *some* reference value"—true enough!) You'll also find a page of links called Internet Resources to Help Persuade Your Board of Trustees for Internet Access or a Library Web Site and a good selection of How to Stay Current in Cyberspace pointers. There's even a link to the daily *Dilbert* comic strip. ("I promise I won't tell your boss.") Jenny Levine is the Internet development specialist for the North Suburban Library System in Illinois.

IMHO . . .

. . . is a classic Internet acronym that stands for *In My Humble Opinion*. As a technical information specialist, Internet trainer and consultant, and someone who writes about the Internet on a regular basis, I turn to certain resources again and again.

A few of my favorite sites offer one-stop-shopping access to a whole bunch of Internet-accessible library catalogs:

- Eric Lease Morgan's Online Catalogs with Webbed Interfaces (**http://www.lib.ncsu.edu/ staff/morgan/alcuin/wwwed-catalogs.html**)
- Peter Scott's WebCATS: Library Catalogs on the World Wide Web (**http://library.usask.ca/ hywebcat/**)
- Scott's Hytelnet on the World Wide Web collection of telnet-accessible library catalogs (**http://library.usask.ca/hytelnet/**)—closing down, unfortunately.
- The gopher-based collection of links to library catalogs and library science resources at **gopher://peg.cwis.uci.edu:7000/11/gopher. welcome/peg/LIBRARIES/**

The following are some of my other top choices.

LIBRARY OF CONGRESS
WWW/Z39.50 GATEWAY

Yes, I do Windows. What I don't do is cataloging. I go instead (**http://lcweb.loc.gov/z3950/ gateway.html**) to the LC and other Z39.50-compliant catalogs. (The national standard Z39.50 defines a protocol for computer-to-computer information retrieval; Z39.50 makes it possible for a user in one system to search and retrieve informa-

tion from other Z39.50-compliant systems without knowing the unique search syntax used by those other systems.) I also double-check citations here when I'm sending out interlibrary loans and use it to see if a newer edition of some book I'm thinking of purchasing has been published yet.

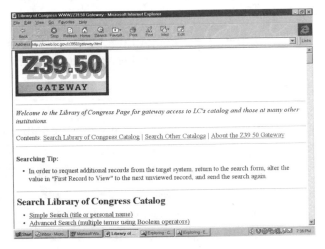

Here you'll find Web-based access not only to the Library of Congress database but also to library catalogs at scores of other institutions—from Acadia University in Nova Scotia to Yale University in Connecticut.

CARL UNCOVER WEB

Search the CARL UnCover Web database (**http:// uncweb.carl.org/**) of seventeen thousand periodicals and get citations. It's one of those amazing free treasures that make the Internet such a joy.

If you need an article in a hurry, you can order it right online with CARL UnCover Web.

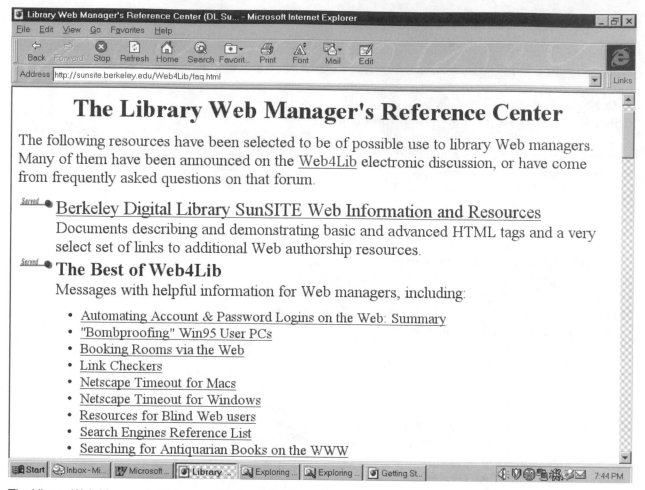

The Library Web Manager's Reference Center (**http://sunsite.berkeley.edu/Web4Lib/faq.html**) is Roy Tennant's resource for library Web managers, an offshoot from the Web4Lib e-mail discussion list, with tons of information about library uses of the Internet. You can link to the searchable Web4Lib archives, too.

PROFESSIONAL ORGANIZATIONS IN THE INFORMATION SCIENCES

At **http://witlioof.sjsu.edu/organizations.html**, one-stop shopping is provided for professional library and information science association Web sites. Why waste time searching around for these yourself?

ST. JOSEPH COUNTY PUBLIC LIBRARY'S LIST OF PUBLIC LIBRARIES WITH INTERNET SERVICES

Want to get an idea how many public libraries are still running gopher servers? Is your institution thinking about putting up a Web page? Look here (**http://sjcpl.lib.in.us/homepage/PublicLibraries/PublicLibraryServers.html**) to see what other libraries are doing. (And then take a look at Eric Schnell's Writing for the Web: A Primer for Librarians, at **http://bones.med.ohio-state.edu/eric/papers/primer/webdocs.html**.)

LIBRARY JOB POSTINGS ON THE INTERNET

If you're a librarian looking for work, Library Job Postings on the Internet (**http://www.sils.umich.edu/~nesbeitt/libraryjobs.html**), by Sarah L. Nesbeitt, Maxwell Library, Bridgewater State College, appears to be the most comprehensive source of library and information science employment listings and related pointers. Browse geographically or by type of library or position. The site is updated frequently.

What Journalists (and News Researchers) Know

Every working journalist plays his or her own version of Beat the Clock. Always, always, always, there's a deadline looming. Generally speaking, it's a profession in which there is no such thing as the luxury of time. Especially time to spend wandering around the Internet, that out-of-control info–flea market, searching in vain for a critical statistic, an appropriate expert source, the background material for that series. . . .

Almost from the beginning, journalists approached the Internet with a staunch "where's the beef?" attitude. And this mind-set persisted as those in the journalism profession were motivated to create their own Internet resources. Which is what makes so many of those resources worthwhile. By and large, you won't find eye candy or long lists of marginally useful links on journo Web sites. You'll find pointers to sites that offer *content*—content that has some practical value.

Barbara's News Researcher's Page

It seems appropriate, somehow, to segue from librarianship to journalism with a Web site created by folks who have a foot in each professional

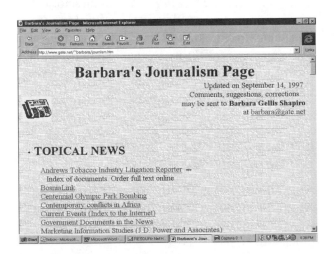

Barbara's Journalism Page, a subset of Barbara's News Researcher's Page, offers a very comprehensive collection of journalism and news-related links, including a number of links to news *archives* on the Web, which can sometimes be difficult to track down.

world. Barbara Gellis Shapiro, a systems trainer and librarian at the *Palm Beach Post* (**http://www.pbpost.com/**), has created a not-very-fancy but quite comprehensive and user-friendly news researcher's page (**http://www.gate.net/~barbara/**). You can browse the alphabetical list of topics and subtopics or use one of two quick-jump options. The page is updated regularly, and Shapiro places little New graphics next to recently added resources, which makes it easy for regular users (this is a Web site designed for a specific audience) to pick out the fresh stuff in each category.

The Poynter Institute for Media Studies and Other News Library Resources

For another take on news library Web pages, take a look at the Poynter Institute for Media Studies Library Research Center (**http://www.poynter.org/research/research.htm**).

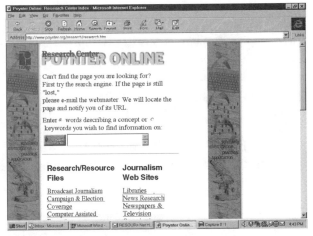

Poynter is a media research and continuing education institution; its research page is simple but elegant.

Very strong on resources dealing with contemporary issues in journalism, Poynter offers a number of relevant bibliographies on topics like media ethics, race and gender, world press, youth and the media. Many items cited in these bibliographies are available full text via live links. The Hot News/Hot Research section features pointers (with annotations) to Web sites that provide background information on current news topics.

For a well-designed, comprehensive academic journalism library, try Columbia University (**http://www.columbia.edu/acis/documentation/journ/journnew.html**), which I find somewhat easier to navigate than the more elaborate, frames-based University of North Carolina School of Journalism and Mass Communications Library (**http://sunsite.unc.edu/journalism/**). And while we're on the subject, the Special Libraries Association News Division home page (**http://sunsite.unc.edu/slanews/**), with an interesting array of resources, is worth a visit. Take a look at the Expert Sources link under Top Internet Sites for Journalists, (**http://sunsite.unc.edu/slanews/internet/experts.html**), compiled by Kitty Bennett of the *St. Petersburg Times* (**http://www.sptimes.com/**). There's also a good bibliography of essential reference books for news libraries here (**http://sunsite.unc.edu/slanews/reference/books.html**).

The Beat Page et Al.

Shawn McIntosh, at the *Dallas Morning News* (**http://www.dallasnews.com/**), organized the collection of resources on his Beat Page (**http://www.reporter.org/beat/**) according to the traditional breakdown of daily news reporting beats—e.g., business, defense, education, politics, etc. This makes the page very easy to navigate—clean interface, no huge graphics to load. Alas, you won't find helpful annotations for the various

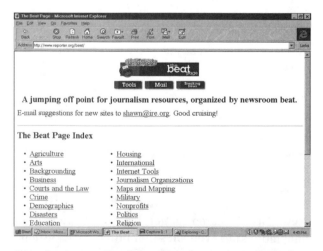

Organized according to traditional newsroom "beats," the Beat Page is simple to navigate.

links, a feature you tend to find more often on Web sites created by librarians.

Cool feature? The three buttons at the top—Tools, Mail, Breaking News. Tools include links to Internet search and navigation tools, journalism organizations, basic reference tools, etc. Mail features information about and live e-mail links to journalism-related Internet mailing lists (plus STUMPERS, the "difficult reference question" list for librarians). Finally, Breaking News has pointers to the appropriate sections of the CNN, CBS, AP, and other Web sites.

A somewhat-less-elaborate take on the same theme is the Reporter's Internet Survival Guide (**http://www.qns.com/~casey/**), created and maintained by Patrick Casey, who is with the Associated Press in Oklahoma City. Ditto for Scoop Cybersleuth's Internet Guide (**http://scoop.evansville.net/**), from the *Evansville (Indiana) Courier* (**http://www.evansville.net/newsweb/**). There's a nice collection of pointers to resources for children under the Kids Room link (**http://www.evansville.net/kidsroom.html**).

Dean Tudor, a journalism professor at Ryerson Polytechnic University in Toronto, keeps an extensive list of computer-assisted reporting links at **http://www.ryerson.ca/~dtudor/carcarr.htm**, including a selection of pointers to Canadian-oriented resources. Julian Sher, a producer with the Canadian Broadcasting Corporation's investigative TV show *The Fifth Estate,* a director of the Computer Assisted Reporting caucus of the Canadian Association of Journalists, and the Net columnist for *MEDIA* magazine, maintains an excellent site called Journalism Net (**http://www.journalismnet.com/**).

Finding Data on the Internet: A Journalist's Guide

Are journalists cynical? Here's what Robert Niles, creator of Finding Data on the Internet: A Journalist's Guide (**http://nilesonline.com/data/links.shtml**), has to say:

> [Y]ou can use the Internet to check facts and download reputable data on everything from aircraft safety to campaign contributions, medical research to crime statistics . . . you name it. Don't end up being the next Pierre Salinger.

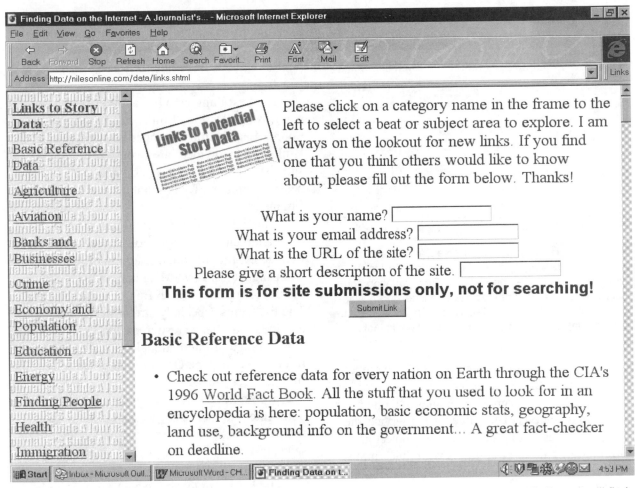

Although Finding Data on the Internet was created to meet the needs of journalists, researchers of all types will find it to be a handy jump station for diverse sources of statistical information.

Learn how to take advantage of the Internet before someone uses it to take advantage of you.

Salinger, of course, was taken in by a free-floating Internet rumor about TWA Flight 800 supposedly being shot down, in the summer of 1996, by an enemy missile. This scandal sparked an ongoing debate about how rumors spread—and get squelched—on the Internet.

Niles has selected a variety of high-quality Internet-accessible sources of hard facts and statistics, mainly from the U.S. government. He has arranged these conveniently by topic—from agriculture to weather—and added small annotations to each link. What's more, Niles offers a very readable and informative introduction to basic statistics, Statistics Every Writer Should Know

(**http://nilesonline.com/stats/**), in which he defines basic statistical terms and explains how not to get "taken in" by numbers. I can't think of *anybody* who would not learn something from reading this. Bravo!

David Milliron's Links to Searchable Databases

In the "just the facts, ma'am" department, we have David Milliron's Links to Searchable Databases (**http://www.lib.msu.edu/corby/reference/milliron.htm**). Milliron is a special projects editor with Gannett News Service, and he compiled these links in the early summer of 1996; Kate Corby, a bibliographer and reference librarian at Michigan State University, turned Milliron's links

David Milliron's Links to Searchable Databases includes unusual, interesting stuff like the Aviation Medical Examiners Database, the National Transportation and Safety Board's Accident Reports and Briefs, FAA Aviation Airworthiness Alerts, Calculators Online, toxic substances databases, and lots of people-finding tools.

into a Web page and updated them in September 1996. Most of these are fairly stable resources maintained by government agencies and other large organizations. The value-added service she performed was to organize them by subject area into kind of a table of contents with quick jumps. As a result, this is a very handy one-stop-shopping site to a whole raft of useful (free) reference sources and databases.

KSG One-Stop Journalist Shop

Adrianne Kaufmann, at Harvard University's John F. Kennedy School of Government (KSG), is responsible for the KSG One-Stop Journalist Shop (**http://ksgwww.harvard.edu/~ksgpress/journpg.htm**). The collection of links isn't as large as those at some other sites, but there are some good writing resources and a nice Perspectives on Journalism section, with links to professional journals, essays, and media criticism.

MediaSource

MediaSource (**http://www.mediasource.com/**) is a large commercial site with diverse and rather interesting offerings. The proprietors are attempting to build "an on-line shopping mall . . . for

journalists." What's really going on is that companies, law firms, and others are being encouraged to include (for a fee) their press kits and other public relations materials for journalists to browse (for free).

The best thing here by far right now is an extensive collection of links called Journalists' Source List (**http://www.mediasource.com/Links.html**), divided into twenty sometimes-surprising categories: Art and Architecture; Business; Computers; Demographics and Population; Engineering and Science; 50 States; Geography; Government, Politics and Political Science; History; Humanities; Information References and Resources; International; Journalism; Languages and Linguistics; Law; Medicine and Health; Music; Religions; Search Engines; and Sports. The list seems especially strong in business, engineering, and science resources and also in links to a wide range of international resources, including foreign newspapers. Obscure but potentially useful resources are scatted throughout the list—I, for one, would never have thought to check the Stockholm International Peace Research Institute (**http://www.sipri.se/**) for information about arms sales, production, military expenditures, chemical and biological weapons, etc.

The list is not terribly easy to use—another case of one long page that requires a significant amount of scrolling. Jumps are provided, however, from the major topic headings. And it's pretty interesting to browse.

The New York Times *Navigator*

In the words of the developer and maintainer of this resource, Rich Meislin, senior editor for information and technology for the *New York Times:*

> Navigator is the home page used by the newsroom of The New York Times for forays into the Web. Its primary intent was to give reporters and editors new to the Web a solid starting point for a wide range of journalistic functions without forcing each of them to spend time hacking around blindly to find a useful set of links of their own. Its secondary purpose was to show people that there's a lot of fun and useful stuff going on out there.

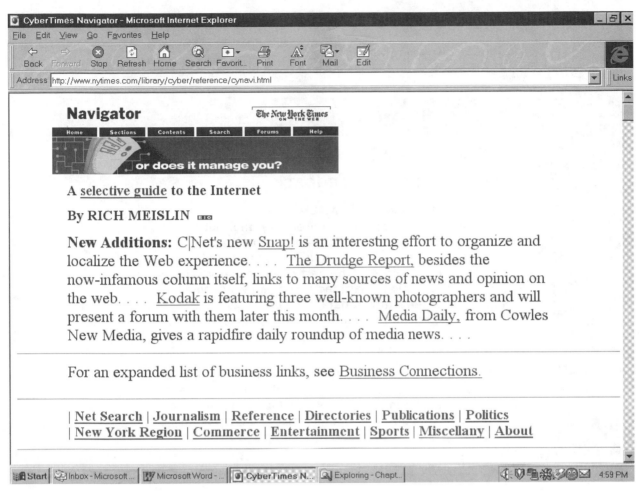

Note that you must register to access the *New York Times* Navigator as well as other parts of the newspaper's Web site, but it's free and definitely worth the small effort.

Look to the newspaper itself as an example of what you *won't* find here—lots of glitzy graphics and strange special effects. Navigator (**http://www.nytimes.com/library/cyber/reference/cynavi.html**) is basically a list of resources that Meislin feels represent the best of what the Web has to offer. The list is divided into ten major categories: Net Search, Journalism, Reference, Publications, Politics, New York Region, Commerce, Entertainment, Sports, and Miscellany. For each site included under each category, there's a brief annotation as to what it offers. It's frequently updated, too, so it's a good place to check for the latest and greatest of what's new and worthwhile.

Wired Cybrarian

Okay, since you've stuck with me through this whole long chapter, I'll share a secret with you. My favorite virtual reference desk was *not* created by librarians. It was created by Roderick Simpson, an associate producer for Wired Online, the cyberspace component of *Wired* magazine.

Granted, *Wired* sometimes makes me want to scream because of its hip pretentiousness—or rush to the ophthalmologist when its off-the-wall typography collides head-on with my middle-aged eyes. But Wired Cybrarian (**http://www.wired.com/cybrarian/**), a research tool built especially for the editorial staff of the magazine, features a

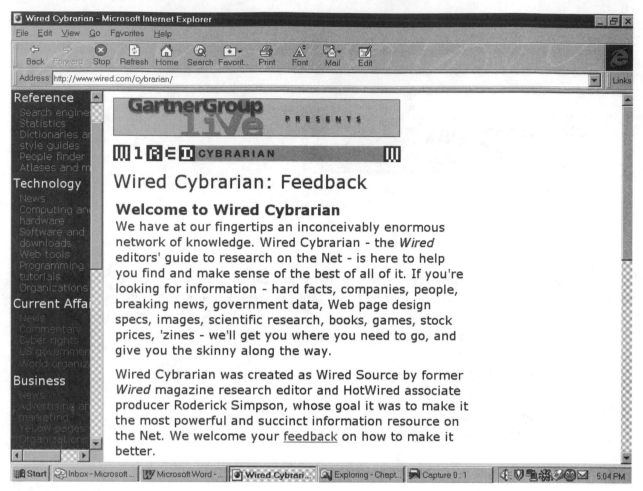

Every link in the Wired Cybrarian collection of reference links is annotated.

handpicked collection of pointers to excellent resources of all types. The design is subdued; navigation is easy via a small table-of-contents-type frame on the left side that delineates the main subject categories: search engines, indexes, reference desk, People Finder, news (papers, wires, personalized services), magazines, Web zines, Press Pass (of interest to journalists), Cyber Rights (telecommunications issues), Net and Tech Organizations, business, stock market, companies, government, politics, science (very extensive), libraries(!), education, television, music, film, literature, and fine arts.

Every link is annotated. In some cases, it's possible to search a remote resource right from Wired Source, via text or drop-down boxes. The site is well maintained and regularly updated; new things are added and dead things are removed on a continuing basis. Users can suggest potential additions via an online form.

[A]s the Net continues to expand and change, as new tools and indices are developed, Wired Source will change with it.

And it will continue to be near the top of my personal bookmark list for a long time.

5

Major Web Search Engines

The Big Guns

What's Here?

AltaVista

Excite

HotBot

Infoseek

Lycos

Open Text Index

WebCrawler

Northern Light

In the course of writing this book, I posted queries to a few Internet mailing lists where large numbers of Net-savvy people hang out (CARR-L, NETTRAIN, Web4Lib). One of the questions I asked was "Which search engine do you use most often and why?" What I got back was no clear consensus, except for the fact that virtually no experienced Internet searcher relies on just a single Web search engine. "I just keep moving from one to another until I find what I need" was definitely the modus operandi of choice.

There were some definite favorites. AltaVista probably got the most votes, followed closely by Infoseek. As of November 1997, HotBot's popularity was up considerably, due largely to an increase in the size of its database and its revamped, user-friendly interface. Several people mentioned specifically that they did not like WebCrawler at all, although a couple of folks raved about it. A few people said they liked to start with the search engine in Yahoo! (discussed in detail in chapter 3) simply because the number of hits returned was smaller, due to the limited size of Yahoo!'s database. Others complained that Yahoo! had gotten "too commercial" or was too full of "dead links." Meanwhile, a newcomer to the search scene, Northern Light (**http://www.nlsearch.com/**), has been garnering rave reviews due to its precision and the organized way it presents its results, including hits from commercial, non-Web-based sources that are available online for very nominal fees.

Receiving too few hits is almost always less of a problem with Web search tools than receiving too many hits. You can definitely improve your search results if you take the time to learn the ins and outs of the different search engines. All of them offer extensive online help, but the average

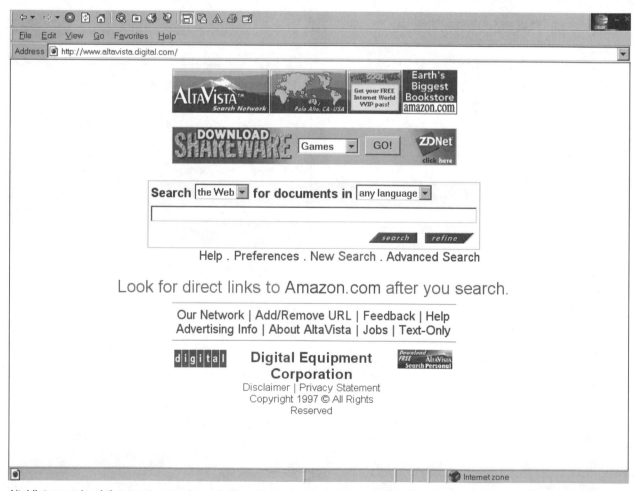

AltaVista received the most votes in my informal survey on search engines. It recently added a rudimentary language translation feature.

person doesn't bother to read it. No, more typically, some poor yutz planning his spring break types the word *Florida* into AltaVista and gets back seven million hits. But we know better. Or at least we will after we finish this chapter.

I certainly don't plan to get into a whole tutorial about the research process in this chapter. Nor do I propose to include a lot of geeky details about the technical workings of search engines. They all function in a similar manner. Each incorporates a software program called a spider or a robot that travels continually from server to server all around the Web, scanning URLs, page titles, and, sometimes, every word and image on every page, building a massive index. Because each one of these big guns employs proprietary ("secret") algorithms to build its index, running the identical search on all of them will produce vastly different results, which is why search pros tend not to fixate on any one search engine.

You don't need to know a whole lot about this stuff in order to use one of these tools to find something fast. You *do* need to know about the different options these search engines offer, since that's how you can fine-tune your query to optimize your results. But you can safely ignore the self-serving chest-thumping you'll find in the documentation at every one of these sites. Aw, shucks . . . wouldn't the Web be dull without a little hype?

AltaVista

It's big. It's fast. And it has a ton of bells and whistles. If I can't find it with AltaVista (**http://www.altavista.digital.com/**), my knee-jerk conclusion is that it can't be found on the Web. One of the things I like best about AltaVista is the number of nifty options available from its simple search interface alone.

You can do a quick phrase search by enclosing your keywords in quotation marks: "*fins to the left.*"

You can mandate that a particular word appear in each document in the search results by putting a plus sign (+) in front of it. Or, conversely, exclude a particular word by putting a minus sign (−) in front of it. (Be sure not to leave any space

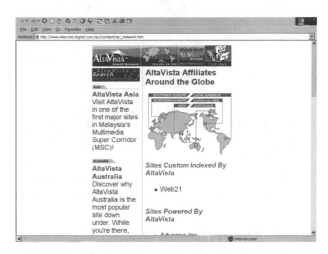

AltaVista got a face-lift in summer 1997. In 1998 it announced plans to add a directory service by partnering with Switchboard. AltaVista also has a network of mirror sites now, one on each continent except Antarctica. While penguins may be out of luck, you can choose the closest server.

between + or − and the word.) For example: *orange +juice −blossom.*

You can take advantage of case sensitivity. If you capitalize the first letter of your keywords, your results will include only pages where the words are likewise capitalized. (If you don't capitalize, you get back results that include both capitalized and lowercase keywords.) For example: "*Grand Old Flag.*"

You can use the wild-card character (*), even in the middle of keywords, provided three actual letters precede it: *Johns*n.*

And you can take advantage of a wide range of "constraining searches," as described in the online help (**http://www.altavista.digital.com/av/content/help.htm**):

- *anchor:click-here.* Matches pages with the phrase *click here* in the text of a hyperlink.
- *applet:NervousText.* Matches pages containing the name of the Java applet class found in an applet tag; in this case, NervousText.
- *object:Marquee.* Matches pages containing the name of the ActiveX object found in an object tag; in this case, Marquee.
- *host:digital.com.* Matches pages with the phrase *digital.com* in the host name of the Web server.

- *image:comet.jpg.* Matches pages with *comet. jpg* in an image tag.
- *link:thomas.gov.* Matches pages that contain at least one link to a page with *thomas.gov* in its URL.
- *text:algol68.* Matches pages that contain *algol68* in any part of the visible text of a page (the word is not in a link or an image, for example).
- *title:"The Wall Street Journal."* Matches pages with the phrase *The Wall Street Journal* in the title.
- *url:home.html.* Matches pages with the terms *home* and *html* together in the page's URL.

AltaVista also lets you search the archives of fourteen thousand Usenet newsgroups, incorporating even more constraining searches:

- *from:napoleon@elba.com.* Matches news articles with *napoleon@elba.com* in the From field.
- *subject:"for sale."* Matches news articles with the phrase *for sale* in the Subject field. (You can combine this with a word or phrase. For example, *subject:"for sale" "victorian chamber pots."*)
- *newsgroups:rec.humor.* Matches news articles posted (or cross-posted) in newsgroups with *rec.humor* in the name.
- *summary:invest*.* Matches news articles with the word *invest, investment, investiture,* etc., in the summary.
- *keywords:NASA.* Matches news articles with the word *NASA* in all caps in the keyword list.

Keep in mind that AltaVista archives Usenet postings for only a couple of weeks. If you need to go further back in time, use DejaNews. (See chapter 8.)

Remember, that's just AltaVista's simple search form. Try the advanced search form for some real power! The rules for defining words and phrases, capitalization, and wild cards are the same in advanced as in simple searches. You can use the same series of constraining searches detailed above. You must, however, use the actual Boolean operators—AND, OR, NOT, and NEAR—in the advanced search form. (Using NEAR retrieves documents in which, by default, the keywords are within ten words of each other.) Boolean operators can be typed in upper- or lower-

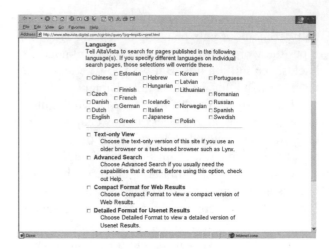

Besides a cleaner interface, the AltaVista folks have added a few new features to the advanced search form. Now there's a drop-down box that allows you to choose from twenty-five different languages, and your search results will include only documents published in that language. You can also customize AltaVista by using a Preferences feature to tell it to always present your results in a particular language, format, and level of detail.

case, or you can use the symbol & for AND, | for OR, ! for NOT, and ~ for NEAR. (If one of your keywords is the same as a Boolean operator, you need to enclose the keyword in parentheses.) You can construct a fairly complex search by using parentheses to group search expressions. As per the online help documents (**http://www.altavista. digital.com/av/content/help.htm**):

gold OR *silver* AND *platinum*
gold OR (*silver* AND *platinum*)
(*gold* OR *silver*) AND *platinum*

The first two queries are equivalent. They return documents containing both *silver* and *platinum,* together with documents containing *gold.* If you want the search to find documents containing *platinum* and, in addition, in the same document, either *gold* or *silver,* you must use the third query pattern.

NOT *gold* AND *silver*
(NOT *gold*) AND *silver*
NOT (*gold* AND *silver*)

The first two queries are equivalent. They return documents containing *silver* but not *gold.* If you want the search to eliminate documents that contain both *gold* and *silver,* you must use the third query pattern.

gold NEAR *silver* AND *platinum*
(gold NEAR *silver)* AND *platinum*
(gold NEAR *silver)* AND *(gold* NEAR *platinum)*

The first two queries are equivalent. They return documents containing *gold* located close to *silver,* and, in addition, in the same document, the word *platinum.* If you want the search to find documents containing *gold* located close to *silver* and, in addition, in the same document, *gold* close to *platinum,* you must use the third query pattern.

NOT *gold* NEAR *silver*
NOT *(gold* NEAR *silver)*
silver AND NOT *(gold* NEAR *silver)*

The first two queries are equivalent. They eliminate from the search all documents containing *silver* located close to *gold.* If you want the search to find documents containing *silver* but want to eliminate those that contain *gold* located close to *silver,* you must use the third query pattern.

gold NEAR *silver* OR *platinum*
(gold NEAR *silver)* OR *platinum*

The two queries above are equivalent. They find documents containing *gold* located close to *silver,* together with documents containing *platinum.*

gold NEAR *(silver* OR *platinum)*
(gold NEAR *silver)* OR *(gold* NEAR *platinum)*

The two queries above are equivalent. They find documents containing *gold* located close to *silver,* together with documents containing *gold* located close to *platinum.*

You can use the Ranking text box to type in words or phrases that are especially important to your query. What this means is that documents containing those specific words or phrases will be ranked higher in your search results list—the best stuff should be right on the first screen of hits. The Start Date and End Date boxes allow you to restrict your search to a particular time period—useful, for example, if you're trying to track down information about a specific news event.

If you really, really like AltaVista, you can get yourself a copy of AltaVista Personal Search, which will index your hard drive and allow you to perform AltaVista–style searches on the full text of its contents, as well as provide direct access to AltaVista's Web and Usenet searching. It's free for the downloading at **http://www.altavista.digital.com/av/content/searchpx.htm**.

Excite

Excite (**http://www.excite.com/**) has been in somewhat of an acquisitive mode, wheeling and dealing with online services, search sites, and content providers. It acquired WebCrawler (see below) from America Online in November 1996 and, in late January 1997, succeeded in getting Netscape to make WebCrawler a featured search engine for surfers who click on Navigator's Search button, superseding Magellan (see chapter 3). Excite had already purchased Magellan's directory of reviewed sites earlier in 1996. All three entities were still operating as stand-alone tools in August 1997. And Excite's search engine technology powers AOL Netfind (**http://www.aol.com/netfind/home.html**), the default search engine for AOL's millions of subscribers.

Excite now offers what it calls a Channel Interface—essentially an enhanced subject tree that brings different forms of information together under the appropriate topic—e.g., business news and stock quotes and relevant Web sites, etc. An Excite search box appears on every page.

In an effort to differentiate themselves from their competitors, most of the major Web search engines and directories have been adding a variety of special services. Excite is one of the most feature laden, offering:

- **Excite Reviews.** Professionally written reviews cover more than sixty thousand Web sites in sixteen subject categories found in every channel under the Web Guide heading.
- **Excite City.Net.** Organized, searchable collection of links to about seventeen thousand Web sites provides information on approximately four thousand cities worldwide, found under the Travel and Regional Channel.
- **Excite Newstracker.** Roughly three hundred current Web-based news sources (**http://nt. excite.com/sources.html**) are scanned for articles relevant to your interests (you can choose up to twenty different subjects) and delivered directly to your desktop. It's accessible from the News Channel.
- **Instant Info.** A single link that takes you to yellow and white pages directories, an e-mail directory, interactive maps, a database of about 200,000 shareware programs, and a variety of other basic reference sources, like a dictionary, thesaurus, etc.

So how does Excite stack up as a Web search engine? It offers a few unique options. You have your choice, typing in a few keywords or phrasing your search as a natural language query—just type your question in plain English. Excite employs something it calls Intelligent Concept Extraction (ICE) to find relationships that exist between words and ideas. This means your search results will include not only documents containing exact keywords, but also documents containing words related to the concepts Excite thinks you're searching for, as per the online documentation:

> Suppose you enter *elderly people financial concerns* in the query box. In addition to finding sites containing those exact words, the search engine will find sites mentioning the economic status of retired people and the financial concerns of senior citizens.

You can search any of four databases by making a choice from a drop-down box: the Web (Excite claims a database of more than fifty million sites);

the eighty thousand Excite Review sites (not a bad choice, actually); Usenet newsgroup postings (à la AltaVista); and Usenet classified ads (if you want to buy or sell something or check prices).

By default, Excite returns your search results ranked by relevance, with those documents it considers most relevant closest to the top. Next to each item in the hit list is a More Like This link. If one of the items retrieved by Excite is particularly relevant to your query, clicking on this link will, essentially, revise your search on the fly, running it over again with the document you've chosen as a prime example of what you're looking for. This sounds good in theory. In practice—at least in my personal experience—Excite seems to shuffle the search results around and bunch near the top of the list other hits located on the same server as the More Like This document. More often than not, these don't really seem related to the subject of my original query.

Tips for searching with Excite: When searching for proper names, be sure to capitalize the first letter of each name. Advanced Search uses the same text box as Excite's basic search. Clicking on the Advanced Search link merely brings up instructions for using advanced features: (1) Type Boolean operators AND, OR, and NOT in all caps; (2) place a plus sign (+) in front of words that must be included and a minus sign (−) in front of words that must be excluded, as with AltaVista; (3) use parentheses to group portions of

If you click on the List by Web Site link, your search results list will compress to show the names of the actual sites included in the hit list and the relevant documents within each one.

Boolean queries together, as with AltaVista; and (4) enter all forms of a word to ensure retrieving all possible results; truncation is not supported.

HotBot

HotBot (**http://www.hotbot.com/**) began life as the Inktomi search engine developed at the University of California at Berkeley. In 1996, it joined forces with HotWired, the online component of *Wired* magazine and, like so many sites before it, went commercial.

What's neat about HotBot is that it's highly customizable—both in terms of each individual search *and* your overall preferred interface. You select the search parameters you prefer and then click Save My Settings. Now, every time you return to HotBot, the search page should appear

exactly as you prefer it on your screen. (Although, if necessary, you can also click on Load My Settings to pull up the last search page you saved as the default.)

By the way, if you're annoyed by the bright green background (which shouldn't be a total shock to anyone who reads the dead-tree edition of *Wired*), you can always go to Options/General Preferences/Colors in Netscape Navigator's toolbar and make sure the box next to Always Use My Colors, Overriding Document is checked.

First you select the database you're interested in searching from a list at the left of the screen; default is the Web, which is what you get at the top-level URL; other choices are Usenet, top news sites, classified ads, domain names, shareware, and—very interesting—discussion groups, which are the topical forums to which users contribute on various Web sites. These are typically hosted

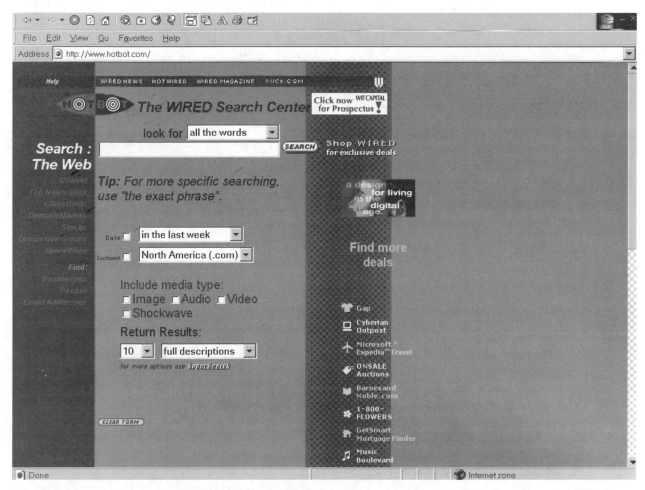

Although you can't see it in this gray-scale picture, HotBot's bright green and blue and red interface advertises its heritage; *Wired* magazine is its most prominent parent.

by e-zines, news outlets, sports sites, etc. This last option is provided by one of HotBot's "partners," Forum One, a guide to online forums (**http://www.forumone.com/**).

HotBot's main Web search screen now offers five drop-down boxes to start customizing the query you enter in the text box:

- **Look For.** All the words, any of the words, exact phrase, the page title, the person, links to this URL, or—for all ye olde-tyme searchers—Boolean phrase
- **Date Constraining Options.** In the last week, in the last two weeks, in the last month, in the last three months, in the last six months, in the last year, in the last two years
- **Continent.** North America (choose among .com, .net, .edu, .org, or .gov domains, or search them all), Europe, Southeast Asia, India and Asia, South America, Oceania
- **Number of Results Returned.** Ten, twenty-five, fifty, one hundred
- **Format of Results.** Full descriptions, brief descriptions, URLs only

All the usual Boolean operators are supported: AND, OR, NOT (or &, |, !); parentheses for nesting search terms and expressions; and quotations to enclose phrases. Proximity searching—e.g., NEAR—is not available.

For more options, click on Super Search (a

HotBot's Super Search offers a myriad of other form-based options that you can use to further refine your query. You can even search for Java applets, Visual Basic scripts, and ActiveX controls.

tiny link found just below the drop-down menus that allow you to customize your results). This produces a search form with more drop-down boxes and a myriad of other options.

Two additional drop-down menus allow you to specify whether a retrieved Document Must Contain, Should Contain, or Must Not Contain certain keywords. Generally speaking, Should Contain will rank pages higher if they match the required constraint, but it won't make that constraint an absolute requirement. Note that you can use a minus sign (−) prefix in the main search box as a shortcut for Must Not Contain or a plus sign (+) for Must Contain. This is just like using these tags with AltaVista or Excite, discussed above.

As of early 1998, HotBot still did not support truncation or wild cards. An extensive help FAQ available at the site (**http://help.hotbot.com/faq/index.html**) suggests typing all possible forms of a word into a search box and then selecting the Any of the Words search option (Boolean OR).

Under the Date section, you can target your search by selecting documents by the date they were published on the Web. Clicking Anytime tells HotBot to search all documents, regardless of the date they first appeared on the Web. Selecting After or Before from the drop-down box lets you specify only documents published on the Web after or before a certain date. Selecting Within the Last allows you to specify a time span, up to the present date.

Location allows you to target searches by country or Internet domain name. Selecting Anywhere tells HotBot to search all Web sites, everywhere on earth, in every Net domain. Or you narrow your search to a specific Internet domain, suffix, or geographic location.

And, finally, you can include Media Type to restrict a search to images or to pages that contain JavaScript, ShockWave, VRML, or audio enhancements. You can also search for certain types of files by typing in the appropriate extension suffix—e.g., *.txt, .jpg, .gif, .pdf.*

It's actually much more difficult to describe HotBot than it is to use it, since the interface consists largely of drop-down boxes, check boxes, radio buttons, etc. Your results are returned to you ranked by relevance. Once the set of matching documents has been identified, the scores are "normalized" so that no document scores over 100 percent. If HotBot considers all the documents to be poor matches, it still gives the best of the poor matches a score of 99 percent. The online documentation is quite enlightening (note particularly "spoofing" below). Relevancy scores are based on a number of criteria:

- **Word frequency in document.** In general, the more often a query word occurs in the document, the higher the score. However, the obscurity of the word also has an impact. Common words like *the* contribute less to the score than rare and discriminating words like *tiki.*
- **Search words in title.** Pages that use your search terms in the title will be ranked significantly higher than documents that contain the search term in the text only.
- **Search words in keywords.** Pages that use your search terms in the "keywords" META tag (an optional feature added to HTML documents by their creators) will be weighted higher than text words but not as high as title words.
- **Document length.** When the search words appear frequently in a short document, the page will be ranked higher than when the words appear in a long document.
- **Spoofing (or index spamming).** It has become popular for people to create pages that maliciously "spoof" search engines into returning pages that are irrelevant to the search at hand or that rank higher than their relevance and content warrant. Common examples of spoofing are duplicating words thousands of times in comments or keywords or including large numbers of "invisible" words in a tiny font or in the same color as the background color of the page. Such spoofing lowers a page's ranking in HotBot in two ways: first, the document length is bigger; second, if HotBot recognizes a common spoofing technique, it will severely penalize a page's ranking.

Be sure to check out the Cybrarian subject tree at the bottom of the home page. The sites found here are considered by *Wired* magazine editors to be *la crème de la Net.*

Infoseek

Infoseek (**http://www.infoseek.com/**) always seems to rate fairly well when the mainstream computer magazines test and review Web search engines. It routinely gets praised not only for ease of use, but also for the relevancy of its search results. Although it was getting a little long in the tooth in mid-1997, a fall update added new features such as topical "channels" and increased access to current news sources. Although not the glitziest or most comprehensive search engine on the Net, Infoseek does fill a niche as a good all-around site for people who prefer one-stop shopping for the bulk of their information query needs. For one thing, there's an excellent variety of useful services available here: e-mail news delivery (via Infobeat, at **http://www.infobeat.com/**); Infoseek Investor, which allows you to set up and track a personalized investment portfolio; U.S. and international company information (via Hoover's Online, at **http://www.hoovers.com/**); Imageseek browsing or searching for pictures, logos, and cartoons; and the ability to search in several foreign languages or by geographic region.

News searching here can be especially fruitful, since Infoseek taps into a variety of top-notch Web-based sources: Business Wire, PR Newswire, Reuters, CNN, *Chicago Tribune, Los Angeles Times,* MSNBC, the *New York Times,* San Jose *Mercury News, USA Today,* and the *Washington Post.*

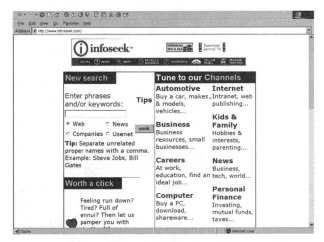

Infoseek is less glitzy than some of the other major search engines, although a face-lift and the addition of several new features have pumped some new life into it. I've found you can get pretty good results by typing in a specific phrase rather than several disjointed keywords.

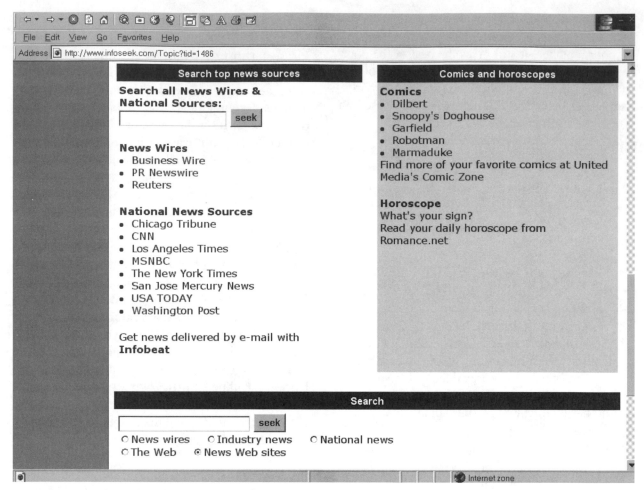

File   Edit   View   Go   Favorites   Help

Address http://www.infoseek.com/Topic?tid=1486

Search top news sources

Search all News Wires & National Sources:

[   ] seek

News Wires
• Business Wire
• PR Newswire
• Reuters

National News Sources
• Chicago Tribune
• CNN
• Los Angeles Times
• MSNBC
• The New York Times
• San Jose Mercury News
• USA TODAY
• Washington Post

Get news delivered by e-mail with **Infobeat**

Comics and horoscopes

Comics
• Dilbert
• Snoopy's Doghouse
• Garfield
• Robotman
• Marmaduke
Find more of your favorite comics at United Media's Comic Zone

Horoscope
What's your sign?
Read your daily horoscope from Romance.net

Search

[   ] seek
○ News wires   ○ Industry news   ○ National news
○ The Web   ⊙ News Web sites

Internet zone

Infoseek's News Channel incorporates the opportunity to search news wires, industry news, news Web sites, and national news—individually or simultaneously.

"No Boolean operators needed" is one of Infoseek's main bragging points. Rather, it touts a variety of "advanced search features," which seem to be available in one form or another at most major search sites. Since you can't build an advanced query through the use of Boolean operators or an equivalent interface (à la HotBot), Infoseek is not the best choice if your search topic is complex. On the other hand, it seems to do a good job with simple keyword and phrase queries—definitions of words or concepts. I've gotten excellent results by typing a simple natural language question into the text box—e.g., *What is photosynthesis?* Inevitably, one or more good hits appear quite high in the results list. Depending upon your subject, the search results are often enhanced by the addition of pointers to related topics and news articles from Infoseek's directory of more than "500,000 of the best pages on Web."

The so-called Infoseek Select Sites are tagged with a red check mark. Your results may also include some Best Bets—links to home pages or to Hoover's capsule information for companies— that are relevant to your search. Finally, on each page of results, you're offered the opportunity either to begin a new search or enter a refined search of the results already retrieved.

Some syntax tips for searching with Infoseek:

• Capitalize names of people and places.
• Enclose phrases in double quotation marks (*"light pollution"*) or, alternatively, use hyphens between words that must appear next to each other (*stupid-pet-tricks*).
• Use a plus sign (+) in front of words that must appear in results, or use a minus sign (−) to exclude words.

- Here's a weird bit of syntax for all you Unix geeks: "Use a pipe (|) to search a certain set of results only. This command is used to narrow search results by searching for one word or phrase, and then within that set of results searching for another word or phrase (*dogs | Dalmations*)."
- To search for a page containing a specific link or URL, use *link:* or *url:* (*link:www.infoseek. com* or *url:http://www.infoseek.com*).
- To search for a specific site and its related pages, use *site:* (*site:microsoft.com*).
- To search for a site by specific title, use *title:* (*title: "Cool Site of the Day"*). Don't forget the double quotation marks if the title is a phrase.

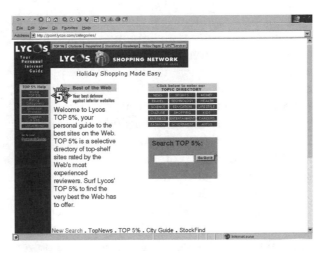

The Lycos Top 5% editorial staff bases its reviews on a site's content, presentation, and experience.

Lycos

Lycos (**http://www.lycos.com/**)—its name comes from the first five letters of the Latin words for *wolf spider*—got its start at Carnegie-Mellon University in 1994. It was really the first large-scale Web search tool, and those of us who were on the Internet at the time may recall that its instant popularity often made it difficult to access. Well, the evolution of Lycos parallels that of so many other Web-related products and services. Lycos is now Lycos, Inc., and—like Excite, Infoseek, et al.—has sucked up a number of other online resources in its effort to become a one-stop Web "information station."

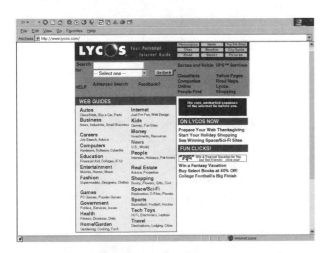

Lycos has been revamped and turbocharged, but its user interface—particularly for the comprehensive directory—can be inconsistent and confusing.

Top 5% Sites (**http://point.lycos.com/ categories/**) used to be a freestanding directory of reviewed and rated Web sites called Point: The Top Sites on the Web. Almost everyone who's done any amount of Web surfing has run across one of those ubiquitous Top 5% logos.

Having been incorporated into the Lycos service, Top 5% is "a selective directory of top-shelf sites rated by the Web's most experienced reviewers"—the editorial staff at Lycos Top 5%. You can browse the catalog in typical subject tree fashion, click on the page title links to read the reviews, and then jump directly to the sites via links on their review pages. You can also choose to search the Top 5% Sites via a drop-down box on Lycos's query form.

Sites are rated on a scale of 1 to 50, on the basis of content (breadth, depth, thoroughness, accuracy, currency), presentation (aesthetics), and experience (overall worth). The ratings—as is the rule with virtually all services of this type—are highly subjective.

There's also a typical mix of other directories and services here—World City Guide (**http:// cityguide.lycos.com/**) offers pointers to more than 7,500 Web sites from 400 U.S. cities; PeopleFind (**http://www.lycos.com/peoplefind/**) is your usual telephone white pages and e-mail directory search; StockFind (**http://www.stockfind. newsalert.com/**) provides quotes on a fifteen-minute-delayed basis during trading hours, plus recent news announcements issued by the company for which you've requested a quote; CompaniesOnline (**http://www.companiesonline.com/**) allows you to search a Dun & Bradstreet database of information on more than 60,000 U.S. public and private companies; and RoadMaps (**http://www.lycos.com/roadmap.html**) generates maps on the fly and driving directions for U.S. addresses. Lycos TopNews (**http://lnews.lycos.com/headlines/TopNews/**) offers the latest news, sports, and weather from a variety of Internet-based news sources.

Lycos has slimmed down its previously cumbersome interface. The mechanics of searching have been simplified, but new features add more power. To search the Web with Lycos, you choose between the simple search form that appears on the site's home page and a Lycos Pro custom search form, which you reach by clicking on the Advanced Search link below the simple search text box.

For a simple search, first use the drop-down menu to decide where to search—the Web is the default, but you could also choose sounds, pictures, personal home pages, or—weirdly—United Parcel Service tracking numbers. You can also choose to restrict your search to those sites included in the Top 5%.

In the text box, type your search words or phrases (use quotation marks around phrases), and click the Go Get It button. Here are some of Lycos's suggestions for fine-tuning your search:

- Use keywords that are as specific as possible.
- Use phrase searching for full names (*"Michael Eisner"*).

- Use the minus sign (−) in front of any word or phrase to screen out that term (*Rico −Puerto*).
- Likewise, use the plus sign (+) to identify must-have words or phrases (*Florida +beaches*).

A Lycos Pro (advanced) search starts out like a simple search. You click on the drop-down menu next to the word Search. There you can choose to target the Web (the default), pictures, sounds, the Top 5% sites, stock symbols, personal home pages, books, recipes(!), or Usenet newsgroup postings. Your next step is choosing how you'd like to search, using another drop-down menu:

- All the Words: Boolean AND (also the default choice)
- Any of the Words: Boolean OR (documents that include all of the words will be ranked higher on the results list)
- All the Words (Good Match)
- All the Words (Near Match)
- All the Words (Close Match)
- All the Words (Strong Match)
- The Exact Phrase: All the words must appear in the order you specify.
- Natural Language Query: Type in your question exactly as you might phrase it if you were asking a human being.

If you're using a Web browser with Java support, give the Lycos Pro Java Power Panel a try. It allows you to use sliding bars to adjust the importance to your query of such factors as matching every keyword, frequency of keyword appearance,

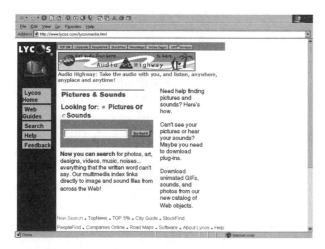

Lycos also lets you look for pictures and sounds on a separate search form if you choose.

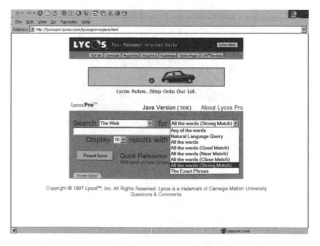

My advice? Start with All The Words (Strong Match) and then keep backing off if you don't get enough results—alas, seldom a problem when searching the Web.

appearance of keyword in page title, appearance of keyword early in page, proximity of keywords to each other, and whether or not keywords appear in exact order.

Lycos also supports an extensive set of Boolean operators including AND, OR, NOT, ADJ, NEAR, FAR, and BEFORE. An extensive help page for using these operators is available at **http://www.lycos.com/help/boolean-help.html**.

Open Text Index

Open Text (**http://index.opentext.net/**) created something of a scandal on the Internet in 1996 when it introduced a "feature" called "preferred listings." In exchange for a fee—reported to be upward of two thousand dollars—Open Text would bump the payee's Web page up to the top of a search results listing. The tag "preferred" was originally appended next to these "sponsored" listings, which some people felt was a false indication of quality. This was eventually changed to "advertisement" or "paid listing." Nonetheless, some users set about organizing a boycott, which was officially called off in November 1996, when Open Text dropped the preferred listing service. According to Open Text's FAQ:

> For a few weeks, the Open Text Index also experimented with "preferred listings" which inserted advertisements into the result list. Since these advertisements caused some confusion over what was a real result and what was not, the Open Text Index has stopped this practice.

Open Text, unfortunately, appears to have fallen behind its competitors, particularly in terms of the sophistication of its interface and the accu-

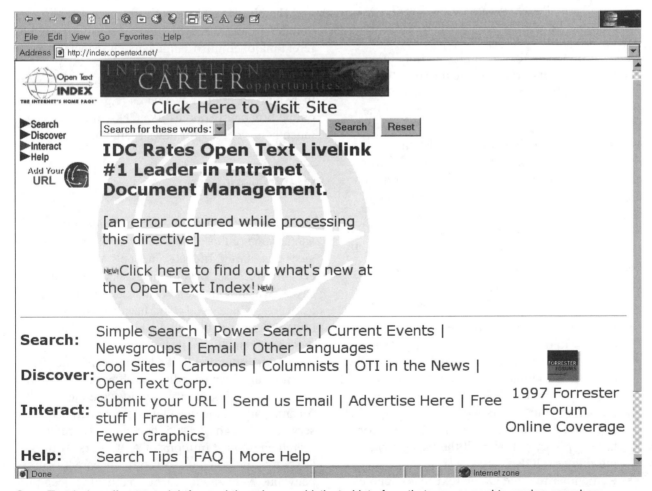

Open Text Index offers a straightforward though unsophisticated interface that may appeal to novice searchers.

racy and comprehensiveness of its results. It's easy enough to use—drop-down menus allow you to construct Boolean AND/OR/NOT/NEAR searches, and permit you to specify where you want a keyword to appear—e.g., in the page title. Truncation and wild cards are not supported. If you want to include results containing all forms of a word, you must perform an OR search—i.e., *child or children or childless or childlike,* etc.

The Simple Search form on Open Text's main page is pretty limited. A drop-down box lets you choose to search for These Words or This Phrase. The Power Search form is much more flexible. It's also easy to use because you can structure your search entirely through the use of drop-down boxes. The drop-down boxes on the left side allow you to join your keywords with AND, OR, BUT NOT, NEAR (within eighty characters before or after the keyword on the previous line), and *followed by* (within eighty characters after the keyword on the previous line). The boxes on the right side allow you to specify where a particular keyword should be found within a document—Anywhere, Summary (as assigned to each page in its database by Open Text; includes its title, first heading, and some important text extracted from the page), Title, First Heading (searches only first-level headings as assigned by the author of the Web page), and URL.

All of these options may sound somewhat confusing and, if you're not completely comfortable with Boolean searching, don't go wild with the drop-down boxes. Open Text doesn't let you use parentheses to group search expressions; it reads the expressions you construct with the drop-down boxes strictly from left to right, in order. By the way, you can enter only one keyword in each text box.

Open Text offers the following search tips:

- Keep in mind that the Boolean operators are applied in the order they appear. For example, if the first line's Search For field contains *donkey* and its operator is OR, and the second line has *horse* and BUT NOT, and the third line has *mule*, your results will include all the Web pages that contain *donkey* and all pages containing *horse,* but with all the pages containing *mule* excluded.
- Remember that the Open Text Index ignores case and some punctuation.

- Use plurals or other word endings. Due to an upgrade of the search engine, the Open Text Index does not take care of plurals. If you are looking for information on a disease, search for *disease* and *diseases.*
- If your search is in English, search for both British and American spellings. For example, you could search for *labour* OR *labor.* (Open Text is a Canadian corporation.)

What else is available at Open Text?

- Searching for e-mail addresses, via the Four11 directory (See chapter 7.)
- Searching Usenet newsgroup postings via DejaNews (See chapter 8.)
- A selection of "cool sites."
- A selection of links to cartoon sites ("Take a load off," suggests Open Text.)
- A selection of links to columnists—from John Dvorak (*PC Magazine*) to Martha Stewart ("the goddess of the home")

There's also a Current Events page that allows you the option to search simultaneously in ten different major English-language newspapers. It's not terribly flexible, though. You can only search for This Exact Phrase or All of These Words. And there's no access to news wires (e.g., Reuters) or online broadcast sources like CNN. Infoseek is a much better choice for news searching.

WebCrawler

WebCrawler (**http://www.webcrawler.com/**) is another one of those now-commercial Internet services that started life as someone's academic project—in this case, Brian Pinkerton, at the University of Washington. It's been around about as long as Lycos—since 1994—but hasn't aged with quite the same degree of sophistication. Also, its database is much smaller.

On the other hand, it's had a recent face-lift and it's very user-friendly, which has contributed to its ongoing popularity—besides the fact that it became part of America Online's now-defunct GNN service in March of 1995, becoming the default search engine for millions of AOL users. Well, GNN may be gone, dissolved by its parent company, but WebCrawler carries on, having been purchased from AOL in November 1996 by Excite.

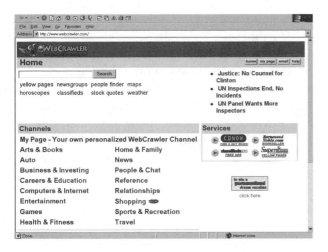

WebCrawler's clean, simple interface contributes to its popularity—especially among novice users.

Excite cut a deal with Netscape to give WebCrawler a spot on the Netscape Net Search page—the default Net Search jump station for the zillions of folks worldwide who use the Netscape Navigator browser.

Location, location, location. From AOL to Netscape, WebCrawler has definitely benefited from its ongoing exposure to heavy Net traffic. So despite its shortcomings as a search tool, it's remained popular—a problem in and of itself, as it's often difficult to access and slow to respond. And yet many people—some of them sophisticated searchers I interviewed in the course of researching this book—claim they get highly relevant results from WebCrawler. So it's definitely worth a closer look.

Operator	Example	Finds
AND	gardening AND vegetables	pages that include both of the words—e.g., pages containing both *gardening* and *vegetables*
OR	whales OR cetaceans	pages that include either of the words or both—e.g., pages containing *whales* OR those containing *cetaceans* OR those containing both *whales* and *cetaceans* (Note: WebCrawler performs OR searching by default so it is not necessary to explicitly specify an OR search.)
NOT	science NOT fiction	pages that include the first word but not the second—e.g., pages containing *science* but not *fiction*
NEAR	arthritis NEAR/25 nutrition	pages in which both words appear within twenty-five words of each other in either direction—e.g., pages containing the words *arthritis* and *nutrition* within twenty-five words of one another (Note: If you do not specify a range, as in the example, the search will return pages in which the two words are next to each other, in any order.)
ADJ	global ADJ warming	pages in which the two words appear next to each other in that order—e.g., pages containing *global warming*
"..."	"1996 World Series Champions"	pages containing the phrase *1996 World Series Champions;* for two-word phrases—"*animal magnetism*" and *animal* ADJ *magnetism* have the same effect
(...)	Homer NOT (Simpson OR Alaska)	pages containing the first word NOT either of the other two—e.g., pages containing *Homer* but NOT *Homer Simpson* or *Homer Alaska* (Parentheses simplify the creation of complex queries and can be used in combination with any of the search operators on this list.)

Although you won't find as many technically sophisticated bells and whistles here, WebCrawler's search options have steadily improved. It manages to produce pretty decent results for the casual hit-and-run Web surfer—"WebCrawler understands plain English and is programmed with novice users in mind"—and yet it still provides extensive support for a variety of Boolean operators, as detailed in the help files.

As mentioned previously, WebCrawler has a smaller database than the other big guns. I could not find documentation on-site that included an exact figure; in various articles and research papers about search engines, I've seen numbers ranging from a low of 150,000 documents to a high of 1.8 million separate entries. Go figure.

But quantity, as any serious researcher knows, is much less important than quality. A few relevant hits are almost always much more desirable than a whole bunch of marginal results. And an FAQ available at the site—there's extensive online documentation—included some information to indicate that WebCrawler's database is, in fact, monitored for quality:

> We have been noticing recently that more and more Web publishers have been "spamming"—including unsolicited, extra, or irrelevant information on their pages, usually in the form of word lists—to make search engines display them at the top of their listings. We strongly discourage this practice. Our aim is to provide the best index to the Internet that we can, and spamming actively interferes with that goal.
>
> To create a better searching environment, and to foster a more level playing field for everyone, we have started removing offending pages from our index and screening new submissions. If you think that your page may have disappeared from or didn't get into WebCrawler for this reason, we hope that you will remove the spam from your page and resubmit your URL to us so that we can index it properly.

WebCrawler offers just one search form, from which you can run a simple natural language query or use the full range of Boolean syntax. You can use drop-down boxes to choose how your results will be displayed:

1. **Titles, or summaries, or detailed format.** The short format gives you a list of titles of Web resources that match your query. The detailed format provides titles plus summaries, URLs, numerical relevancy scores, and the option of viewing similar pages for each result returned.

2. **Number of results per page.** Using the second choice box, you can choose to view search results ten, twenty-five, or one hundred at a time.

Results are provided in order of relevance, with the most relevant resources first. The icons to the left of the results provide a graphical indication of how relevant each link is to your search. "WebCrawler computes the relevance score for a particular document by considering how many times the terms in your search occur in that document. The more frequent, the more relevant. Another consideration is how unique to the document a given search word is. If the word occurs in only a few documents, its occurrence in a particular document makes it more relevant." To reduce the strain on system resources, WebCrawler restricts search results to a maximum of one hundred hits at a time. At the bottom of each results page is a button that you can click on to get the entire list of results, but you'll pretty much be wasting your time unless you've narrowed down your query first.

What else is offered by WebCrawler? The standard search engine cornucopia of services.

WebCrawler Maps. Include a U.S. city in your search, and WebCrawler will offer to retrieve an interactive map of that city (via MapQuest, **http://www.mapquest.com**) along with your search results.

WebCrawler Guide. This is a subject tree of sites that have been reviewed by editors. It

WebCrawler Guide offers a brief, helpful review for each site included. Additionally, a Search the Web for More Like This link for each entry makes it easy for you to mine for additional sites on the same topic.

includes a link to the WebCrawler Guide Top 50, "the fifty most-accessed links in the guide" for a recent week. Hint: Chat sites are wildly popular. (See chapter 3.)

E-mail and Address Lookups. Utilize free e-mail addresses via Excite.

Northern Light

Northern Light (**http://www.nlsearch.com/**) is the new kid on the block in the realm of major Internet search engines. Introduced in August 1997, it was created with the assistance of real, live librarians. Its database of Web resources is very large—on a par with AltaVista and HotBot. Additionally, it offers a Special Collection of full-text articles from about 1,800 proprietary sources, including journals, reviews, books, magazines, and news

wires. You can search the Web database, the Special Collection, or both simultaneously. While there is no charge to click through to documents in your results list that are available on the "public" Web, full text of documents from the Special Collection is instantly available for fees ranging from one dollar to four dollars. These are delivered online—with a money-back guarantee that can be exercised up to thirty days after you've purchased a document. You can either set up a member account that lets you pay as you go, or you can ante up a nominal monthly subscription fee, which entitles you to view a fixed number of full-text Special Collection documents.

While Northern Light doesn't have the extensive list of extra features available at most of the other search mega-sites, it offers something very special in the way it presents search results. According to the Northern Light FAQ

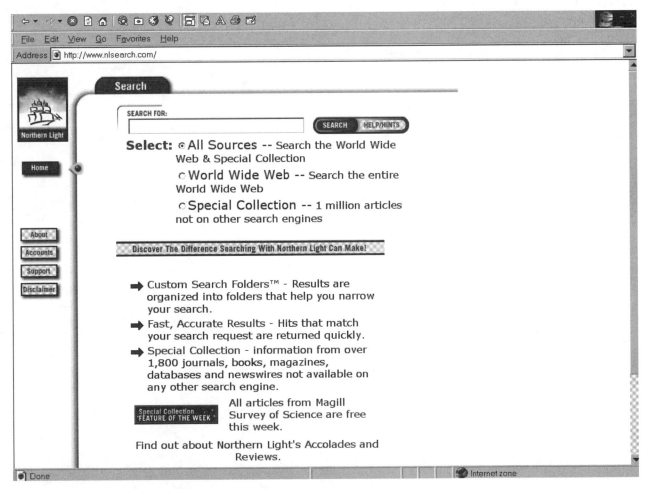

Northern Light, the newest of the Web's major search engines, appears to be quite technologically advanced. It is fast, uncannily accurate, and organizes results into folders for easier browsing.

(**http://www.northernlight.com/docs/annafaq. htm**), hits are "dynamically organized" into Custom Folders—sorted by subject, source, or document type. Click on any folder that looks topically promising and you can quickly review the relevant results.

Northern Light's query-building capabilities are fairly limited, compared to most of the top search engines. Full Boolean searching was not supported as of November 1997, although it was a promised addition for the future. Both OR and NOT are available, for broadening or restricting the scope of a search, respectively. Phrase searching is accomplished by enclosing the words within double quotation marks (*"light pollution"*). A plus sign (+) can be used to indicate words that must be present in the resulting documents, and a minus sign (−) for words that must not be present (+*hiking* −*hitchhiking* or +*dolphins* −*NFL*).

Northern Light's ease of use, accuracy, and sophisticated results interface make it very much worth a spot high on your personal bookmark list. It will be interesting to see how this site develops.

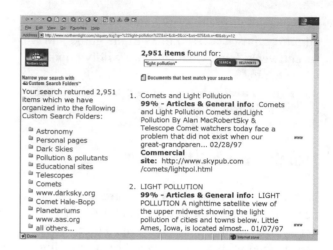

Northern Light organizes your search results into a series of Custom Folders, found on the left side of the screen. This greatly facilitates browsing, since you can quickly view items returned in what you perceive to be the most relevant topic areas.

6

When One Is Not Enough

All-in-One Pages, Parallel Search Engines, Software Tools

What's Here?

Search Engine Collections

All-in-One Search Page
The Internet Sleuth
Search.Com

Parallel Search Engines

Cyber 411
MetaCrawler
SavvySearch
If You *Still* Want More . . .

Software Tools

Those who remember the days when virtually no decent tool existed for searching the Internet are often overwhelmed by the wealth of choices available today. Most people pick one or two favorites and use them again and again. Alas, the serious Internet researcher can't afford to take such a casual approach. But who can keep track of all these things?

You don't have to. Take advantage of the work others have done in creating all-in-one search pages, which are basically jump stations to all sorts of Internet search services, categorized by subject into a user-friendly interface. Try searching a number of the big guns (see chapter 5) simultaneously, with one of the parallel search tools, and learn the advantages and disadvantages of this one-shot approach. And finally, you might want to download and experiment with one or more of a growing number of client software programs that you load on your computer and use to run your query on a number of search engines simultaneously. Some of these are quite customizable and are capable of processing your search results in a fairly sophisticated manner.

Search Engine Collections

These are basically user-friendly collections of existing search services that offer a simple forms-based opportunity to perform searches on the tools of your choice from one convenient location. Typically, though, you can't take advantage of the advanced features of the various search tools this way, but all of these pages provide direct links to the search sites themselves. The best of these are well worth visiting, as you're bound to discover at least one very useful search service—often subject specific—that you never knew existed. The three sites described below, All-in-One Search Page, the Internet Sleuth, and Search.Com, are those I've found particularly useful. But there are many others out there, and you may well find one you like better.

All-in-One Search Page

William Cross, the developer and maintainer of this excellent resource, at (**http://www.albany. net/allinone/**), is manager of User Support Services for the Department of State, New York State.

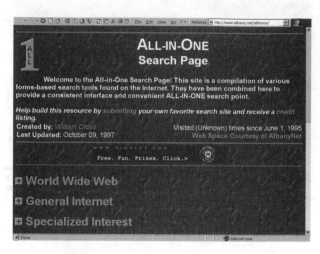

More than two hundred separate search tools can be accessed from a uniform interface at the All-in-One Search Page.

Obviously, he knows the meaning of *user-friendly*. While this site is quite extensive, the separate search services represented are nicely organized, with a uniform interface, and usually include small annotations. Cross updates the pages on a regular basis and actively solicits submissions from Net surfers who know about a search site that isn't included here yet.

The top-level index, available from the main page, includes the following categories:

- World Wide Web (the most extensive section)
- General Internet (search tools for Usenet and other non-Web resources)
- Specialized Interest (small collection of subject-specific search tools)
- Software (for all computing platforms)
- People (telephone, address, and e-mail finding tools)
- News/Weather (major news outlets and weather servers)
- Publications/Literature (mixed bag—government documents, magazines, fine arts, and humanities)
- Technical Reports (mostly computer-oriented)
- Documentation (mostly Internet and Web related)
- Desk Reference (typical ready-reference sources—dictionaries, maps, etc.)
- Other Interesting Searches/Services (fun to browse—airline schedules, CD music titles, movie reviews, tax forms, recipes, health information)

Under each major topic, the search tools are arranged alphabetically. Enter your keywords into the text boxes provided by Cross—some of which have drop-down menus to customize various aspects of your query—and click the adjacent Search button. Voilà! Didn't get what you wanted? Go to the next search tool on the list. Or click on the name of any search tool to link directly to its home site, where all of its advanced features will be available to you.

The Internet Sleuth

A *very* extensive search jump station, the Internet Sleuth (**http://www.isleuth.com/**) provides access to more than 1,800 *separate* searchable databases but is extremely well organized, with plenty of on-line documentation. You can browse the available search engines, which are categorized in standard subject tree fashion: Arts, Business, Computers, Education, Employment, Entertainment, Environment, Government, Health—General, Internet, Law, News, Recreation, Reference, Regional, Sciences, Shopping, Social Sciences, Society, Sports, Travel, and Veterinary/Zoology. Most of the main headings include one or more subcategories.

If you arrive here and you're not sure where to go next, use the Search the Sleuth text box in the upper right. Typing in the word *recipes*, for instance, brings up an extensive list of possible databases. Each one is annotated so you know what your search is likely to find. Dive in and have a ball!

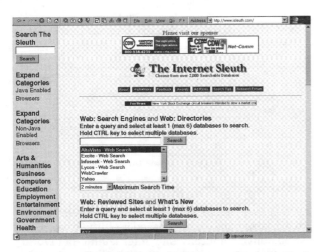

The Internet Sleuth includes its own search engine that allows you to determine which of its 1,800-plus databases are most appropriate for your query.

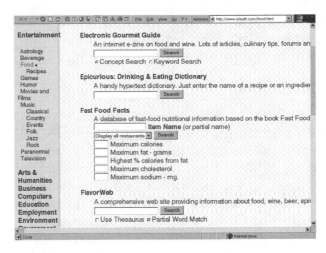

Eat, drink, and be merry! The Internet Sleuth allows you to search a large variety of food and beverage recipe databases.

If you sort of know what you're looking for, the best strategy is to use the subject tree and click on the broad category that offers the most likely possibility. Most categories offer a Quick Search option right off the bat. This is a convenient way to run your search through several databases simultaneously—usually, a maximum of ten. Use the scroll box to make your selections. (Hold down the Control key—Command on the Mac—to select multiple databases.)

There are certain limitations here. Since you're searching multiple databases, each with its own syntax and idiosyncrasies, you have no real way of knowing how multiple keywords will be treated. Therefore, according to the Sleuth, "Best results are achieved by using one query word only." Which means this strategy is probably best for a very broad search or if—hallelujah—you're familiar with the syntax of each search tool you're tapping into. But it's also a very fast way to find out which individual databases might be the most useful to you.

The Sleuth has attempted to include information about how to search each database. If you still can't get decent results, you can click on the name of the search tool and link directly to its home site where, presumably, more extensive instructions and options will be available.

Believe it or not, this site is the work of one extremely talented woman—Sally Elliot, of Ormond Beach, Florida. She also offers an Information Research Forum here—an interactive bulletin board where you can ask specific search-related questions or provide assistance to other users, right along with Elliot herself.

Search.Com

At Search.Com (**http://www.search.com/**), we have yet another ambitious offering from those prolific folks at C|Net, the computer TV network people. While it doesn't include as many search-able databases as the Internet Sleuth, it provides excellent documentation in the form of feature articles that tell you when and how to use the various tools you'll find here. You have several options:

CUSTOMIZED ACCESS TO THE ALTAVISTA SEARCH ENGINE

Search.Com provides step-by-step instructions and help, plus links to advanced search features.

EXPRESS SEARCH

Drop-down boxes at the beginning of each subject category let you choose from an abbreviated selection of the most appropriate databases, type in a query, and get back quick results. Handy for experienced searchers who find themselves using a few search tools regularly.

CATEGORIES AND SHORTCUTS

Basically a subject tree approach to search tools, à la the Internet Sleuth. Click on the category of

your choice—Arts, Automotive, Business, Computers, Directories, Education, Employment, Entertainment, Finance, Games, Government, Health, Housing, Legal, Lifestyle, News, People, Politics, Reference, Science, Shopping, Sports, Travel, Usenet, Web—on the yellow bar at the left side of each page.

THE WHOLE LIST

Click on A–Z List on the yellow bar, and you can view the entire list of searchable databases available at this site.

FIND A SEARCH

Use Search.Com's internal search tool to find the appropriate databases for your query.

PERSONALIZE SEARCH.COM

Click Personalize on the ubiquitous yellow bar. Select the categories you're interested in, select the search engines you like in each category, and then arrange them in the order in which you'd like to see them. (Search.Com puts a little icon next to its favorite choices, many of which are also C|Net related.) Fill out a registration form, and you're all set. Next time you visit Search.Com, click on the Your Page menu link to get to your personalized search page. Ain't life great?

C|Net's Search.Com is well organized and contains lots of helpful documentation.

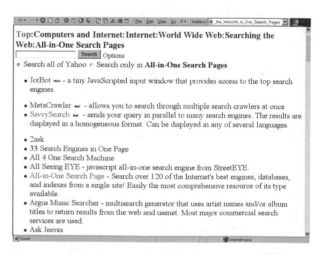

If you *still* want more, scores of all-in-one search pages are available from— you guessed it—**http://www. yahoo.com/Computers_and_Internet/Internet/World_ Wide_Web/Searching_the_Web/All_in_One_Search_ Pages/**!

Parallel Search Engines

The idea is intriguing. Why go from one major search engine to the next, typing your same query over and over again? Wouldn't it be faster and more convenient to type your query once and run it through a whole slew of search engines at the same time?

So far, this is an idea that has played better in theory than in practice. The two major problems with the parallel search approach are speed and accuracy. Since these tools rely on what are already busy major search sites, it almost always takes a long time to run your search. If it takes too long at any individual search site, your mega-search will "time out," resulting in an incomplete set of results. Also, since the individual search engines each have their own unique syntax, way of handling Boolean operators, etc., you will probably not be able to make your parallel search query as specific as you would if using each search engine's advanced options. And these tools do not yet approach the level of sophistication that commercial alternatives (e.g., Dialog OneSearch) offer with regard to duplicate detection and removal, so your parallel search engine results will likely contain at least some duplicate hits.

So are these mega-search engines actually useful at all? They can be handy for quick single-keyword searches of unique or specialized terms—the kind of search where you're wondering if you're likely to find anything at all on the Internet. It can't hurt to take a quick look at three of these sites: Cyber 411, MetaCrawler, and SavvySearch.

Cyber 411

Simple interface, few choices here at Cyber 411 (**http://cyber411.com/**). A drop-down box on the right allows you to choose between searching on a word or words (OR is the default Boolean operator) or searching on a phrase (if supported by the individual search engines that will run your actual query). A drop-down box on the left allows you to select either a Hyper search, which will display results from each search engine as they are received, or a Fast search, which will first collect the results from all the search engines and then collate them to remove duplicate hits.

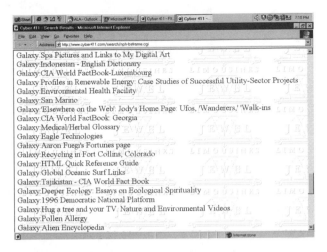

I don't know about Cyber 411. I searched on the phrase *light pollution* and got back some very strange results, particularly from the Galaxy search engine.

Cyber 411 makes a claim of "Fifteen Search Engines—One Query," but documentation at the site did not identify the fifteen search engines used. Several test searches in early 1998 did not return results from more than eight different search engines—Infoseek, Excite, Lycos, Yahoo!, AltaVista, Galaxy, Aliweb, and Point Search (now part of Lycos).

A quirky add-on feature here is the Dictionary/Thesaurus, where you can look up the definition of a keyword you typed in and also get a list of synonyms. Presumably, you use this when your initial query gets bad or skimpy results.

MetaCrawler

MetaCrawler (**http://www.metacrawler.com/**) is another child of academia—the same institution, as a matter of fact, where WebCrawler originated, the University of Washington. While it doesn't query as many search engines as does Cyber 411, it offers more configurability and search options, which overall produce better search results.

MetaCrawler searches AltaVista, Excite, Galaxy, HotBot, Infoseek, Lycos, Open Text, WebCrawler, and Yahoo! If you have a Java-enabled browser, you can watch the progress of your search, request more results under certain circumstances, and click a button to jump right back to the search form and modify your query. When you arrive at MetaCrawler for the first time,

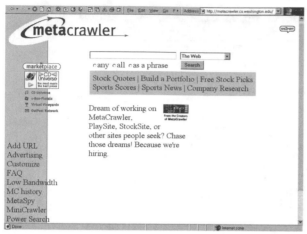

Developed in 1994 at the University of Washington, MetaCrawler is now operated by go2net, Inc., a Seattle-based Internet content and technology company.

click on Customize right away. This brings up a page with various check boxes that allow you to configure the search form—high or low bandwidth interface, default method (any, all, or phrase search), filtering of results by domain origin (.edu only, for instance), number of results per page, maximum amount of time to wait for results, maximum number of results from each source, and Sticky, which means your search preferences will "follow you" around MetaCrawler.

MetaCrawler supports the Boolean operators AND and OR, plus phrase searching, via a series of three radio buttons on the search form. Type your query in the Search For text box and then choose A Phrase; All of These Words; or Any of These Words. The familiar plus (+) and minus (−) signs may also be used here, in front of keywords that *must* appear in the resulting search documents or keywords that *must not* appear. However, notes the MetaCrawler documentation, "not all sources queried support these features. They are, therefore, only suggestions that MetaCrawler will use when tailoring each source's query."

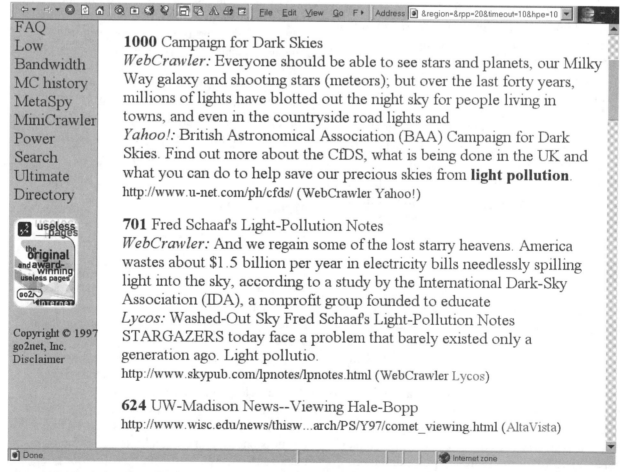

After MetaCrawler finishes running your query through its target search engines, it loads and collates the results, removing duplicates.

SavvySearch

SavvySearch (**http://guaraldi.cs.colostate.edu:2000/**) takes an interesting approach to the parallel search process. Unlike with MetaCrawler and Cyber 411, you can select a category or categories to search in by turning on the Sources and Types of Information function on the main search page. By clicking in check boxes, you can choose from among Web Indexes, Web Directories, Usenet News, Software, People, Reference (dictionaries, etc.), Entertainment, and Technical Reports. Savvy decides which databases to search, based on your choices; this is your Search Plan, which you get to see after your results come back. As the on-site documentation (which is plentiful and excellent) explains:

> When you submit your query, the fitness of each target search engine is ranked. Information from past searches is used to make an educated guess as to which search engines will perform best with your query specifically. These rankings are further adjusted using information about the current turn-around time of each search engine. If a search engine is excessively slow or broken (or there is a prob-

When I searched for *light pollution* here, I chose WWW Resources, Technical Reports, and Usenet News. It took SavvySearch almost four minutes to run this search through its search plan choices of WebCrawler, DejaNews, and Infoseek and then collate and display the results. (And this was at 11:15 P.M. It's even slower during the busy daylight hours.) I received a total of twenty hits, most of which were relevant. The false drops (bad hits) seemed mainly to come from WebCrawler.

lem with the SavvySearch interface to that particular search engine), it will receive a much lower rank. The search plan displays the ranked search engines in order, with the most appropriate and fastest ones toward the left (or top). The number of search engines simultaneously queried, or concurrency value, is dependent on our local load and Internet conditions. It is almost always 2, 3, 4, or 5 search engines. Users often find what they want in the first step. If you don't find anything useful you can continue querying more search engines by selecting any other step.

Savvy claims to be querying a long list of search engines, including some rather obscure or narrowly focused ones: Aliweb, AltaVista, CSTR (the unified Computer Science Technical Report server at Indiana University), DejaNews, Excite, EINET Galaxy (now Tradewave Galaxy), Four11 (the e-mail and address directory), FTPSearch95 (Norwegian server that searches FTP sites), Infoseek, InReference (a site that provides searchable newsgroup archives), Internet Movie Database (for reviews and other cinema-related information), LinkStar (a business directory), LookUP! (Four11), Lycos, Magellan, NlightN (a directory containing a hybrid mix of fee and free information), Pathfinder (Time-Life), Point Search (now part of Lycos), Shareware.com (C|Net's software search engine), Tribal Voice, WebCrawler, WhoWhere? (e-mail directory), Yellow Pages, and Yahoo!

Keep in mind when constructing a keyword search here that Savvy is not case sensitive and doesn't support the plus (+) or minus (−) operators. Also, according to the documentation, "Small words (i.e., the, it, for, etc.) are typically ignored, but you can use numbers and most symbols." A drop-down box allows you to choose ten, twenty, thirty, forty, or fifty hits from each search engine queried, but, as Savvy reminds you, "this is not a guarantee of how many results you will get from each because some queries don't retrieve anything, and some search engines limit the maximum number of results they're willing to return." You can also choose to check off the Integrate Results box on the search form, which is recommended. "When selected," Savvy explains, "duplicate results are combined, and results are not separated by search engine. While this format is easier to interpret, the tradeoff is that you must wait until all search engines report (up to 45 seconds) before seeing any results." You can also opt for a brief, normal, or "verbose" results display, common with other large search tools.

If You Still *Want More . . .*

Several other parallel search engines are out there for you to try. The unfortunately named Dogpile (**http://www.dogpile.com/**) uses Arfie technology to work its way through twenty-three different search engines, hitting on three at a time, apparently for speed. Boolean capabilities are supported, and an advanced search option allows you to customize sources and save this customization for return visits.

Highway 61 (**http://highway61.com/**) is what some might call a meta-search engine with attitude. Like most similar services, it submits your query simultaneously to AltaVista, Excite, Infoseek, Lycos, WebCrawler, and Yahoo! Boolean AND and OR are supported. Unlike similar services, Highway 61 prompts you to set a maximum time-out compatible with your individual patience level. You can also indicate how many hits you'd like returned from each source. The option Lots will bring back 35 to 75, while Bury Me will retrieve 60 to 125. As the documentation wryly notes, "This is an inexact science." Results are ranked according to "how many sites a link was found at, how those sites ranked it, and the current temperature in downtown Natchez, Mississippi, one of the hot spots on the real Highway 61!"

Inference Find (**http://m5.inference.com/ifind/**) bills itself as "the Intelligent and Fast Parallel Web Search." It simultaneously searches WebCrawler, Yahoo!, Lycos, AltaVista, Infoseek, and Excite, pulls the maximum number of results from each, removes duplicate hits, and then employs clustering—grouping related items together to make them easier to weed through.

ProFusion (**http://www.designlab.ukans.edu/profusion/**), an interesting project of the University of Kansas Design Lab, queries AltaVista, Excite, Infoseek, Lycos, Open Text, and WebCrawler. You can either choose to run your search in all of them, pick the ones you want, or let ProFusion pick the best three. When your

search results come back, it will check up to the first fifty links to make sure they are valid. This can be time-consuming, though, and ProFusion is one of the slower parallel search services to begin with. One unique feature: you can register your regular queries—along with your name, e-mail address, and a password—and ProFusion will run them for you periodically, letting you know when there are new results.

Software Tools

An up-and-coming category of software is the variety of Internet search client programs that you load on your own computer. These typically provide parallel searching of the big guns, followed by manipulation of the search results to a greater or lesser extent, for better functionality. Some do the job better than others. Some are overly complex. Some are relatively expensive, and some are free. Visit the Web site for the latest prices. All offer at least a downloadable demo. So try them out and see if one meets your needs.

ECHOSEARCH

In addition to Web searching, EchoSearch (**http://www.iconovex.com/**) also searches Usenet newsgroup articles and supports a variety of Boolean operators. It displays search results within your browser and automatically downloads documents to your computer so you don't have to go back out onto the Web.

INTERNET FASTFIND

Coming to you from Symantec, the Norton Utilities people, Internet FastFind (**http://service. symantec.com/iff/faq_iff.html**) includes a variety of Internet utilities, including a file finder, Patch-Connect (surveys your computer and lets you track down new patches and drivers for your system's hardware and software), Notify (which will let you know if there have been any changes to your favorite Web sites), and WebLaunch (which brings up an icon-laden view of your bookmark file and allows you to launch your browser by clicking on the site of your choice). WebFind is the parallel search component that simultaneously hits the big gun search engines, collects all results on a single page, and allows you to sort them by relevance or by Web site.

WEBCOMPASS

By Quarterdeck, WebCompass (**http://www.quarterdeck.com/qdeck/products/webcompass/**) arranges your searches topically, in a window that resembles the Windows 95 Explorer view. It's designed to let you build up archives of searches, which you can refresh as needed, with the Web-Compass agents. And you can easily sift through the results using a variety of options, such as page names and descriptions, the search engines listing each page, and each URL. It comes configured to search thirty-five different engines, and you can add new ones or delete old ones at any time, including search engines for FTP and gopher sites.

WEBSEEKER

Offered by the ForeFront Group, the same folks who developed WebWhacker, the popular offline browser, WebSeeker (**http://www.bluesquirrel.com/seeker/**) comes configured to use twenty-three search engines, allows you to schedule unattended searches, monitors Web pages for changes, removes duplicate hits, and checks to see that the URLs it retrieves are "still alive." It will also, on request, download the text of each URL to your hard drive.

WEBFERRET

A popular number, as far as most of us are concerned, is "free." And that's the price of WebFerret (**http://www.webferret.com/netferret/webferret.htm**), part of a suite of Internet utilities. The suite includes search tools for e-mail addresses, files,

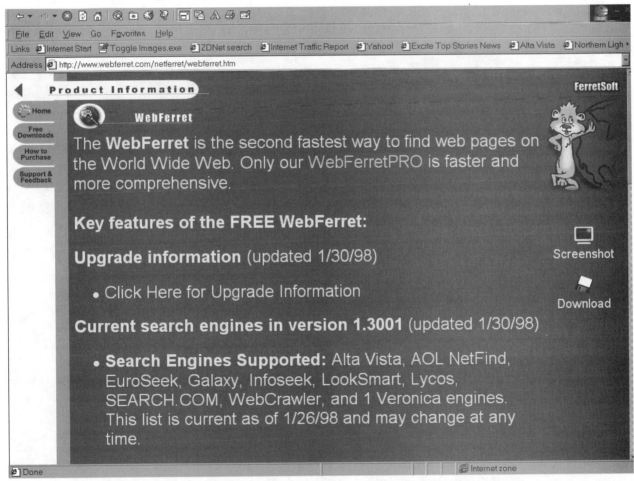

The people at FerretSoft, which makes a suite of utilities, promise that the WebFerret component will always remain free to all takers.

Usenet newsgroup articles, phone numbers, and Internet Relay Chat users. While not as elaborate as some of the other products discussed here, it's fast and easy. Start up the program from the Win 95 Start > Find option, enter a keyword, and hit Enter (or the Find Now button.) It supports phrase searching, gopherspace searching, and removes duplicate hits. Hey, the price is right! Give it a try. A commercial version, WebFerret PRO, is slightly more feature laden.

Similar products are being developed constantly. You'll find a good, up-to-date selection under the Browser SearchBots category at TUCOWS (**http://www.tucows.com/**).

7

Doing the Private Eye Thing

Using Internet Resources to Find People

Major E-Mail Address Databases

You've heard it before. Probably lots of times. But the reason certain phrases become clichés is because they contain more than a small measure of truth.

Q. How can I find someone's e-mail address?

A. Pick up the phone, call, and ask!

That's the easy way. As a matter of fact, it used to be pretty much the only way. But as the Internet burst into the mainstream and people from all walks of life made their way online, a variety of useful alternatives have popped up to address the need to track down individual e-mail addresses.

It's important to understand that no single source will fit the bill. There is no such thing as a central repository of e-mail addresses—a comprehensive white pages for the Net, as it were. Some e-mail address directories are known as white pages, but as you'll see farther along in this chapter, these are almost always restricted to a single institution—usually academic. A few attempts have been made to publish hard-copy Internet e-mail address directories, but even more than most print directories about the Net, these are out of date well before they hit the shelves of your favorite local compu-bookstore.

People come and go on the Net all the time. They change jobs; they move; they graduate; they switch Internet providers. A somewhat-smarmy little book appeared several years ago called *E-Mail Addresses of the Rich and Famous,* by Seth Godin (**http://www.nctweb.com/books/richfam. html**). It was a relatively inexpensive paperback, and I'm sure a lot of copies were sold to people desperate to find out how to reach their favorite celebrities—most of whom were *not* listed. As one reviewer stated, "90% of the names listed are for people I've never heard of so they must be rich."

Like Shirley D. Kennedy, whose e-mail address apparently was appropriated by Godin from a newspaper column she used to write. And who, sad to say, is unlikely to become either rich *or* famous unless you tell all your friends to rush out and buy a copy of this book, and persuade Oprah to review it on her show. (And thank you very much!) To top it all off, the e-mail address

listed for me in that slender volume was one I had ceased using years ago. Moral of story? Print directories of e-mail addresses suck!

Online directories are another matter. Sort of. They are still plagued with the "nobody lives here anymore" problem, and none can claim to be totally comprehensive. What this means is you'll probably have to use multiple resources, and yet there is no guarantee of success. While some people have multiple e-mail addresses, plenty of folks out there don't even have *one* (although you can give the street address and phone directories discussed below a try). Many institutions do not make their e-mail address directories available to the public—most corporations, for example (although IBM has put up a convenient search interface to theirs at **http://whois.ibm.com/**), and membership organizations that generate income by selling their directories. There are a few ways of tracking down some of these individual e-mail addresses, but you need to be creative.

If you're reasonably certain that someone does, in fact, have an active electronic-mail account, the easiest way to find his or her address—outside of picking up the phone, assuming you've already got the number—is to try one or more of the large Web-based e-mail directories. Keep in mind that their databases are not identical. Despite the differences in database size, searching each directory is likely to turn up unique entries. So don't hesitate to try all of them.

Bigfoot

Bigfoot (**http://www.bigfoot.com/**) has somewhere between eight and nine million entries in its database, but it doesn't offer some of the sophisticated search features of the other large commercial e-mail directories. The simple search option on the main page has just one text block into which you type as much of a person's name as you know.

Bigfoot's advanced search form—pretty much the equivalent of the basic search form at most of the other sites discussed here—permits searching by first name, last name, street address, city, state, or e-mail address (handy for reverse lookups). As with most of the other directories discussed here, the database entries come from public sources—

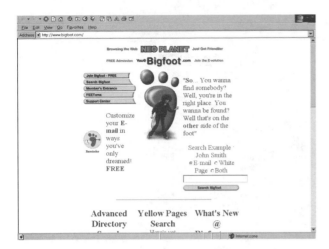

Bigfoot's main page offers a simple search option.

probably Usenet (see below)—and users who register themselves.

There's also a white-pages phone directory here—data are provided by ProCD, the CD-ROM phone-book people. On Bigfoot's advanced search form, users have their choice of clicking on two buttons: E-Mail Info or White Pages Info. This means you can search both databases from the same screen—a small but convenient option.

Four11 Directory Services

The Four11 Directory Service (**http://www. four11.com/**) claims a database of more than ten million "unique e-mail address listings." Where do these listings come from? About a million people have gone ahead and registered themselves here. Whole bunches of other folks were "auto-registered" by their Internet service providers. The rest of the addresses come from "public sources (primarily Usenet)." In 1996, Four11 merged with LookUP!—another directory service, which likely added to the database as well.

There are two levels of service here. Search options for unregistered users include all the ones you'd expect—first name, last name, Internet domain, city, state, and country—and one very nifty feature, SmartName. Click in the Smart-Name check box, and the search engine will look for *Bill, Billy,* and *Will* as well as *William.*

As an incentive to get people to add themselves to the database, Four11 offers a few enhanced search features for registered users, including the following:

Group Connections permits searching the database by common interests, past and current organizations, past high schools, favorite "Web hangouts," and research topics of interest.

Sleeper Searches runs your searches automatically as new entries are added to the directory and forwards results to your own e-mail address.

A higher limit is available on the number of names that can be returned from an e-mail search. Unregistered users are limited to fifty hits, while registered users can receive up to two hundred. (Four11 says it places these numerical limits on search names "in order to make it more difficult for people to abuse the . . . database for marketing purposes.")

The Alternative Names Feature permits inclusion of maiden names, husband and wife names, nicknames, alternative name spellings, and alternative name combinations in your database entry, which provides more options for people searching for you.

Other things worth knowing about searching Four11:

All search fields are optional (although some search fields need to be used with other search fields). If your search criteria match too many entries, you will be asked to narrow your search. Don't bother entering a middle name or initial, as the search won't support this.

Searches are "NOT cAsE SeNsItIvE." *Mary, mary,* and *MARY* are equivalent.

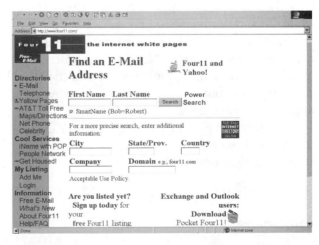

Four11 is an e-mail directory with plenty of bells and whistles.

All search criteria are ANDed together (as opposed to ORed). Therefore, for an entry to match, it must satisfy all search criteria—e.g., First Name AND Last Name AND City.

In some cases, very common words (*a, the, in, at,* etc.), punctuation marks, and symbols are ignored.

An asterisk (*) at the end of a name or word is interpreted as the wild-card character. It can only be used at the end of a word, not the beginning or middle.

Four11 claims that three thousand people a day add themselves to the database and that e-mail addresses are verified at least once a year. (Registered users may log in and update their own information at any time.) Documentation claims that the database also includes non-U.S. e-mail addresses.

Other resources available at Four11 are a U.S. white pages telephone directory search, an e-mail directory for U.S. senators and representatives, and a serendipitous offering called Celebrities on the Net—somewhat of a misnomer, since e-mail addresses aren't available for the vast majority of celebrities listed, only snail-mail addresses, usually for studios, etc.

If you use one of the various Internet telephone software programs—or you're curious about Internet telephony in general—check out the particularly extensive Net Phone section here. You can browse through directories of folks who use the various software packages and are eager to yak with you—including folks who are online with their Net phones right then and there, in real time. Click on someone to give him or her a "ring." You'll also find download links to working demo versions of various Net Phone products. You'll find this same resource at some of the other directory sites, but it seems particularly extensive and easy to navigate here.

Incidentally, Four11 was acquired by Yahoo! in late 1997, so you can now use the directory from **http://yahoofour11.com/**.

InfoSpace

Billing itself as "the Most Innovative Directory on the Internet," InfoSpace (**http://www.infospace.**

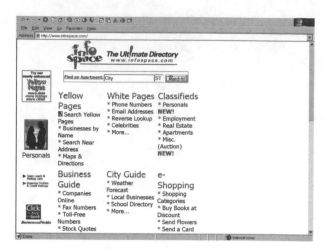

The force behind InfoSpace is a former product manager for the Microsoft Network.

com/) has integrated white and yellow pages of directories together and claims to include "more than 112 million people in the U.S."

InfoSpace licenses proprietary data from companies such as Harris Publishing, which aggregates information on federal, state, and municipal employees. Regional phone-book data are also included.

Proprietary search tools and database technology allow for bells and whistles galore. Users can click on a street address on a Web page and be shown via an on-the-fly map where that site is in the real world. It's also possible to do such things as specify an intersection and ask to be shown nearby hotels, restaurants, stores, schools, etc.

You can get corporate profiles as well as links to the sites of any business in the database that has a Web presence. And there's a wealth of government information, including a search tool for officials, right down to the municipal level. The address and telephone directory search results (data provided by ProCD) contain "click here to dial" links. All you have to do is put your Touch-Tone telephone handset in front of your computer's multimedia speakers while the number's tones are being played. (I guess they're assuming you have a second phone line.) Click on the person's name and you can do an immediate search in the directory to see if they have an e-mail address.

InfoSpace offers the following advice for e-mail address searching:

- You must enter a first or a last name.
- You may enter as many or as few fields as you choose.

- If there are more than one hundred results, you will not see any of them. You need to provide more information to narrow your search.
- In the United States only, when the results appear, you can click on the name to get more information on that person. If the information is available, you will get a list of possible addresses and phone numbers for that person.
- Choose a province or state only if searching for someone in Canada or the United States.
- You may add, change, or delete your e-mail listing with InfoSpace at any time if you have a digital ID (an electronic means of identification involving encryption).
- If you are not allowed to do any more searches, you may request to increase your quota by sending a request to quota@infospace.com.

These last two points, obviously having to do with quality, accuracy, and quantity control, are somewhat confusing. At the time I checked this site, there was just a bit of documentation online—including a link users could follow to read about and obtain a digital ID from Verisign (**http://digitalid.verisign.com/**).

Internet Address Finder

The Internet Address Finder, IAF (**http://www.iaf.net/**), with upward of 5.8 million entries and growing, is a service similar to Four11, with fewer bells and whistles. Like Four11, it uses public databases (Usenet again) as the source of its entries; a self-registration option is also available. You can search here by first name, last name, organization, and domain. You can also do an e-mail address reverse lookup.

When you view your search results, keep in mind that Organization refers to the *owner* of the person's e-mail address domain rather than the individual's institutional affiliation (unless they happen to be the same). In other words, if someone's e-mail address is janedoe@aol.com, the listed organization will be America Online. In all probability, Jane Doe doesn't actually work there. The results display will also show the date the record was last updated—a nice feature—and a

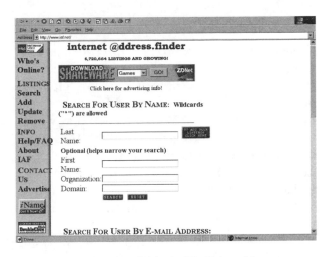

Where do the Internet Address Finder's entries come from? Basically, from the same places as other directories: "The Internet Address Finder gets its information about you from public information available through the Internet, primarily through perusal of Usenet news postings. Thus, if you've ever posted a message to a news group on the 'Net, it's likely that you will be in our database."

guess at the organization's Web site, with a live link to the site. Inevitably, IAF makes its guess by adding *www* to the domain name to the left of the @ sign in the e-mail address. Quite often, this is dead wrong.

Some hints for searching in Internet Address Finder:

- All fields are case insensitive.
- Enter as much information as you can to narrow your search. This will make your search run much faster.
- You may use the wild-card character (*) in any field, especially if you are uncertain of the spelling of a name.
- An entry is always required in the last name field (except for reverse e-mail address lookups).
- If a person's name has a suffix (e.g., *Jr., Sr., II,* etc.), you may want to append the wild-card character (*) to the last name, so that all variants will be found.
- If you know a user's e-mail address, use the reverse lookup search. Obviously, this will be very fast and quite precise.

Usenet Addresses Database

Usenet is a collection of online discussion groups that are accessible from a humongous number of Internet sites, usually through your own Internet provider. Usenet has been around for a long time—actually, since before the Internet as we know it. The address database itself (**http://usenet-addresses.mit.edu/**) is clearly delineated. You can search here by given name, surname, Isolated Name, Organization, or Arbitrary Text. Isolated Name can be confusing; the documentation says:

> By "Isolated Name," we mean that a first name and last name were not both included when the person posted to Usenet. The person may have included initials instead of their first name or last name, for example. The person may also have entirely omitted their first name

or last name. Another possibility is that the person posted using a nickname or pseudonym. Finally, it's possible that this isolated name is the person's full legal name, especially if the person is from a culture that does not have separate first and last names. Here are some examples:

- "Mrs. Rayburn" <principal@grant-ave.edu>—(Isolated Name: Rayburn)

- Gus <gus@fire.mayfield.st.us>—(Isolated Name: Gus)

- Lumpy <c_rutherford@mayfield.edu>—(Isolated Name: Lumpy)

- Ivanhoe <knight1@river-don.or.uk>—(Isolated Name: Ivanhoe)

Organization is the entity through which the person has the computer account that was used for

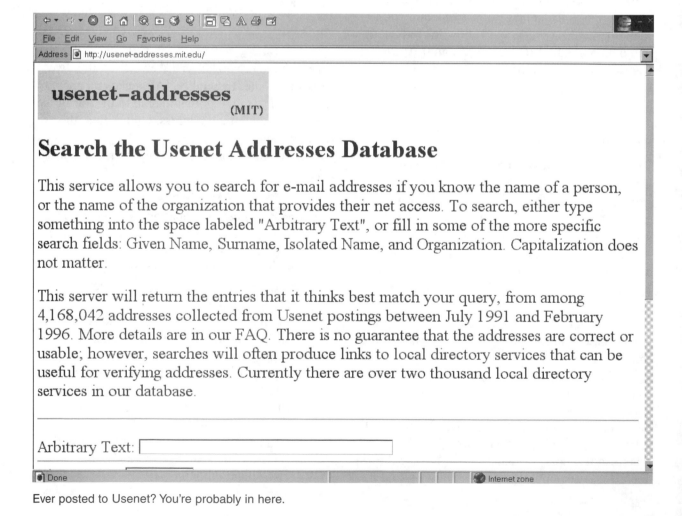

Ever posted to Usenet? You're probably in here.

posting—i.e., place of employment, school, or commercial Internet provider.

Arbitrary Text is part of a person's name or the name of his or her organization. According to the on-screen help, "It is usually not useful to type in the person's username, 'screen name,' or other account identifier."

Obviously, with so few options, this is not a difficult database to search. Just as obviously, since it's derived from only one specific source, it is fraught with limitations. Lots of folks don't use their "real" names when posting to Usenet, and it is heavily used by college students, who are extremely mobile, so you'll find more out-of-date addresses here than in most e-mail databases. If someone doesn't participate in Usenet discussions, you won't find his or her e-mail address in here at all, although some e-mail lists are gatewayed to Usenet.

On the other hand, search results will often contain links to servers that are local to the target of the inquiry, which can be used to verify addresses. And since results are displayed in reverse chronological order, it's possible to see which e-mail address is the most current one for a particular user.

WhoWhere?

WhoWhere? (**http://www.whowhere.com/**) calls itself "the most comprehensive and popular directory on the Net." It boasts more than 10 million e-mail listings, 1.5 million registered users, and 80 million U.S. residential listings. It also says WhoWhere? is "consistently featured among the top 25 most-visited sites on the World Wide Web" according to a Web site at **http://www.100hot.com/**.

With the basic search form, you enter just as much as you know of a person's name and the person's Internet domain, if you happen to know or suspect what it is. The results are displayed ten at a time, color coded as highly relevant, probably relevant, or possibly relevant, with the latter two classifications using fuzzy logic—i.e., *Baker* equals *Barker* equals *Becker,* etc. (Personally, I'm wondering how useful the probably relevant and especially the possibly relevant matches are, since most people looking for someone's e-mail address already know the person's name.) There's also a

When I searched WhoWhere? for myself, I got the shock of my life. Out of all the directories discussed here, WhoWhere? was the one that turned up the most e-mail addresses for me—including some from short-term consulting and sys-admin jobs. Yikes! Obviously, WhoWhere? is vacuuming up e-mail addresses from all over the Net.

hot link to the Web site of the person's Internet provider. (I suspect that they do the WWW-guess thing—adding www. to the front of the domain part of someone's e-mail address—as InfoSpace does.)

An advanced search form allows the kind of options available at Four11 et al., where you can search on personal profile information—here it's called WhoWhere? Communities Advanced Search. Of course, these detail-oriented options are completely useless if the person you're looking for hasn't registered with the database and coughed up the appropriate information online. Surprisingly enough, many people do—and if their names turn up in your search results, you can click on a More Details link and read all about them. You might even find a WhoWhere? pen pal: "WhoWhere? Pen Pals are people who would like to receive e-mail from others who share their interests. On their listing pages, a line will appear that says 'I'm a WhoWhere? Pen Pal.' You may write to them by clicking on their e-mail address." As someone who deals with an avalanche of e-mail in the course of earning a living, I can't imagine actually wanting *more* e-mail, but apparently plenty of people out there feel differently.

If your search is fruitless, you can turn to WhoWhere's E-Mail Wizard, which employs fuzzy logic to try to get results of some sort. Or you can click on the We'll Call You link, and, in the manner of Four11, WhoWhere? will continue running your search against new directory listings, notifying you by e-mail if and when it finds whom it thinks you were seeking.

Other features here? A street address and phone directory with 90 million listings. The ability to search the Geocities (**http://www.geocities. com/**) collection of about 300,000 personal home pages, a directory like Four11's of pointers to Internet phone users, a directory of companies that have Web sites (plus stock prices), a toll-free directory, a yellow pages directory with online mapping, and WhoWhere? EDGAR (**http://edgar.whowhere. com/EDGAR**).

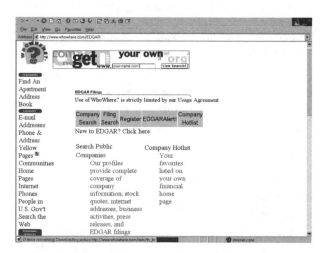

WhoWhere? EDGAR is an enhanced version of the Securities and Exchange Commission's EDGAR database of financial filings.

WhoWhere? EDGAR is cool! It's an enhanced version of the Securities and Exchange Commission's EDGAR database of financial filings for publicly traded companies. You'll find an assortment of other information—Web site addresses, stock quotes, press releases, what have you. Apparently, the WhoWhere? folks are adding to the databases all the time. If you register with WhoWhere? EDGAR, you can set up a personal page with links to companies you're interested in following. You can also set up an Edgaralert! that notifies you when new filings show up in the database. Doing competitive intelligence? This is a nifty tool!

Okay, So Who's Best?

Hard to say. When I searched on my own name, WhoWhere? produced the most listings by far, except some of them were e-mail addresses that don't exist for me anymore and haven't for a while, so I have my doubts that the database entries are being verified, as Four11 claims to be doing. InfoSpace is getting its information from a variety of commercial sources, which should produce a higher-quality database, and the site is unique in the way it manages to combine information from its various databases so you can link to related information from the results of a single search. But there's *so much* here that a confusion factor is created. Bigfoot doesn't offer as much in the way of bells and whistles, but it's fast and convenient if you want to search both e-mail and telephone white pages directories from one screen. The Usenet database, which derives from a limited source, contains the most out-of-date addresses.

When all is said and done, of course, every experienced researcher knows that the best database is the one in which you find the information you need. And since each of the directory databases discussed here is unique, the best strategy is to keep trying one after another until you find what you're seeking.

Are these various directory services making this information available free over the Internet out of the goodness of their virtual hearts? What do you think? It's fairly obvious they're trying to sell advertising, based on their popularity with Web surfers (a common "business model" on the Net these days), and they're licensing their services to various other sites and search engines, so the whole Web-based directory business gets more incestuous every time another one of these deals is closed.

Keep in mind that these sites are also attempting to collect as much information about you as they can. That's why they encourage you to register and fill out a detailed profile form. Amazingly, many people do. Personally, I don't have a problem with my e-mail address's being public information. I use it as a contact point for people who read what I write for publication. And my telephone directory information is already publicly available, since I refuse to enrich the coffers of the local telco by paying to be unlisted.

But I'm not too keen on offering more personal information, like my interests, my profession, where I went to school, what Web sites I like, etc. I have a very real fear of being pursued to the ends of the earth by aggressive peddlers of binoculars and field guides should I reveal in one of these directories that I am interested in birding. The directory providers realize that this is a common fear, and they do address the issue in various ways—making it extremely difficult to retrieve massive numbers of listings, for instance, to curb abuse by direct marketers. They also claim not to sell their data.

On the other hand, AT&T's AnyWho Directory (**http://www.anywho.com/**) will spew forth the names, addresses, and phone numbers of everyone who lives on a particular street. The data come from phone books. Just enter the name of the street and the city and state in the form and click the search button. Telemarketers' heaven!

All of these directories, with the possible exception of the Usenet database, will remove your listing if you request it (although the how-to information is sometimes not easy to find), and there are procedures for updating incorrect information about yourself. Some offer an option to keep your e-mail address private, while still allowing others to get in touch with you by forwarding a notice that such and such a person has tried to contact you.

This is a classic example of one of cyberspace's hottest issues—the right to privacy versus access to information. Let's face it—comprehensive and accurate online e-mail directories are useful, increasingly so as e-mail becomes more and more universal. But we already know how telephone directory information is abused by direct marketers, and e-mail spamming (sending huge amounts of unsolicited, usually commercial, e-mail messages) is turning into a problem of epic proportions. Also, it's another avenue for stalkers—the abusive ex-husband trying to track down his former wife, for example.

It seems to me that information professions have a particularly strong stake in seeing that information like this is used responsibly, lest these resources vanish. Although you can't control the behavior of other people, don't become part of the problem yourself.

Other Sources of E-Mail Addresses

As noted previously, there's no one central repository for e-mail addresses. The biggies are a good place to start, and they're easy enough to use, but they're not your only option. Here are some other resources worth trying.

LOCATE

Know the phone number of the person whose e-mail address you're seeking. Try typing it in 411 Locate (**http://www.411locate.com/**) to see if you get anything back. (I couldn't find myself here, however, despite the fact that I have several e-mail addresses and my phone number is listed.) The database must be small. Users are encouraged to register.

LYCOS, ALTAVISTA, EXCITE, ET AL.

Most of the major Web search sites offer some sort of people-finding option now, although they tend to license the directory databases from one of the major services discussed above.

HOUSERNET

Most of the personal home pages in this directory (**http://www.housernet.com/**) include the e-mail addresses of their creators. While it's not the only resource of this type (and Housernet links to sev-

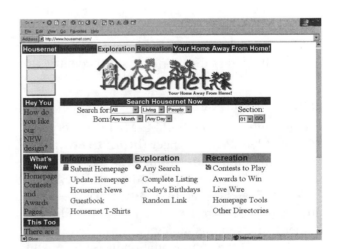

Peruse other people's home pages here.

eral others at **http://www.housernet.com/explore/docs/other.html**), it does offer some fairly unique features, which may come in handy who knows when. For instance, you can search for the home pages of people in particular age groups or of people who were born on the same day as you. Those interested in enhancing their social lives might be interested in combining the age option with the search by gender and marital status options. A lot of other stuff goes on at this site, not all of which is comprehensible to me. It appears that the site's creator is attempting to build a virtual community of sorts here. One major inconvenience is that, as of early 1998, the home page directory was divided into thirty-four(!) separate parts, and a user had to search each part individually. Boo! Hiss!

THE PEOPLE PAGE

One individual's "snapshot of humanity," the People Page (**http://www.peoplepage.com/**) provides no definitive information about the size of the database, although it doesn't compare to the big directories discussed earlier. But you can browse alphabetically by last name and find not only e-mail addresses but links to personal Web pages as well.

WORLD E-MAIL DIRECTORY

With a distinctive international flavor, this directory (**http://www.worldemail.com/**) boasts 12 million e-mail addresses and more than 140 million business and phone addresses. While searching for myself produced a big goose egg, it may be a valuable resource for non-U.S. e-mail addresses, as it has an extensive collection of links to e-mail address directories in other countries.

OTHER RESOURCES

A site similar to the World E-Mail Directory is Global Meta-People Finder (**http://trendy.net/sites/peoplefind/index.html**). Another non-U.S. resource in which I didn't find myself is ESP (E-Mail Search Program) at **http://www.esp.co.uk/**, although there are more than two million other listings in this directory.

Some of the commercial online services and major Internet providers allow you to search for member home pages:

- America Online (**http://home.aol.com/**)
- CompuServe/Sprynet (**http://www.sprynet.com/ourworld/searchow/**)
- Delphi (**http://www.delphi.com/dir-html/simple_web_search.html**)
- Earthlink (**http://www.earthlink.net/company/free_web_pages.html**)
- Mindspring (**http://www.mindspring.com/dbase/**)

Telephone Directories

When Switchboard (**http://www.switchboard.com/**) hit the Web in February 1996, it was unique. With some 90 million residential address and telephone listings, provided by Database America (**http://www.databaseamerica.com/html/index.htm**), it was very much the online equivalent of that somewhat-more-traditional reference tool, the CD-ROM phone directory.

By mid-1997, it contained more than 106 million residential listings and 11 million business listings, attracting something in the neighborhood of 800,000 searches a day. The database also contains some e-mail addresses, if people have added them to their individual listings. You can register your e-mail address without having it made public in the directory by using Switchboard's Knock Knock service:

> The "Show e-mail address as Knock-Knock" feature lets you selectively divulge your e-mail address. If you login to modify your list-

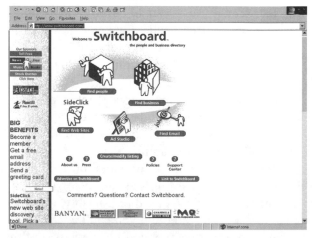

According to its maintainers, Switchboard logs more than five million lookups for people and businesses each week.

ing you can choose this option. Then, when someone wants your e-mail address, they search for you and click the "Knock-Knock" link under your listing (which appears in lieu of your e-mail address). They must login (so Switchboard knows that they are who they say they are), and they write a brief e-mail note that Switchboard forwards to you. When you read the note, you decide whether to reply to that person and hence divulge your e-mail address.

Note that you don't get a log-in name and password unless you register (free).

Searching here is a no-brainer: first name, last name (required), city, state, via a nice, clean interface. This is a wonderful site to show a person who's never been on the Web before (providing you can actually *find* one), since it's very easy to use and the utility of the information is readily apparent.

Switchboard is no longer the only game in town, however. Most of the Web search sites offer similar services now, licensed through one or another directory provider, and so do most of the major e-mail directory services mentioned above.

Canada 411 (**http://canada411.sympatico.ca/**) is an equivalent service for that nation's residential white pages, with more than ten million listings that include those sometimes-elusive Canadian postal codes. Naturally, it's available in both English and French.

There are a number of Web sites with links to large numbers of online telephone directories—from various organizations, government entities, and lots of non-U.S. countries. If such resources are likely to be useful to you on even an occasional basis, have a look:

TELEPHONE DIRECTORIES ON THE WEB

At (**http://www.contractjobs.com/tel/**):

> Only links to directories that make some attempt to be complete (preferably official telco directories) are included. I [Robert Heare, creator and maintainer of this resource] don't list the numerous directories of "businesses on the web." Selective business directories are mostly listed only when there is no telephone directory for that country online. Please note that not all types of directory are

present for all countries, some might only have a phone directory, or only a fax directory.

TELEPHONE DIRECTORIES ON THE NET

Not to be confused with Telephone Directories on the Web, above, this site (**http://www.procd.com/hl/direct.htm**) is provided by those ubiquitous folks at ProCD. There's a ton of stuff here and no search engine—yikes—so use your browser's Find feature (e.g., under the Edit menu on Netscape's toolbar). You can also browse; the list is subdivided by categories: Businesses and Organizations, City and Government Listings, United States Colleges and Universities, Colleges and Universities around the World, and Other Resources, which includes links to university directories on gopher servers, an area-code finder, and a zip-code finder.

YAHOO!

Good old Yahoo! has a bunch of phone directory links at **http://www.yahoo.com/Reference/Phone_Numbers/**, including some oddballs you're not likely to find easily elsewhere. One is El Jefe's Pay Phone Directory (**http://www.televar.com/~eljefe/payfonedir.html**), which provides the numbers of more than 1,800 public phones in the United States (mostly in the state of Washington) and Canada. (Don't ask. Visit the site for an explanation of why this resource is on the Internet.)

Specialized Resources, Tips, and Tricks

Sometimes, the best place to go is a highly specialized resource, like the following:

FOR DOCTORS

At AMA Physician Select (**http://www.ama-assn.org/aps/amahg.htm**), search by name, medical specialty, or disease/condition through a database of more than 650,000 MDs and DOs in the United States and its possessions. Listings offer information about the physician's specialty, credentials, office address and phone number, medical school and year of graduation, and graduate medical education.

FOR LAWYERS

Yes, Martindale-Hubbell Law Directory (**http://lawyers.martindale.com/marhub/**) is online! Search by name, firm name, city, county, state, country. Listings provide information about the attorney's job title, practice areas, education, year admitted to the bar, and year of birth, plus office address and phone number. Or try West's Legal Directory (**http://www.wld.com/**), which offers an advanced search form that allows you to search by eighteen different fields, including unusual ones like Courts Admitted to Practice and Publications, Classes Taught, Affiliations.

FOR COLLEGE INFORMATION

College E-Mail Addresses (**http://www.qucis.queensu.ca/FAQs/email/college.html**) is actually a FAQ document, with instructions on how to find addresses at a broad range of schools, from Abilene Christian University to York University. Also included are collections of links to university home pages around the world, plus some general hints and tips on e-mail address finding.

FOR ADOPTEES AND BIRTH PARENTS

Angry Grandma's Adoptee's Links Page (**http://www.ior.com/~laswi/bookmark.htm**) has a fairly comprehensive collection of links to sites on the Net devoted to reuniting adoptees and their birth parents.

FOR CELEBRITIES

The collection of information at How to Contact a Celebrity (**http://www.islandnet.com/~luree/howto.html**) is a good place to start.

FOR EXPERTS

Looking for an acknowledged expert in a certain discipline? Try ProfNet Experts Database (**http://www.profnet.com/ped.html/**), which offers profiles of more than two thousand individuals whom public information officers on college campuses have identified as leading experts in their fields. ProfNet started as a service to link journalists with public information officers of universities, medical centers, national laboratories, nonprofit organizations, corporations, and government agencies—a source of experts in a wide range of fields. In general, journalist-oriented sites often provide excellent leads to resources for tracking people down (see chapter 4).

FOR DEAD PEOPLE

Try the Dead People Server (**http://www.city-net.com/~/mann/dps/**) for celebrities, mostly. "It's really fun" (Pat Paulsen). The Obituary Page (**http://catless.ncl.ac.uk/obituary/**) lists mainly average people whose friends and relatives have submitted online memorials (free). It includes links to other online obituary pages. Besides the Social Security Death Index (**http://www.ancestry.com/SSDI/Main.htm**) at the Ancestry HomeTown, a major genealogy site, there's a database of American marriage records (1800s and earlier) at **http://www.ancestry.com/marriage/** and a number of other biographical databases.

FOR TRANSPORTATION PROFESSIONALS

The netAddress Book of Transportation Professionals (**http://dragon.princeton.edu/~dhb/TRANSPORT_NAB/**) includes a variety of folks—DOT officials, engineers, municipal transit authority workers, shipping and trucking people, professors. The search form is primitive—click next to a letter of the alphabet, click the Process This Request button, and your results will be a list of everyone in the directory whose last name begins with that letter of the alphabet—with e-mail addresses and links to Web sites, if any.

FOR HISTORICAL FIGURES

Historical biographical databases on the Internet range in quality from pitiful to magnificent. Best to start hunting for these in specific subject areas—science, mathematics, women, etc. Or try a couple of the best history meta-sites:

- Horus's History Links (**http://www.ucr.edu/h-gig/horuslinks.html**)
- The HistoryNet, National Historical Society (**http://www.thehistorynet.com/home.htm**)
- University of Kansas Index of Resources for Historians (**http://kuhttp.cc.ukans.edu/history/index.html**)

FOR PROFESSIONALS

Lots of specialized professional directories are found on the Internet, especially in the areas of science, technology, and education—any discipline where collaborative research is the modus operandi and researchers want to find each other. These are most easily located by searching in the specific subject area and following links to professional associations or universities with particularly strong teaching departments in that subject area.

Meta-Sites and Resources for People Finding

The sheer number and variety of people-finding resources on the Net are proof positive that what most people really like to do online is communicate with one another—for better or for worse! Note that the name in parentheses after a site's title in the list below is that of the site's creator.

- A Stalking We Go! (Glen L. Roberts)—**http://www.glr.com/stalk.html**
- CULTURE-People-Lists—directories, home pages (John December, Computer-Mediated Communications)—**http://www.december.com/cmc/info/culture-people-lists.html**
- FAQ: How to Find People's E-Mail Addresses—**http://www.qucis.queensu.ca/FAQs/email/finding.html**
- Gopher-based directory of e-mail address servers at universities and research institutions around the world (must be searched individually)—**gopher://merlot.gdb.org:70/11/phonebooks** (Web-based interface to this resource—**http://home.cdsnet.net/~zachbo/others.html**)
- INTERNET-Searching-People (John December, Computer-Mediated Communications)—**http://www.december.com/cmc/info/internet-searching-people.html**
- InterNIC (Internet Network Information Center) White Pages Directory Services—**http://ds.internic.net/ds/dspgwp.html**
- Magnum P.I. in Cyberspace (NetGuide Live)—**http://www.netguide.com:10101/knowhow/snapguides/friend/index.html**
- NAIS Private Investigator's Link List (Ralph D. Thomas, National Association of Investigative Specialists)—**http://www.pimall.com/nais/links.html**

- Training: Finding E-Mail Addresses (U.S. Region 2 EPA NY Library)—**http://www.epa.gov/Region2/library/mailhelp.htm**
- Webgator: Investigative Resources on the Web (David Guss)—**http://www.inil.com/users/dguss/wgator.htm**

Hints and Tips

One often-overlooked source of e-mail addresses is Internet mailing lists. When you subscribe to a magazine, for example, the publisher often sells its mailing list to direct marketers. While maintainers of electronic mailing lists don't do this (to the best of my knowledge, and I'd certainly like to hear about it if anyone has verifiable evidence to the contrary), e-mail subscription lists are available—although in many cases, they're only lists of e-mail addresses without names attached. (Of course, you can use one of the reverse lookup tools available at the major e-mail address directory services if you find any likely suspects while scanning the list of addresses.)

The first thing we're assuming here is that the person whose e-mail address you're trying to track down is, in fact, on the Internet. What do you know about the person? What's his or her profession? Any hobbies or other special interests? Start by heading over to one of the large directories of Internet mailing lists (see chapter 8). If the person you're looking for is a microbiologist, for example, search for mailing lists having to do with microbiology. If you know the person is a ham radio operator, search for ham radio mailing lists. You get the picture.

Not surprisingly, e-mail is the tool used to obtain a list of e-mail addresses for the people subscribing to a particular mailing list. Exactly what you do depends on the software being used to manage the administrative functions of the list.

For lists running on the powerful LISTSERV software (i.e., to subscribe, you send a message to listserv@hostname.domain), send an e-mail message to the LISTSERV address (*not* the mailing list address—you want this message to go to the computer managing the list, not to the members of the list). Leave the subject line of the message blank. In the body of the message, type *review listname*, where *listname* is the name of the mailing list you want to search.

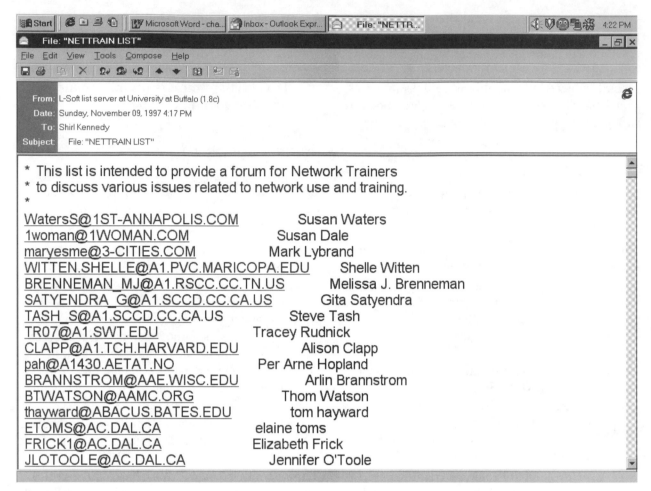

To search NETTRAIN, the e-mail list for Internet trainers, type *review nettrain* in a message to the listserver.

What you'll get back is a list of e-mail addresses, sometimes with names, depending on how things are set up on the host computer. A couple of caveats: Some lists don't allow themselves to be *review*-ed unless you are a subscriber to that list. If you're really gung ho, go ahead and subscribe (see chapter 8). You can always unsubscribe later. Also, some list members *conceal* themselves, a command option supported by the LISTSERV software. This means the names and e-mail addresses of these folks won't show up when someone sends off a *review* message.

For lists running on Majordomo, a public-domain mailing list management program, your message goes to majordomo@hostname.domain. Leave the subject line blank and type *who listname* in the body of the message, where *listname* is the name of the mailing list in which you're interested.

For mailing lists running on other software packages:

- Listproc (listproc@hostname.domain): Recipients (listname)
- Mailbase (mailbase@hostname.domain): Review (listname)
- Mailserv (mailserve@hostname.domain): Send/List (listname)

Most of this information came from Discussion Lists: Mailing List Manager Commands, by Jim Milles (**http://lawwww.cwru.edu/cwrulaw/ faculty/milles/mailser.htm**).

An increasingly popular pastime on the Web—at least for certain types of individuals—is ego surfing. As the major search engine databases get larger and larger, sometimes it's irresistible to plug in your own name and see how many hits come back. Well, why not try plugging in the name of the person you're interested in finding? It's simple enough, and what have you got to lose? Start with the big guns—AltaVista, HotBot, Infoseek (see chapter 5). Try both the Web option and the Usenet database option. If you suspect the person might regularly participate in Usenet newsgroup discussions, head straight for DejaNews (see chapter 8).

Do you know where the person works? Try prowling the organization's Web site. Universities are quite likely to have student-faculty-staff directories online. Corporations usually don't make this information available on the Internet, although you might get lucky. Some companies, particularly high-tech outfits, run a server for employee Web pages, and you may be able to track someone down by searching for those.

You can find out when and in which state someone's social security number was issued at the Informus Corporation site (**http://www.informus.com/ssnlkup.html**). Informus does pre-employment screenings for a fee. This SSN lookup service is free; all you get, however, is a year and a state.

Finger is a nifty little Unix-based utility that allows you to look for a user by log-in name or full name on a particular host computer (see chapter 9). The service will return information stored about the user in question. The results that you get from a finger search will vary because differing sites implement the command differently. Some sites have disabled the finger command for security reasons. If this is not the case, however, the usual response to a finger request is brief, describ-

If you're a command line kind of person, finger can be used from almost any Unix shell account. But if you don't have access to an account like this, a Web-based interface is Finger Gateway, at **http://www.cs.indiana.edu:800/finger/gateway/**.

ing the site to which you issued the command and, possibly, something about the user.

Some systems will tell you if the user you have fingered is logged in at the moment. Some systems will tell you if the user has unread e-mail waiting. Sometimes you will see a line that says, "No plan." This does not mean that the user has no plans. It means that the program is unable to display a file named plan that may be stored in the home directory of the user. Some sites return responses with partial matches. If you finger th@hostname.domain, you may receive a list of active users who have the character string *th* somewhere in their user or full name. Fingering @hostname.domain with nothing to the left of the @ sign will sometimes return a list of active users at that particular host.

8

Mailing Lists and Usenet Newsgroups

The Heart and Soul of the Internet

It's easy to forget about the Internet's "people" resources, but they're just as important (if not more so) as the computers that are available. Far from being a machine-dominated wasteland, where anti-social misfits sporting pocket protectors flail away at keyboards, the Internet is a friendly place to meet people just like you.

—Ed Krol, *The Whole Internet User's Guide and Catalog*

What's Here?

Scammers and Stalkers and Scumbags . . . Oh, My!

Internet Mailing Lists: Finding Them, Joining Them, Mining Their Resources

Usenet Newsgroups
  DejaNews
  Reference.COM

Just the FAQs, Ma'am

Scammers and Stalkers and Scumbags . . . Oh, My!

Okay. I plead guilty, guilty, guilty. I once wrote a monthly column for a large daily newspaper about "information technology"—mainly about the Internet. That was just four or so years ago, but already the hype was beginning to get out of control. And the powers-that-be were buying into it. They became much less interested in practical uses of the Internet and much more eager to see columns about the sensational aspects—online stalkers, pedophiles, etc. After a gut-wrenching experience writing about a "stalker" on a major online service, I decided it was time to fold my editorial tent and move on. I found a much better fit writing for *Information Today* (**http://www. infotoday.com/**), a professional publication for the electronic information industry.

If you're unfamiliar or inexperienced with the Internet, you could get a very distorted picture of cyberspace based on what you read in the popular media or watch on the boob tube. All you have to do is log on, and filthy pictures pop up on your monitor. Pedophiles lurk behind every electron, seeking to prey on your children. Fast-buck artists are trying to get their virtual hands on your wallet. Hate groups, religious extremists, anarchists, and fringe political organizations are In Your Face all over the Web.

Certainly, all this stuff is out there, but, by and large, unless you go looking for trouble, you're unlikely to find it—or if you do, it's simple to hit the Delete key or click on to the next Web site.

In six years on the Internet, I've never had what I would consider to be a bad experience. Granted, I've run into a few nuts. Heck, there's also a crazy sidewalk preacher—pacing back and forth, spouting scripture—in front of my favorite local Chinese restaurant. But overwhelmingly, the folks I've met on the Internet have been kind, funny, helpful, supportive. If you know where to ask and how to ask, you can get an amazing amount of assistance, especially from your professional colleagues, no matter how far-flung. Many, many times, a quick e-mail or even a phone call can save you hours of searching—online or in the stacks somewhere.

Internet Mailing Lists: Finding Them, Joining Them, Mining Their Resources

Despite all the hype connected with the World Wide Web, e-mail is *still* the most frequently used Internet tool for the vast majority of Netizens. As a matter of fact, even if the only Internet access you have is an e-mail account, you can still tap almost every other resource out there—FTP sites, search engines, directories. It may not be fast, elegant, or easy, but it *can* be done. Curious? Check out Bob Rankin's Accessing the Internet by E-Mail FAQ at **ftp://rtfm.mit.edu/pub/ usenet/news.answers/internet-services/access- via-email**.

Nevertheless, what most of us do with e-mail is *communicate*. E-mail communication takes either of two forms: one to one (a message to my boss) or one to many (a message to a group of people).

Internet mailing lists—which are, essentially, e-mail-based discussion groups—are an excellent example of the latter.

There are, quite literally, thousands of mailing lists out there, on virtually every topic imaginable. I doubt if there's a single professional group anywhere without at least one relevant mailing list devoted to the concerns of its practitioners. If you think I'm kidding, take a look at these real-life examples, with their descriptions extracted from a mailing list search tool:

> LIFEGARD is an unmoderated discussion list for Lifeguards, dealing with any issue they feel is worthy of discussion, with relation to their job. Such topics have included first aid, equipment, rescue procedures, staffing trouble, facility design, uniforms, textbooks, training, in-services, and others.
>
> Plumbers-L is an unmoderated open discussion list for all plumbers and plumbing contractors. The list also welcomes manufacturers and suppliers to join in an atmosphere of open, noncommercial communication. Plumbers-L is intended to be a forum for free-flowing conversation and shared experiences that benefit our trade and our livelihoods.

MINISTRY is a discussion list for ministers and for those interested in the pursuit of ministry. It's a conversational list rather than strictly academically motivated. In this way, ministers can get a "feel" for how other ministers work in places other than their own congregations, and people in the pursuit of ministry can find out one of the hardest things to really know: What is it to be a minister?

DOM_BIRD is a discussion group about the general health and husbandry of fancy or unusual breeds of chickens, pigeons, ducks, guinea fowl, pheasants, peafowl, etc. and the commercial production of ostriches and emus, etc.

CLOCKS is a discussion list dealing with any and all aspects of clock and watch work. The list's primary goal is to discuss the collecting, construction, and repair of both clocks and watches. Included also are topics on the history of time keeping, wooden movements, water clocks, antique and modern clocks, etc. Of great interest is information about suppliers of repair and construction parts and techniques, information, books, newsletters, national and local associations. Another interest is the use of clock/watch tools, such as the watchmakers lathe, bushing replacement, time regulation, etc.

You get the general idea. Think of how amazing this is: Internet mailing lists allow anyone with an e-mail account to network with colleagues all over the world. If you need advice on a professional problem, if you want unbiased evaluations of a product or service, if you have a job opening to fill, if you are looking for hints and tips on how to do something specific, sign onto the appropriate mailing list, and the world is your oyster.

Drew Smith (**http://www.cas.usf.edu/lis/faculty/smithd.html**), an instructor in the School of Library and Information Science at the University of South Florida, describes to students in his Internet classes a real-life example of productive mailing list use. Prior to his arrival at USF, Smith was a computer user services consultant at another university. Faculty members there were complaining because the systems people were requiring

password changes every thirty days for security reasons. Smith wanted to know what the rule was at other academic institutions. So he sent off a query to a mailing list for—surprise—academic computing user services staff. Within a day or so, he received about twenty-five replies. He was able to plug the data into a comparison table and show the powers-that-be how many colleges required password changes every thirty days, every sixty days, every ninety days, and so forth. "Even if I knew who all these people were and had their phone numbers," Smith says of his fellow list members, "when would I have had the time to call them?"

Thanks to a variety of excellent search tools, it's easier than ever to track down relevant professional mailing lists—as well as lists devoted to just about any avocational passion you might have. If you're a library professional, the first place to go is Library-Oriented Lists and Electronic Serials, at **http://info.lib.uh.edu/liblists/liblists.htm**.

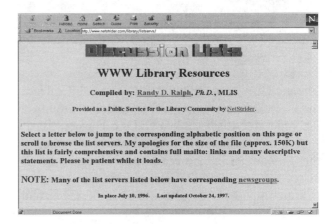

An alternative to Library-Oriented Lists and Electronic Serials is the Discussion Lists page at Randy Ralph's WWW Library Resources site, **http://www.netstrider.com/library/listservs/**.

Probably the most convenient one-stop-shopping spot for mailing list search tools is Inter-Links (**http://alabanza.com/kabacoff/Inter-Links/listserv/subscribe.html**). Here you'll find pointers to the major mailing list directories—the Directory of Scholarly E-Lists, the huge list of Internet

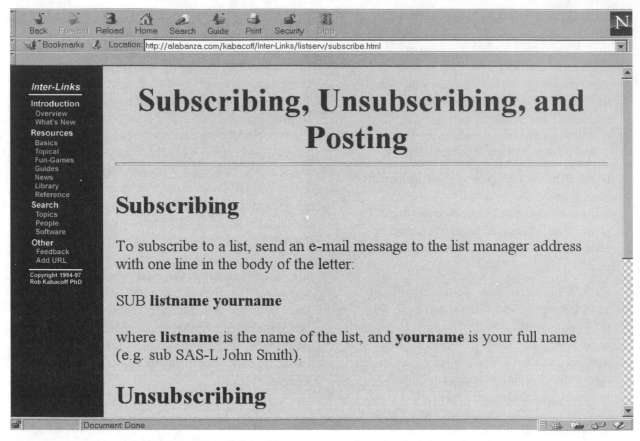

Not only can you search for mailing lists at Inter-Links, you can also learn how to participate.

Interest Groups maintained at Dartmouth College, the Liszt Directory of Email Discussion Groups, the venerable List of Lists, and the Tile.net List of Internet Discussion Groups. Keyword searching these resources is a no-brainer, and Inter-Links also offers a good collection of help files on how to sign on and off lists, how to post messages, and other fine points of list etiquette.

Key point to remember: every list has *two* e-mail addresses—the administrative address of the computer running the mailing list software (LISTSERV, Listproc, Majordomo) and the actual mailing list address. Administrative requests—*sign me up, remove me,* etc.—go to the computer's administrative address. To communicate with the other list members, send your message to the mailing list address. This will all make more sense after you've searched for some lists and read the appropriate help files. At any rate, don't ever send administrative requests to the mailing list address. It won't tell the computer running the list management software anything, and it will mark you for-

ever in the eyes of your fellow list members as a clueless newbie! It's the online equivalent of sending one of those "I want to subscribe" cards to every one of, say, *Time* magazine's zillion or so subscribers. A very nice, short-and-sweet primer called Listservers: What They Are and What They Can Do for You, by UCLA's Department of Library and Information Science, is available at **http://www.gslis.ucla.edu/LIS/lab/unote05.html**.

If you can't find what you're looking for via Inter-Links, try CataList, the catalog of LIST-SERV LISTS (**http://www.lsoft.com/lists/listref. html**). L-Soft International, Inc., which maintains this site, is the company behind LISTSERV software, a powerful mailing list management program for host computers. LISTSERV is often tossed around casually in Net-related conversation as a synonym for mailing lists in general, many of which actually run on public-domain software programs such as Listproc or Majordomo rather than via LISTSERV. The people at L-Soft are interested in having you know that LISTSERV is a registered trademark. So as a writer, I'm not allowed to use LISTSERV generically, and you probably shouldn't either. Except what you will find at CataList is, in fact, a directory of almost eleven thousand LISTSERV-managed mailing lists, generated and updated automatically from LISTSERV's LISTS database. You can search for mailing lists of interest here or view lists in alphabetical order (if you're a masochist), by host site or host country. You can also choose to look at lists that currently boast ten thousand subscribers or more or lists with one thousand subscribers or more. There's also information for *list owners*—the folks responsible for individual mailing lists, usually a thankless labor-of-love-type volunteer job.

Stephanie da Silva's list of Publicly Accessible Mailing Lists, at **http://www.neosoft.com/internet/paml/index.html,** is a resource that has gotten better and better over time. You can browse through more than sixty-eight thousand lists by name or subject, and the easy-to-navigate site is updated regularly.

A fair number of mailing list discussions are archived somewhere. There's no central repository for these archives à la DejaNews, the Usenet newsgroup search tool discussed below, although the Reference.COM site, also below, is attempting to create one. Usually, when you sign onto a mailing list, you automatically receive some sort of informational document that tells you about the list (including how to sign off—*vital* information that you should save, lest you end up like poor Charlie on the MTA). Usually, if the list is archived, this welcome message tells you where the archive is and how you can search it. These archives are valuable resources for any number of reasons.

For instance, it's always worth running an archive search before you post a message about some issue on which you'd like the input of the list members. That very topic could have been dis-

Publicly Accessible Mailing Lists is a mom-and-pop undertaking. As described in the introductory material, "Peter da Silva is the typing machine [slave] for these pages. He does the web stuff, but his wife . . . does all the real work."

cussed just prior to the time you joined the list, and you can extract the information from the archives yourself rather than asking the folks on the list to reinvent the wheel for you. There's a collection of links to library-oriented mailing list archives on the Web pages maintained by Southern Connecticut State University's Buley Library and Department of Library Science and Instructional Technology (**http://library.scsu.edu/ libbib.html**).

Some of these archives are Web based with sophisticated keyword searching interfaces. Others are a bit more primitive, ranging from indexes on gopher servers to files on FTP servers. The archives of mailing lists running on LISTSERV software are housed on the host computer itself. To search an archived LISTSERV, send an e-mail message to the LISTSERV address (that's the computer, not the address of the list itself), placing the search commands in the body of the message. Remember that you're actually sending commands to a remote computer rather than a live body, so the whole thing seems a bit cryptic, to put it mildly.

For example, the message:

//

DATABASE SEARCH DD=RULES

//RULES DD *

SEARCH *phrase* IN *listname*

INDEX

/*

will return all articles from the mailing list *listname* that contain the text *phrase*. The e-mail message you'll get back from the computer will contain a list of numbered articles matching your search criterion, along with their subject lines.

You use the article numbers to send a second message to the computer, requesting the ones you wish to read:

//

DATABASE SEARCH DD=RULES

//RULES DD *

SEARCH phrase IN *listname*

PRINT ALL OF *numberlist*

/*

Back will come a message with the contents of the articles indicated by your *numberlist* (e.g., PRINT ALL OF 112, 115, 137, 218). It ain't slick, but it's eminently doable!

Usenet Newsgroups

Asking experienced Internet users to define Usenet is a lot like that well-known poem "The Blind Men and the Elephant." How they feel about this amorphous mass of discussion groups depends a lot on their individual perspectives.

If mailing lists serve as the prime example of one-to-many communication on the Internet, Usenet colorfully illustrates the concept of many-to-many communication. By various estimates, there are somewhere between twenty-five and thirty thousand different Usenet newsgroups, organized into somewhat of a hierarchy based on content and, sometimes, place of origin. The word *news* is more or less irrelevant here. Generally speaking, we're talking bulletin board–style message forums, not news à la CNN.

For a user-friendly directory, which presents newsgroups under more familiar subject headings, take a look at CyberFiber's Newsgroups, at **http:// www.cyberfiber.com/news/**. And Randy D. Ralph

Usenet Hierarchy

Bionet	research biology
bit.listserv	forums originating as mailing lists
biz	business
comp	computers and related subjects
misc	forums that don't fit elsewhere
news	forums about Usenet itself
rec	hobbies, games, sports, etc.
sci	science other than research biology
soc	"social" groups—often ethnic
talk	politics and related topics
alt	controversial and unusual topics

The groups themselves are organized into a category. subject.details format. For example, the newsgroup rec.arts.books.children would be in the *recreational* part of the top hierarchy as above, in the *arts* subject area, featuring discussions about *books,* more specifically about books for *children.*

has put together a nice listing of newsgroups having to do with libraries, information science, books, and reading at **http://www.netstrider.com/library/newsgroups/**.

Newsgroups don't operate via e-mail. You don't sign on, as with mailing lists, so the discussion doesn't come to you in the form of e-mail messages in your in box. Rather, you use a client software program called a news reader to access a newsfeed on a computer—usually operated by your Internet provider—running a software program called a news server. The newsfeed is almost like a living organism that travels from news server to news server, all around the globe. It's much like that childhood game you may have played, Whisper down the Aisle. You whispered something in the ear of the person sitting next to you, he or she then whispered it to the person sitting on the other side, and so on. It's been estimated that it takes about three days for an individual Usenet message to propagate itself all around the globe.

Due to the dynamic nature of the Net in general, and of Usenet in particular, determining exactly how big it is can be difficult; current estimates indicate about half a million member sites worldwide, through which about twenty million people post an average of a hundred thousand messages *a day*. That's a lot of chatter. As you might expect, not all of it is highly productive. Usenet has been called an online cocktail party by some, and an online bar fight by others. From an information-quality standpoint, Patrick Crispen, creator of the Internet Roadmap Tutorial (**http://internic.net:80/nic-support/roadmap96/syllabus.html/**), offers the following caveat:

> You should be warned that the information on Usenet is of *much* lower quality. Anybody with an opinion can post anything in a Usenet newsgroup, whether they know what they're talking about or not. If you want to bet your grade in school or your company's or organization's future on information you get from

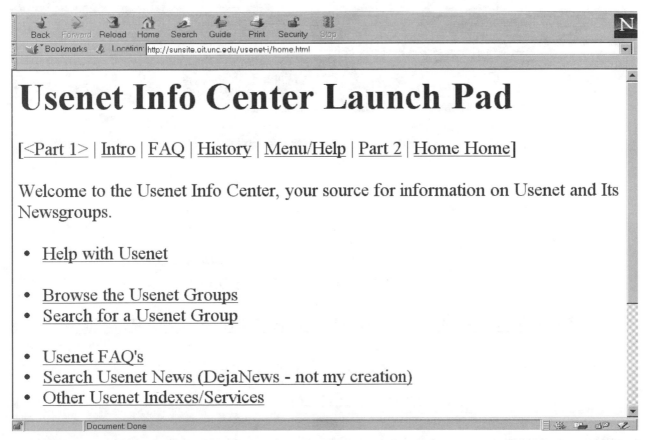

If you're interested in learning all the nitty-gritty details of Usenet, go right to the Usenet Info Center Launch Pad, at **http://sunsite.oit.unc.edu/usenet-i/home.html**.

Usenet, please e-mail me first—I have some bargains in real estate (including a great price for a bridge in Brooklyn) I'd like to discuss with you.

Nonetheless, if you learn the ins and outs of Usenet, you'll find it to be a unique source of information that you can tap judiciously. For one thing, it's an excellent place to find people who are knowledgeable within a particular subject area. Many of the sci-tech newsgroups—in the comp. or the sci. part of the hierarchy—are virtual home to a variety of experts who make it their business to keep discussions within the group strictly on topic. You can post a question in these groups and check back a little later to find one or more authoritative answers waiting for you. Or you can skim through messages, noting the e-mail addresses of participants who seem particularly savvy, and send off a private e-message or two with your query. A simple keyword search tool for finding newsgroups of interest is available at **http://www.cen.uiuc.edu/cgi-bin/ find-news**.

Be advised that Usenet has a unique culture and "netiquette," and it's wise not to go charging into any newsgroups like the proverbial bull in a virtual china shop, lest you offend the very folks who might be able to help you. To get the lay of the land, take a look at:

- Usenet Newsgroup Information for Beginners (**http://www.geocities.com/ResearchTriangle/8211/**)
- SELF-DISCIPLINE: Towards Better News Discussions (**http://www.eiffel.com/discipline/**)
- Usenet: The Global Watering Hole (**http://www.eff.org/papers/eegtti/eeg_68.html**)
- A Primer on How to Work with the Usenet Community (**ftp://rtfm.mit.edu/pub/usenet/news.announce.newusers/A_Primer_on_How_to_Work_with_the_Usenet_Community**)
- Emily Postnews Answers Your Questions on Netiquette—worth reading for entertainment

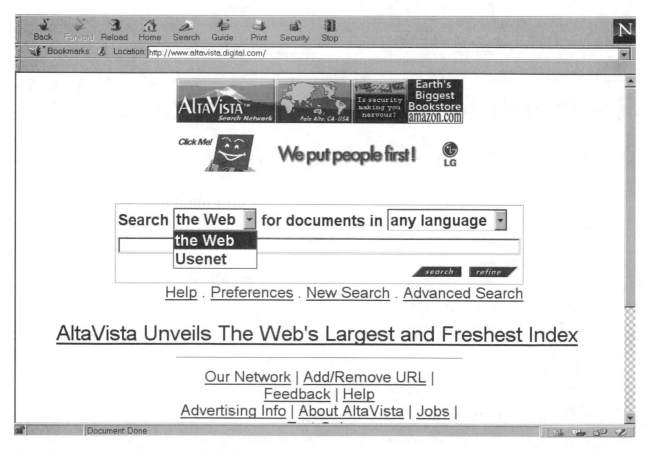

Most of the major search engines offer a Usenet searching option either by a check box or a drop-down menu.

value alone (**ftp://rtfm.mit.edu/pub/usenet/
news.announce.newusers/Emily_Postnews_
Answers_Your_Questions_on_Netiquette**)

Some other things to know about Usenet: Not every Internet provider gets the full twenty thousand–plus newsgroup feed. For one thing, there are entire hierarchies of groups in foreign languages or that are specific to a particular geographic area or organization. For another thing, particularly true if your Internet access is through a nonacademic employer, you may not receive the "nonserious" hierarchies like the alt. or rec. groups. The alt. hierarchy in particular is where most of the controversial groups are (i.e., sex, drugs, and rock and roll). Some of these groups consist of nothing but messages containing encoded images—usually not family oriented— that you can download, decode, and view on your own computer. Since the legal situation vis-à-vis this kind of stuff is far from straightforward, some Internet providers don't offer access to it.

Most large providers and academic institutions do get a *full newsfeed* of more than twenty thousand groups. That's a lot of data. It takes at least five gigabytes of disk space to store all this stuff. Which is why Usenet postings don't hang around on your provider's news server indefinitely. Unlike e-mail discussion groups, where the messages stay in your in box until you read or otherwise deal with them, Usenet newsgroup messages "age off"—providers purge the older stuff to make way for new messages. Depending on policy and available disk space, newsgroup messages may be kept for anywhere from two days to two weeks or more. Some sites may ditch the alt. group messages quickly, but hang on to, say, the comp. or sci. groups for a longer time.

What this means is that if you don't read the newsgroups of your choice regularly—your newsreader software keeps track of the groups in which you're interested and which messages you've seen—you're quite likely to miss something. In theory. In practice, the vast majority of this stuff is now archived somewhere, and you can retrieve messages in your area of interest by keyword searching. Even if you don't follow newsgroups at all, searching Usenet is sometimes a good option if you're looking for information on something

extremely topical or cutting edge. Usenet tends to be particularly strong, subjectwise, in computers, the Internet, almost all scientific disciplines, recreational activities, sociology, psychology, and education, both K–12 and higher academia.

DejaNews

For serious Usenet searching, however, DejaNews (**http://www.dejanews.com/**) is the premier tool, targeted specifically toward this vast and often-confusing resource. DejaNews is a very powerful search tool, with a plethora of options and features. Not only can you search for information, but you can also search for people—e.g., anyone who has posted a message to a Usenet group. It's a good way to track down someone's e-mail address if you think he or she may be a Usenet user, which is discussed at length in chapter 7. The site's documentation explains how you can create an "author profile"—"a statistical summary of all the articles residing in our current Usenet database with a particular e-mail address in the From field of the article." A complete profile includes:

- From field e-mail address (often with a name or handle)
- Number of articles posted and range of posting dates

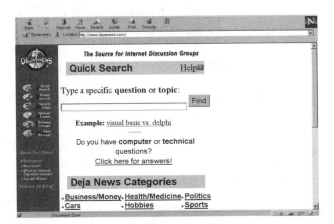

Messages from more than fifteen thousand newsgroups are archived here; documentation at the site (which is extensive, by the way, and well worth reading through if you want to maximize the potential of this resource) indicates that more than five hundred megabytes of new data are collected each and every day. The contents of the archive date back to March 1995.

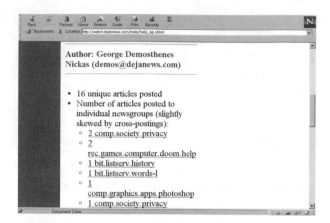

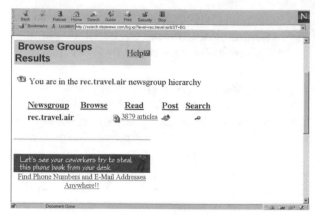

You can do an author profile either by using the Easy Author Profile Form or by clicking on an e-mail address in a DejaNews hit list or article.

- Percentage of articles which were follow-ups to other Usenet articles
- Numerical breakdown of postings to individual newsgroups

While this may be an excellent way to track down folks with a unique area of expertise, there's a definite privacy issue here. You apply for a job. Your prospective employer runs your name through DejaNews and sees that you do a lot of posting to groups in the alt.sex hierarchy. An employer could also search by the domain name of the company—microsoft.com, for instance—and see which employees are using their work-related Internet accounts to post to which newsgroups—and what they're discussing.

While it's not my purpose here to get into a whole rap about the ethics of this particular search tool, you should know that it's relatively easy to forge someone's e-mail address in the header of a newsgroup message. So maybe it isn't *really* your spouse who is posting all that salacious stuff to alt.sex.fetish.feet. The folks at DejaNews do point this out:

> It is important to note that it is possible to forge the e-mail address in the From field. Therefore, articles in our Usenet database and author profiles derived from the headers of these articles may not have actually been sent from the address claimed by the article. Caveat emptor!

By the way, if you don't have access to a news server through your Internet provider, you can post messages to newsgroups from DejaNews, using an online form there. You'll either need to

You can also browse through newsgroups by hierarchy at DejaNews or search for groups of interest by keyword. Then you can actually read the newsgroup messages by typing the names of the groups you're interested in on an online form. Good way to explore Usenet if you're not familiar with it, since everything is pretty much point and click here.

send a confirmation newsletter for each message you wish to post or to register (free) as a DejaNews user, which does away with the need to send confirmation e-mails.

But what you'll usually want to do at DejaNews is search for actual information in its rather-unique database. As Internet guru Hope Tillman, director of libraries at Babson College, Wellesley, Massachusetts, explained in a presentation (**http://www.tiac.net/users/hope/tips/sld001.htm**) done with her husband, Walt Howe of Delphi Internet Services, "DejaNews will point to sources that the other search engines will never find."

Since this is a sophisticated search tool with lots of bells and whistles, it pays to read through the extensive on-site documentation. The Quick Search option is simple enough. Enter your search terms in the text box and click the Find button. Also on the Quick Search page is an Interest Locator search box; type a keyword, click Find, and DejaNews will display those newsgroups likely to contain material of interest to you.

For serious searching, though, what you want is the Power Search form. This offers a wealth of options for refining your query, including Boolean AND/OR, age/date of messages retrieved, number of hits wanted, and schemes for sorting the hits. A bonus option with the Power Search form is the ability to create a Query Filter. You can winnow down extraneous search results by filling in an online form that restricts your search to particular newsgroups, authors, dates, and subjects. Say, for example, you are interested in rockets. You can restrict your search to the sci.space newsgroups so you don't pick up messages about the Houston Rockets basketball team.

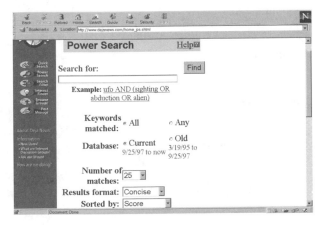

For DejaNews power searches.

Your DejaNews search results are returned in the form of a list of hyperlinked article headings and hyperlinked author names. When you click on a name, you automatically get an author profile, showing which groups that person has posted to and how many messages he or she has submitted. Privacy issues aside again, this can help you avoid messages from spammers—those universally despised individuals who flood every newsgroup with irrelevant messages, usually of a commercial nature. Clicking on the article heading will display the full text of the message, which will likewise

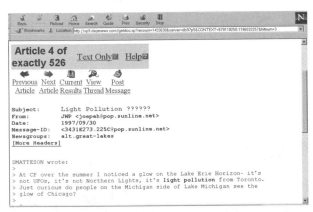

Here's the text of a Usenet item displayed by DejaNews. Notice the highlighted link, *light pollution,* which can take you to other articles related to this *thread* or topic.

provide pointers to other messages in the same *thread*—discussion topic.

Some hints and tips about the DejaNews search syntax:

- AND is the default connector. Either type nothing or use & instead of typing out the actual word. (*Chicken wine* is the same search as *chicken & wine.*)
- OR is represented by |. Unix heads recognize | as the "pipe." (*Chicken | wine* is the proper syntax for an OR search.)
- The symbols &! are the syntax for AND NOT, which is used to exclude words from a search. (*Chicken &! Wine* will eliminate any hits mentioning wine.)
- In DejaNews searches an asterisk (*) is the wildcard character. Be sure to use this if you want hits that include plural forms of the keyword, since the search engine won't produce these automatically. For example, *compan** would be the proper syntax for retrieving hits that include both *company* and *companies*, but you'd also have to use the AND NOT *(&!)* operator to exclude *companion, companionship*, and so on, if you felt it was worth the effort. DejaNews warns that "any search which begins with a wild card will typically result in an error or at least take much longer to process than one that ends in a wild card."
- Parentheses make it possible to combine search elements. For example, in the query *chicken & (wine | rice),* the database would first search for what is inside the parentheses, *wine* or *rice*, and then look for records that also contain *chicken*.
- Braces allow searches on alphabetical ranges of words. The query {*monkey monkeying*} would produce articles containing the words *monkey, monkey's, monkey73, monkeying*, etc.
- If several words are to be searched together as a phrase, enclose them in quotation marks (e.g., *"take this job and shove it"*). The wild-card character (*) cannot be used in phrase searching.
- DejaNews supports the proximity operator ^, which allows you to specify how close one keyword must be to the other. The syntax is *keyword1 ^<distance> keyword2* (e.g., *bogart ^30 maltese*). If a numeral isn't specified— *bogart ^ maltese*—DejaNews assumes a

default distance of five characters. Phrases cannot be used in proximity searching, and wild cards should not be used near the beginning of either keyword.

Stopwords are those words the search engine ignores when doing a search. They're a standard feature of many search engines because they occur so commonly in language that they don't significantly narrow the search. For example, most library cataloging systems ignore the word *the*. A standard DejaNews query must contain one or more nonstopwords. A phrase or proximity search must contain two or more nonstopwords. A complete list of DejaNews's stopwords is available in its online help pages; they include most of the common words you might suspect—*a, and, are, be, for*, etc.—and some that are Usenet specific: *newsgroups, sender, subject*, etc.

It's possible to narrow your searches with context operators, which allow you to zero in on the data you want by making searches based on specific parts of an article (called contexts), such as author, subject, or newsgroup. A context operator before a keyword will cause a search that finds articles with the keyword in the context you specify with the operator:

- Author searching
  (~a): *~a skennedy@pobox.com*

- Subject searching
  (~s): *~s (ibm & layoff)*

- Newsgroup searching
  (~g): *~g sci.space.**
  (retrieves articles only from the five sci.space newsgroups)

- Creation date searching
  (~dc): *~dc 1996/08/05*
  (retrieves all articles posted on August 5, 1996)

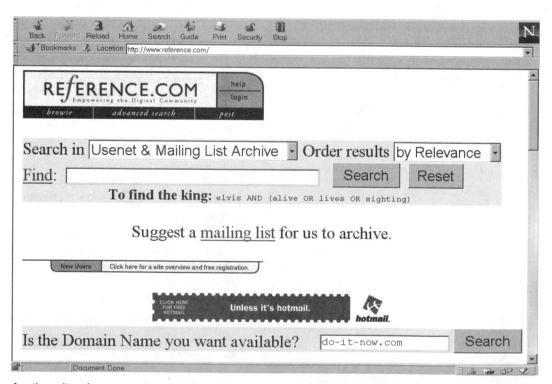

Another site where you can search newsgroup archives is Reference.COM.

Reference.COM

Reference.COM's databases (**http://www. reference.com/**) house the archives of about sixteen thousand newsgroups and—added bonus, since these are harder to come by—the archives of several hundred Internet mailing lists. It's difficult to determine how far back, datewise, the databases go, although the service went "live" in beta form at the end of May 1996. It offers a full range of search features and options, similar to DejaNews, and plenty of documentation is available at the site.

One nifty feature offered here is a "stored query" service. Two types of stored queries are available, according to the site's documentation: passive and active.

Passive queries let you save a frequently run query for future use when you visit the Reference.COM Web site. You can edit passive queries each time you run them, which allows you to use them as customized query templates.

Active queries go one step farther, acting as a clipping service that automatically reruns the same query at an interval you specify. Each time the search is run, you receive an e-mail message that contains the results found since the last search (unless the search produced no hits). Included in the message are a user-defined number of lines for each hit and a URL on the Reference.COM server for retrieving the entire message. (This service actually originated as the Stanford Information Filtering Tool, a well-regarded current-awareness service for Usenet. It was folded into Reference.COM in 1996.)

Just the FAQs, Ma'am

Even experienced Internet researchers sometimes overlook the wealth of information available in Usenet frequently asked questions (FAQs, pronounced either as "F-A-Qs," as an acronym, or "fax"). What's an FAQ? Basically, it's a wonderful example of how the Net takes care of its own.

FAQs are online documents—often quite extensive and containing the collective input of acknowledged experts—that purport to answer all the questions people are likely to ask over and over again in a particular newsgroup. For instance, the folks who participate in soc.genealogy are less than enthusiastic about newbies to the group who post messages like "How do I get started in genealogy?" "How can I access the Mormon databases?" Ad nauseam. An extensive FAQ exists that addresses all these issues—and many, many more. As a matter of fact, there are separate soc.genealogy FAQs available for research in specific ethnic groups.

Although these documents are directed at newcomers to newsgroups (and, indeed, one of the biggest blunders a clueless newbie can commit is to post a message to the group *before* he or she has checked the FAQ to see if the subject was addressed there), they offer a wealth of information to any interested party. Savvy journalists use them to get up to speed quickly on an unfamiliar topic, and they can be a great tool for the reference librarian.

First of all, these documents invariably include the names, e-mail addresses, and, often, professional affiliations of those who contributed to them. Usually, you'll find a date—either when the FAQ was last updated or when it expires. Quite frequently, FAQs include extensive bibliographies of additional resources—books, journals, or other Internet sites. These can often be used to verify an FAQ's information.

FAQs are easy enough to find. The documents are posted to their affiliated newsgroups on a regular schedule, and also to a designated newsgroup called news.answers. The mother of all FAQ repositories is the venerable RTFM archive at MIT (**ftp://rtfm.mit.edu/pub/usenet-by-group/**). (RTFM, by the way, is an acronym for *read the "fine" manual*.) But there are a couple of other Web-accessible FAQ-oriented sites that are somewhat easier to use (and usually less busy than RTFM). One of the best is Infinite Ink Finding and Writing Periodic Postings ("FAQs" and "PIPs"), at **http://www.jazzie.com/ii/internet/ faqs.html**, which offers lots of good background information about FAQs, including pointers to and descriptions of the major archives.

Of course, Yahoo! is always a decent place to start looking: **http://www.yahoo.com/Reference/ FAQs/**. And you can usually manage to unearth

FAQs from the major search engines; most FAQs are available in Web-based hypertext format now, and unless you're going to be printing the thing out, this version is preferable, since there will be live links to the other Internet resources mentioned in the FAQ.

Want to take a look at an FAQ that's a particularly good read? Don't miss the five-parter from alt.folklore.urban (**http://www.cis.ohio-state.edu/ hypertext/faq/usenet/folklore-faq/part1/faq. html**). If nothing in here gives you at least a chuckle, it's time for a major tune-up.

9

Intelligent Life outside the Web

Gopher, Telnet, WAIS, Finger, FTP

What's Here?

Gopher
  What Is It?
  How Do You Use It?
  Veronica and Jughead

Telnet
  What Is It?
  How Do You Use It?
  Hytelnet
  MELVYL

WAIS

Finger

And a Few Words about FTP

Back in the days before point-and-click—before anyone accessed the Internet via a graphical interface—there were still tools and resources that offered value to the researcher. Some (WAIS) were not as easy to use as others (gopher). By and large, these are still available today, although they may be used less often for a variety of reasons. And when we do use them, it's usually through our Web browsers, which "protect" the computer phobic among us from Unix and its associated command-line ugliness.

Since this is a how-to-do-efficient-research book rather than a how-to-do-the-Internet book, I'll spare you the gory details about using these various tools and resources from a Unix command line. Many excellent books are available if you'd like to learn the mechanics. You still can't do much better than the O'Reilly and Associates best-selling classic, *The Whole Internet User's Guide and Catalog,* by Ed Krol (**http://www. ora.com/catalog/twi2/**), although it's ripe for an update.

Anything that's discussed in this chapter can be accessed through a Web browser, although you have to know where to go and what to do when you get there. My objective is to show you the quickest and easiest way to do what you need.

Gopher

What Is It?

When gopher arrived on the Internet scene back in 1991, it was the greatest thing since sliced bread to those of us who'd previously had to track down information by serendipitous rummaging in FTP archives. Created by the academic-computing folks at the University of Minnesota (whose mascot is the Golden Gopher), it is a menu-driven interface through which you can "tunnel" to find what you need—much as you drill down through a subject tree like Yahoo! Except, in most cases, gopher servers were not as nicely organized, at least from a topical standpoint.

Gopher was quickly adopted by libraries, academic institutions and other organizations that wanted a user-friendly way to make information available. Browsing in gopherspace is a no-brainer; you simply choose items from a series of

menus. Because of its linear structure, however, all you can actually do is go up and down the various levels of menus—unlike the World Wide Web, where you can take off in any direction you want.

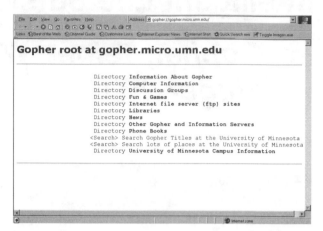

"Mama Gopher" at the University of Minnesota, where it all started.

Although it's fair to say that gopher has pretty much been supplanted as a key Internet navigation tool by the Web, plenty of gopher servers out there still contain good information. And gopher is fast; you're dealing almost exclusively with textual information, so you don't have the retrieval problems associated with those bandwidth-busting multimedia files on the Web.

On the other hand, far too many gopher "ghost towns" are out there, and you have to beware of outdated information. While some institutions dismantled their gopher servers after putting up Web servers, others have essentially

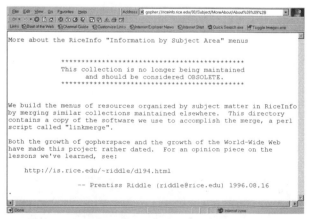

Gopher ghost town, albeit one with a warning label.

condemned their gopher servers to death by benign neglect. Sometimes, but not always, you'll find a disclaimer about the age of the information right on the main gopher menu. So before relying on gopher-based resources, hunt around a bit on the server for some evidence of currency—at least for those subject areas in which this is a critical factor.

How Do You Use It?

As indicated above, the how-to of gopher is not rocket science. If you already know how to mouse your way around the Web, you'll have no trouble clicking your way through the individual gopher menu item links. When you access a gopher server from within a Web browser, you'll see some different menu icons that are pretty self-explanatory. Much more confusing is knowing where to start looking for information in gopherspace if you're not familiar with these resources. While we've already determined that gopher servers are accessible through your Web browser, you need to know that most of the major Web search engines do not index gopherspace. And if your research project demands that you do a deep search of cyberspace, you may well miss something critical if you overlook this part of the Internet—although some experienced Net researchers feel that the odds of turning up a unique, critical resource on a gopher server is diminishing rapidly over time. You have to keep in mind that companies and organizations establishing an Internet presence now almost always go directly to the Web.

In chapter 2, in the discussion of subject trees, we looked briefly at a gopher-based subject tree called Gopher Jewels (**http://galaxy.einet. net/GJ/**). In information science lingo, this is called a "highly edited source." Although additions and modifications to Gopher Jewels came to a halt in late 1994, the folks who maintained it (notably David Riggins of the Texas Department of Commerce's Office of Advanced Technology) exercised quality control over the menu items. As a result, you can get to pretty much all of the worthwhile stuff in gopherspace from here.

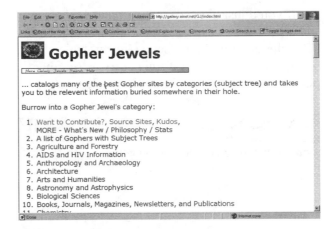

Although Gopher Jewels has been incorporated into Galaxy (**http://galaxy.einet.net/galaxy.html**), the "traditional" Gopher Jewels, browsable and searchable, is still available.

The most convenient way to access Gopher Jewels is via its Webbed interface at Tradewave Galaxy. You can browse the main menu subject tree, or you can search the menu titles of the servers included in Gopher Jewels through a forms-based interface (**http://galaxy.einet.net/gopher/gopher. html**), which offers AND/OR Boolean options.

Invoke the Boolean AND or OR by clicking on either the Any Search Term or All Search Terms buttons.

The real, live gopher-based version of Gopher Jewels is available via the University of Southern California's campus-wide information system (CWIS) gopher (**gopher://cwis.usc.edu/11/ Other_Gophers_and_Information_Resources/ Gopher-Jewels**). An opportunity to search the menus by keyword (with AND/OR Boolean options) is also available here.

If you'd just like to browse around gopherspace and see what's out there, a good jump station is PEG, the Peripatetic, Eclectic Gopher, maintained by the University of California at Irvine (**gopher:// peg.cwis.uci.edu:7000/11/gopher.welcome/peg**).

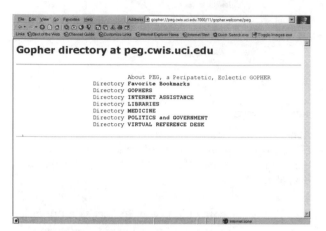

According to the welcome message on the main menu: "PEG went online to the network in spring 1992. In 1995, there were more than 3,000,000 accesses made to PEG from locations around the world. Sometime during spring 1996, the total accesses to date exceeded 10,000,000. In this period, PEG became possibly the most successful (*frequently accessed*) gopher on the Internet."

Eclectic is the operative word here. You'll find gopher-based pointers to everything from issues of the *Bryn Mawr Classical Review* to Big Ugly Smiley (**gopher://geneva.acs.uci.edu:1070/00/ franklin/gleanings/Big%20Ugly%20Smiley**).

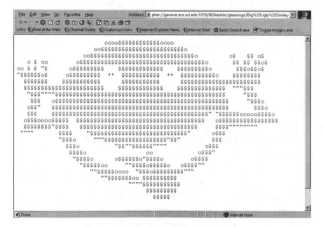

The Big Ugly Smiley is still hanging around in gopherspace.

As a researcher, you'll be glad to know that PEG is checked regularly for dead links, which are scrupulously pruned (although the PEG folks have

no control over the maintenance of the remote servers it links to). There's an excellent collection of U.S. government gophers here; while much of this information has migrated to the Web, some of these servers are still being maintained. If what you're after is text-based information anyhow, the gopher route can be a lot faster than many of the graphics-laden government Web pages.

Believe it or not, in this age of major Web hype, a trickle of new gopher servers onto the Internet persists. You can browse the newest at Washington and Lee University's Netlink Server (**gopher://liberty.uc.wlu.edu/11/internet/ new_internet%09%09%2B**). That's a pretty funky URL; the weirdness is due to Unix directory structures and file names.

Veronica and Jughead

No, there wasn't a mix-up at the publisher. This is not an *Archie* comic book. Veronica and Jughead are the two native gopherspace search tools. A really thorough search of the Internet (as in "Yes, I've checked everything") requires a basic familiarity with them.

Veronica, created at the University of Nevada–Reno in 1992, quickly became the Internet's premier search tool. If you were an Internet user back then, you probably remember how hard it was to get into a public Veronica site.

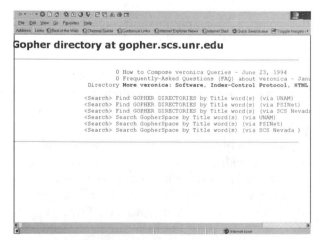

Although its simple keyword-search text box looks pretty primitive by the standards of today's glitzy Web finding tools, Veronica gets the job done.

According to the Veronica FAQ (**gopher:// veronica.scs.unr.edu:70/00/veronica/veronica-faq**), this search tool indexes the information available on "99% + of the world's gopher servers." The index also includes other Internet resources— Web, telnet, FTP, and Usenet—where pointers to them are found on gopher menus. (As with Web search engines, when you do a Veronica query, you are actually searching the database created and indexed by that particular Veronica server.) Although the bulk of gopherspace resources are text based, you can find other file types as well.

ID Number or Letter	Gopher File Type
0	Text file
1	Directory
2	CSO name server (institutional "phone book")
4	Mac HQX file (binhexed Macintosh file)
5	PC binary (usually software)
7	Searchable index
8	Telnet session (remote log-in)
9	Binary file (software, not necessarily PC)
s	Sound
I	Image (other than GIF)
M	MIME multipart/mixed message (e-mail)
T	TN3270 session (remote log-in for IBM mainframes; less common than telnet)
g	GIF image
h	HTML, HyperText Markup Language (Web page)

All gopher file types are identified internally by numbers or letters. This may look like gibberish to you at first glance, but it's actually quite useful, inasmuch as Veronica allows you to restrict your query to a particular file type, as you will see if you keep reading. You can refine your keyword query by specifying only certain types of gopher resources: use the *−t* option in conjunction with the number or letter identifier for the resource type as per the table. For example, if you are looking for a picture of a horse, you type: *−tI horse.* (Do not leave a space between the *−t* tag and the resource type identifier.)

Most public Veronica access menus offer two predefined search types:

1. Searching gopherspace by keywords in titles finds all types of resources (text files as well as other items) whose titles include your specified keywords.

2. Searching gopher Directories Only for keywords in titles finds only gopher directories whose titles contain the specified words. This search can be very useful to locate only those sites offering major holdings of information related to your query—especially useful if you're searching with a very common keyword.

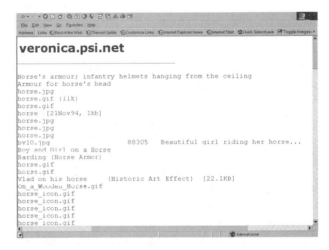

Who would have suspected that gopherspace is full of pictures of horses?

Veronica queries are not case sensitive, and entering multiple keywords can definitely encourage better results. The default Boolean operator is AND, but you can use OR and NOT as well. Phrase searching is not supported—i.e., searching for *grand canyon* will produce the same set of results as searching for *canyon grand*. The Boolean parentheses option is supported: *chicken and (rice or noodles)* will turn up recipes that include *chicken* and *rice* as well as *chicken* and *noodles*. The wild-card character (*) may be used only at the end of keywords.

By default, Veronica limits the number of search results retrieved at one time to a maximum of about 200, but you can change this with the *−m* option: *−m500 AIDS or. HIV.* If you are also using the *−t* option to restrict resource types, it needs its

The best place to start looking for a Veronica server is Yahoo! (**http:// www.yahoo.com/Computers_and_ Internet/Internet/Gopher/Searching/ Veronica/**). Extensive help files are available here as well, including a detailed FAQ.

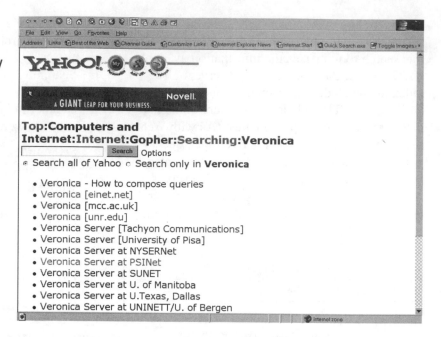

own separate minus sign: *−m500 −tI horse*. Incidentally, you can put the *−m* and *−t* modifiers before or after your keywords.

Why the name *Veronica?* There was already an FTP search tool called Archie, a small word play on *archive.* Then somebody somewhere felt that Veronica needed to be an acronym for something: Very Easy Rodent-Oriented Netwide Index to Computerized Archives.

About a year later, in 1993, Jughead made its appearance, created by Rhett Jones at the University of Utah Computer Center. (Thus we have Jonezy's Universal Gopher Hierarchy Excavation and Display.) Basically, Jughead looks, feels, and works like Veronica, but its scope is much smaller. It indexes only a single gopher server or a particular set of servers. And it doesn't support Veronica's *−t* and *−m* modifiers, although it incorporates two of its own: (1) *?all*, which returns all search results for a particular keyword, with no upper numerical limit; and (2) *?limit#*, which limits results to the number you substitute for *#*.

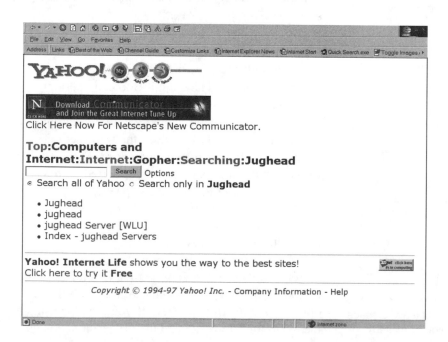

Typically, you will not see the name *Jughead* as a menu item on a server where it's available. What you'll see is something like Keyword Search of UIUC Gopher Menus for a Jughead server that indexes only the gophers at University of Illinois at Urbana–Champaign. Since it's not a global resource, you'll probably only use it if you stumble across an implementation of it on a particular gopher server. But if you're curious, you'll find pointers to Jughead servers— where else—at **http://www.yahoo. com/Computers_and_Internet/ Internet/Gopher/Searching/ Jughead/**.

Telnet

What Is It?

Telnet, otherwise known as remote log-in, is an Internet protocol that allows you to connect to a remote computer and use its resources just as if your own computer were a "dumb terminal" at that physical location. Most commonly, as researchers, we use telnet to browse and search library catalogs, although more and more of these are becoming accessible via a Web interface.

The national standard Z39.50, defining a protocol for computer-to-computer information retrieval, that allows searching a variety of databases from a uniform interface, is being implemented more frequently in automated library systems these days. Still, it's far from universal. (If you'd like to try it, the largest Web-based Z39.50 gateway I know about is at the Library of Congress, **http://lcweb.loc.gov/z3950/gateway. html**.) Using remote library catalogs still may mean logging in via telnet and browsing or searching according to the command syntax of each individual system's proprietary software interface, which is not always very user-friendly.

How Do You Use It?

If you're a dedicated Netscape user, the first thing you need to know about telnet is that Navigator can't handle it alone. It needs a separate "helper application"—which usually means downloading and installing your own telnet program. (Users of Microsoft's Internet Explorer [IE] browser on a Windows 95 platform don't really need to worry about this, as IE already "knows" about the telnet client included in Win 95, which will be launched automatically if a telnet URL is entered in the browser's location box.)

You can find telnet programs at almost any of the major software sites—start with TUCOWS, discussed in chapter 10. Windows users might want to take a look at EWAN, NetTerm, or CRT. For the Mac, there's Comet, NCSA Telnet, or Nifty Telnet.

Once you have your telnet client installed, you have to tell Navigator where to find it. Go to Options/General Preferences and select the Apps tab. Under Supporting Applications, the first item

is Telnet Application. Click the Browse button and cruise your hard drive until you find the executable file that starts up your telnet program—which will be in the folder or directory where you installed it. Highlight it, click Open, and then click OK. Now that Navigator knows where your telnet program is, it will launch that program automatically when you access a telnet URL. (Telnet URLs take the form *telnet://host.domain*.)

```
OSF/1 (fn5.freenet.tlh.fl.us) (ttyqe)

              WELCOME TO TALLAHASSEE FREE-NET


New users enter 'visitor' at the login prompt to explore the system.
If the 'visitor' login asks for a password, just hit 'return'.

Need help? Call the Free-Net help Desk at (904) 921-0822 and leave
a message, or else send electronic mail to problems@freenet.tlh.fl.us

login: █
```

Many free computing networks are telnet accessible.

Hytelnet

Now you've got a working telnet client. How do you go about tracking down library catalogs and other telnet-accessible resources? The easiest way is through Hytelnet (discussed briefly in chapter 2, in the section about Tradewave Galaxy), which houses a mirror of the original site developed and maintained by Peter Scott at the University of Saskatchewan (**http://library. usask.ca/hytelnet/**).

Hytelnet is your basic one-stop-shopping location for telnet resources, including library catalogs organized both geographically and by automated-system software-vendor type—DRA, GEAC, Dynix, etc. The latter arrangement is likely to interest only librarians who work with this stuff. However, the Help Files for Library Catalogs menu item is worth checking because you'll find instructions for negotiating your way around the various proprietary catalog interfaces, some of which can be downright byzantine.

Library catalogs are not the only telnet-accessible Internet resources. Check Hytelnet's Other Resources menu for links to Archie servers

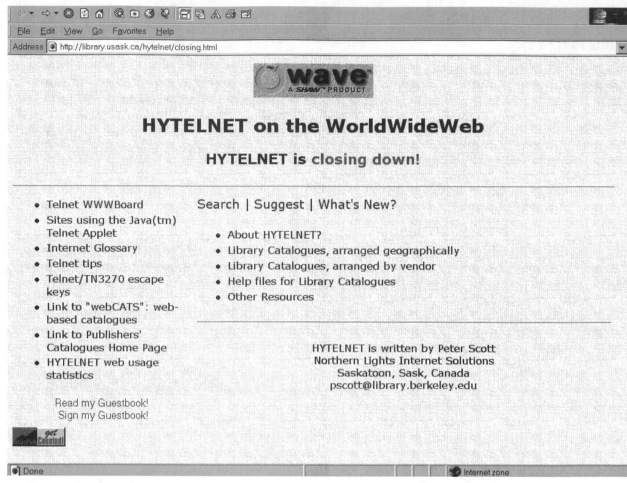

Hytelnet does offer a simple search engine so you can do a quick check to see if a particular library, a certain type of library, or another specific resource is available from there. It's not highly sophisticated, but it can be useful. And if you really don't like telnetting to library catalogs, there's a link to WebCATS, a one-stop-shopping resource for Web-accessible library catalogs also developed by Peter Scott. Alas, Peter Scott has announced that he will be closing down Hytelnet, although he says he is building a new resource that will incorporate "all of the data that currently resides in the Hytelnet files." *Sic transit gloria mundi.*

(for searching FTP archives, see below); bibliographies; free and fee-based databases; Free-Nets and community computing networks; bulletin board systems; NASA databases; Internet network information services; white pages and directory services; and "miscellaneous resources" (including everything from online stores to weather servers). Whereas most of these types of resources have migrated to the Web, some still offer telnet-accessible, text-based interfaces. If you only need a weather forecast and not weather maps, why should you sit there and gnaw your nails while a graphics-intensive Web page loads? And who needs a graphical interface to search a library catalog?

MELVYL

My personal favorite among telnet-accessible library catalogs is the University of California's MELVYL system (**telnet://melvyl.ucop.edu/**). If you've got a system password, it's a gateway to a plethora of proprietary databases. But even if you're not affiliated with the University of California system in any way, it's still a worthwhile resource.

The library database itself is *huge,* containing "approximately 9,377,278 titles representing 14,359,500 holdings for materials in the University of California libraries and the California State Library" (as of early 1998). This includes books, maps, music, and audiovisual resources, such as videos. If you're only interested in newer materials, you can search in MELVYL's ten-year catalog, a subset of the larger database.

Using MELVYL can be confusing due to the variety of options. Fortunately, the system always seems to move pretty fast and provides extensive on-screen help. Also, you can connect from here directly to the Open Access (free) version of CARL UnCover, where you can search about seventeen thousand different magazine and journal titles and retrieve article citations. (UnCover is also available via the Web—**http://uncweb.carl.org/**—and you can order full-text articles online if you've got a credit card.)

And yet if MELVYL were just another large library catalog, I would not have felt a need to talk about it here. It offers a couple of nifty features that I use and that might be useful to you as well: MAIL and UPDATE.

Since it's important to me professionally to know what's available in terms of Internet publications and resources, I'd like to see a comprehensive list of books that have been published about the Internet. One convenient place to obtain this information is Kevin Savetz's Unofficial Internet Book List (**http://www.northcoast.com/savetz/booklist/**). However, this is just a listing of titles with some basic bibliographic information; it doesn't attempt to be selective at all. It's more useful for my purposes to know which Internet books are considered authoritative or useful enough to have been purchased by a well-regarded research institution, like an academic library.

So I telnet to MELVYL, choose the ten-year catalog (I'm not interested in older books about the Internet), and do a subject search (syntax: *find subject internet*). Yikes! MELVYL returns 658 records! I sure don't want to scroll through these on the screen. Still, I'd like to have this information to use as a reference and peruse at my leisure. Mirabile dictu! MELVYL offers me the opportunity to e-mail my search results to myself (*mail to skennedy@reporters.net*). By the time I log off and check my electronic in-box, the information has arrived. I can now save it as a text file and pull it into a word processor for closer examination, text searching, whatever.

Alas, it's fair to assume that the MELVYL system will keep adding Internet-related titles to its collection. Even if I could remember to do it

on a regular basis, I'm not all that keen on the idea of running the same search in MELVYL, picking through the results for new entries, etc. Conveniently, MELVYL keeps tabs on this for me via its UPDATE feature.

To use this feature, be sure you are in the database you want to search, then type *update*. You'll be prompted for your electronic-mail address. Type it in, press Enter, and then you can type up to twenty lines of search and display commands. (Note to librarians: By specifying *display MARC*, you can get results sent to you in MARC format.) There's plenty of on-screen help and prompting. Here's what my update looks like:

TEN-> UPDATE TO skennedy@reporters.net
   TOPIC INTERNET

UPDATE-> FIND SU INTERNET

UPDATE-> AND NOT PUB TYPE NON-
   BOOKS

UPDATE-> DISPLAY LONG (results mailed
   in long format)

UPDATE-> <return>

When you're done editing your update and press that final Return, the system will give you an update ID number. You'll need this information if you want to cancel or modify your update. By default, the MELVYL system will run your update search weekly and e-mail you the results (even if zero new entries have been added) for at least six

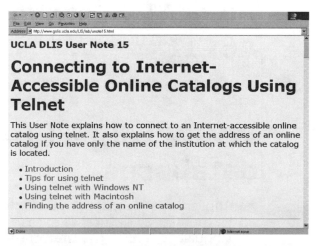

For more information about using telnet, the University of California at Los Angeles Department of Library and Information Science offers an easy-to-follow online tutorial at **http://www.gslis.ucia.edu/LIS/lab/unote15.html**.

months. A month before your update is set to expire, you'll receive a notice giving you the opportunity to renew it.

How can you go wrong? What a convenient way to keep up with books being published in a particular subject area!

WAIS

WAIS, if you haven't already guessed, is an acronym; it stands for *Wide Area Information Service.* Pronounced "waze," this indexing technology began life as a project involving three companies: Apple Computers, Thinking Machines, and Dow Jones. The intent was to encourage creation of a large number of databases that would be searchable over the Internet by paying customers all over the world.

Well, Thinking Machines went bankrupt. And Apple doesn't look all that healthy—and certainly

isn't a leading light in the commercial database business. Dow Jones is doing fine, although not because of its involvement with WAIS.

So why are we even bothering to discuss it here? Because there are still WAIS databases out there, and, as a researcher, you may be motivated to explore them at some point; many contain quite specialized types of information that could be difficult to access in other ways.

To see what's available, try the library at Sweden's Lund University (**http://www.ub2.lu.se/auto_new/UDC.html**), which is one of the easiest places to access and search these databases. The overall topic mix is interesting—everything from Usenet newsgroup archives to poetry and recipe databases. Since the WAIS project itself has been discontinued, Lund is no longer updating this index, and some of the databases themselves are inaccessible when you try clicking on their links. In certain areas—like computers and social sci-

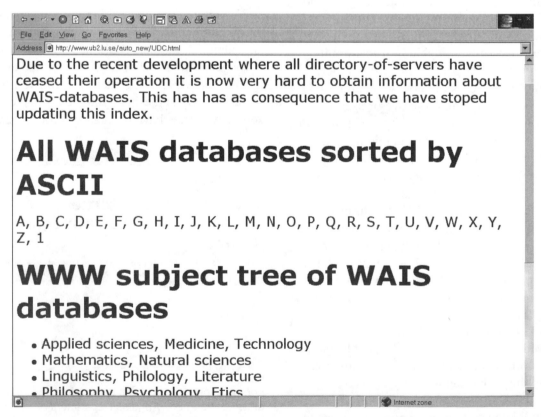

Like many other non-Web-based resources, the WAIS indexes at Sweden's Lund University are no longer being updated.

ences—many WAIS databases were created, and you can search a number of different sources at the same time by checking the boxes next to each source and entering keywords in a text box at the bottom of the page.

WAIS supports the Boolean operators AND, OR, NOT, and also ADJ, if one keyword must follow the other with no other words in between. The wild-card character (*) can be used at the end of words, and search terms can be grouped in parentheses. You can also try rudimentary natural language searching: *who are some Irish poets NOT Yeats*.

When your search results come back, each document is scored on perceived relevance to your question; the highest score is 1,000. Scores are based on word weight (where a keyword appears in a document—higher is better) and other factors.

At any rate, WAIS will probably not be your first choice as an information retrieval tool since, basically, its time has come and gone. But keep in mind that, although the WAIS project itself never came to fruition, the technology is still in use; many Web sites use it to index their own databases and make them keyword searchable.

Finger

The primary purpose of finger, a basic Unix command line utility, was originally to check when other users had last logged in and whether or not they'd read their e-mail. The finger utility also takes advantage of the fact that individual users can create a text file in their home directories called .plan, in which they can place any information they want people to see when their accounts are fingered. Typically, a university professor might include office hours, current research projects, contact phone numbers, etc.

The command line syntax is *finger user@ host.domain*. Sometimes, on a given system, you can display a list of everyone who is currently logged in if you leave off a specific user name: *finger @host.domain*. Keep in mind that finger has been disabled by many system administrators due to privacy and security concerns, but it's still widely available. And it's sometimes used for disseminating certain types of information. Use one of the Finger gateways at Yahoo! (**http://www.**

yahoo.com/computers_and_Internet/Internet/ World_Wide_Web/Gateways/Finger_Gateways/) and try these servers (which seem to come and go):

- Daily almanac of events (**copi@oddjob. uchicago.edu**)
- Daily events at NASA (**nasanews@space. mit.edu**)
- Denver–Boulder area weather information (**weather@rap.ucar.edu**)
- Earthquake bulletin from the U.S. Geological Survey (**quake@gldfs.cr.usgs.gov**)
- SpaceNews (**magliaco@pilot.njin.net**)
- Tropical storm forecast (**forecast@typhoon. atmos.colostate.edu**)
- Weekly trivia (**cyndiw@online1.magnus1. com**)
- Code of the Geeks (**hayden@vax1.mankato. msus.edu**)
- Status of Coke machine, Computer Science Department, Carnegie-Mellon University (**coke@cs.cmu.edu**), or at Rochester Institute of Technology (**drink@csh.rit.edu**)

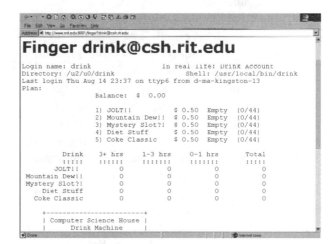

Bummer! Looks like the Computer Science House soda machine at Rochester Institute of Technology is all cleaned out.

And a Few Words about FTP

FTP is an acronym for *file transfer protocol*. It's the tool used for transferring large files—typically software programs, images, etc.—from a remote computer to your own machine. FTP from the Unix command line can be technically challenging, to say the least. But done through a Web browser, it's just another point-and-click experience.

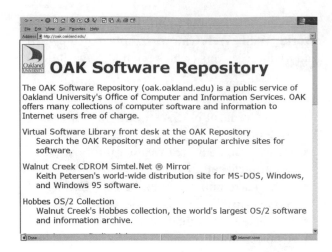

Fortunately for most users, FTP can now be done easily through most Web browsers. And many of the larger FTP archives now have Webbed interfaces anyhow, like the venerable OAK Software Repository (**http://oak. oakland.edu/**).

Plus, for software, the user-friendly sites like TUCOWS (**http://www.tucows.com/**) and Shareware.com (**http://www.shareware.com/**), discussed in chapter 10, can't be beat.

If you have to snag a particular resource from a specific FTP site, it couldn't be easier to do it via your browser. Enter the URL using the syntax *ftp://host.domain/directory-path/filename.* If the site offers anonymous FTP privileges—meaning anyone anywhere on the Internet can log in and use the resources—you'll end up right where you need to go. If, on the other hand, you need to log in with a user name and password (authenticated FTP), use the syntax *ftp://username:password@ host.domain/directory-path/filename.* If you don't want to enter your password directly into the URL, where it'll be visible to anyone walking by (and also in your browser's history list), use the syntax *ftp://username@host.domain.directory-path/filename.* You can type in your password when you are prompted for it.

As an example, let's visit the huge archive of images maintained by the Finnish University and Research Network. In your browser's location box, type *ftp://ftp.funet.fi/pub/pics/* and press Enter. Within seconds—if the server is not overloaded—you should be logged right in and sitting in the proper directory. Scroll down and look at the names of the different directories. If you click on one of the Readme files, you might see an index of what's available here or other information about the server. Choose the directory you want

and click on it. You may see actual file names or more directories (identified by those little folder icons). If you're presented with another list of directories, you'll have to pick one and click on it to move down another level. Finally, you reach a list of file names. Click on the one you want. If it's an image, as in this Finnish directory, it will display in your browser's window. If you decide you want to save it to your hard drive, right-click the picture with your mouse and choose Save Image As . . . from the menu. Choose a directory and a file name, click Save, and the image is yours.

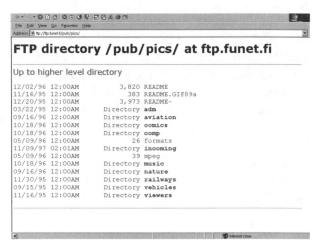

Welcome to FTP.FUNET.FI. You are in the /pub/pics directory, where hundreds of images are available.

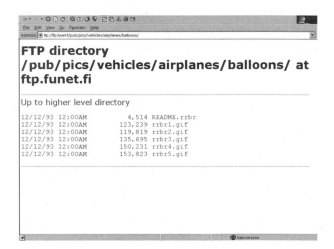

These are all pictures of hot-air balloons.

If you're FTPing software or some other file type that your browser can't display, when you click on the file name, you'll receive a prompt asking how you want to handle it. Choose the Save File option, and you're all set!

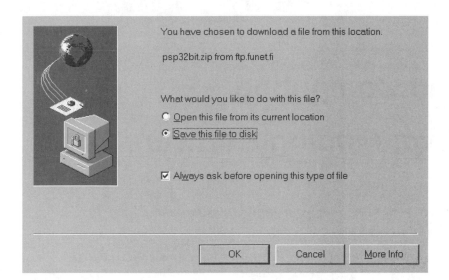

The browser can't handle zipped files, so you'll be prompted to save it to your hard drive, where you can use a file decompression program like WinZip to restore it to its original size and format.

The "old" way of searching for files in FTP sites used a tool called Archie, mentioned above in the discussion of Veronica. In its original text-based version, it's not very user-friendly, especially if you don't know the exact file name of the resource you're looking for. The Web interfaces offering keyword search forms are a bit easier. Check Yahoo! (**http://www.yahoo.com/ Computers_and_Internet/Internet/FTP_Sites/ Searching/Archie/**) for a selection of these.

Perry Rovers is the reigning Internet maven of FTP, and pretty much everything you need to know about it can be found on his FTP-List page (**http:// www.iaehv.nl/users/perry/ftp-list.html**). To get

some idea of the scope of Internet resources residing on FTP servers, take a look at the Anonymous FTP Sitelist, accessible from here. Searchable versions are available in various locations, or you can download a compressed version in *.zip* format. Be forewarned that the uncompressed ASCII version weighs in at more than 1.2 megabytes; it documents more than a thousand different FTP sites.

And finally, if you're interested in learning more about the wealth of Internet resources that exist outside the World Wide Web, there's a one-stop-shopping site called Internet Now. (I like the nonframes version at **http://www.internet-now. com/main3.htm**.)

A niftier way to search FTP sites is via FTP Search (**http://ftpsearch. ntnu.no/**), which offers a configurable forms-based interface that allows you to fine-tune both your query and the results display.

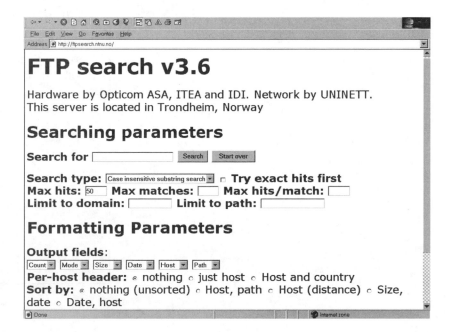

10

Computers and Computing

Finding Help, Finding Software

There's no such thing as a stupid question, but they're the easiest to answer.

—The Tech Support Guy (**http://www.cermak.com/techguy/**)

120

Using the Internet for Technical Support

Your PC starts making ugly grinding sounds. Your telecommunications program won't talk to your modem. Every time you try to install that new application you eagerly brought home from the computer store, your machine locks up. Who ya gonna call?

In most cases, not the manufacturer—unless you've got time on your hands (to sit on hold until your ear withers away) and a fat wallet (because there's no such thing as "toll free" anymore unless you're willing to provide a credit-card number).

There's a good reason that free technical support is rapidly going the way of the dodo bird. Because it ain't free to the manufacturers providing it. It costs a fortune to find, train, and field the live bodies who actually render the service. Computers are being sold as commodities now rather than sophisticated devices requiring a certain level of technical savvy. The great masses of folks trucking their first machines home from Circuit City or Wal-Mart these days are not, by and large, among the technological elite. So the demand for tech support is booming. And those of us who do have a bit of technical savvy and call a vendor for some quick help with a specific issue are often dismayed to find that we know more than the "support" person on the other end of the line.

At the same time manufacturers are making it more difficult to get help by phone, many of them are making it easier than ever to get help online. While customer support bulletin board services reachable by direct modem call have been around for a while, most of the large computer hardware and software companies are now pouring a great deal of time, money, and effort into their Web sites. The results vary—from well-organized and attractive sites that make it easy to find exactly what you need, to overdone eye candy pages that take forever to download and make navigation frustrating. Lots of sites offer an e-mail link so you can actually contact a live tech-support person who probably has more expertise than his or her colleagues manning the phone lines. Alas, my personal experience has been that it's sometimes like sending a message to the Black Hole of Calcutta; many times, you don't even get back an automated response from a "mailbot."

Still, if your problem is such that it's not actually keeping you from getting on the Net to begin with (keeping in mind that the level of tech support from Internet service providers ranges from excellent—my experiences with Mindspring [**http://www.mindspring.com**] have been quite wonderful—to horrendous), you have nothing to lose and everything to gain by taking your initial quest for help out onto the Web.

Vendor Web Sites

How do you find them? Typically these days, the URL is prominently displayed on their packages, their advertising, and the manuals and other literature that come with their products. If not, you can try an educated guess. Whereas most of these companies may not be too eager for you to reach them on the telephone (unless you want to buy something), they are very interested in making themselves visible to the Web-surfing public. Therefore, they are likely to have a fairly obvious URL, in the manner of *http://www.companyname. com*. With most newer Web browsers, all you have to type in the address box is the company name; the browser is "smart enough" to append the rest of the URL to it.

Since Microsoft "owns the desktop," it's not surprising to find that its Web site is an elaborate affair. The amount of stuff available is staggering: downloadable software (demos, patches, upgrades, free products); a searchable Knowledge Base of

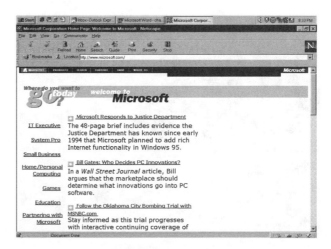

Just typing *microsoft* and pressing Enter will get you to **http://www.microsoft.com/**.

tech-support documents; a series of newsgroups where you can post questions and read ongoing discussions about Microsoft's products. . . . Complete sections of the site are devoted to different groups of customers and software developers. It would be extremely tough to find what you need if it weren't for some sophisticated navigation and search tools.

Click on the Support button on the navigation bar at the top of the main page, and then choose the Support Online link. Use the drop-down menu to select a specific product, and type your question in the text box. Then click Find. Resources available online include FAQs, the Microsoft Knowledge Base (technical papers), feature articles, downloadable software patches and drivers, Microsoft newsgroups, and Troubleshooting Wizards—a series of step-by-step online guides designed to walk you through specific product problems. Other support options are described, but virtually anything involving a live person from Microsoft is going to cost you money.

If you haven't been able to locate a specific company's Web site using the suggestions offered earlier in this section, then give ZDNet's Company Finder (**http://www.zdnet.com/cgi-bin/ texis/cofinder/cofinder/**) a try. ZDNet's parent company is Ziff-Davis Publishing. Its magazines (**http://www5.zdnet.com/findit/mags.html**) dominate the computer sections of newsstands, offering choices for everyone from the newest newbie to the hard-core nerd. Much of its published material—and lots of added features—are available at

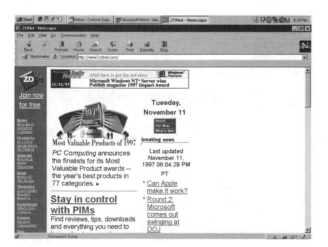

If it has anything to do with computers or computing, Ziff-Davis has it covered.

the various magazines' Web sites. This is a great place to start hunting for product reviews (**http:// www.zdnet.com/products/**), for example. ZDNet (**http://www.zdnet.com/**) is huge, but fairly easy to navigate.

Third-Party Alternatives

ZDNet can serve as a third-party alternative for tech support. Its magazines are full of advice about virtually everything having to do with hardware and software, and its Web site incorporates a search engine with some fairly sophisticated options:

- Standard Boolean operators (AND, OR, and NOT)
- Adjacency operators (NEAR, to specify a numerical word range, and ADJ, to query words next to each other)
- Wild-card characters (* and ?)
- Stemming (*child+* will include hits for *children, childless,* etc.)
- A thesaurus operator (*screen@* will retrieve hits that include synonyms in the database's thesaurus)
- A concept operator (an exclamation point), which "spontaneously generates a list of words related to the word before the operator; searches for, retrieves, and ranks all records containing those related words"

SupportHelp.com (**http://www.supporthelp. com/**) is basically a search engine that allows users to locate telephone support lines, Web sites (with hot links), e-mail addresses, and other contact information for roughly 2,500 technology-based companies. A couple of features are really cool. If you have your Web browser configured to access a news server, there's a hot list of Usenet newsgroups that can provide technical support for specific products or categories of products. (Newsgroups can definitely be a good source of tech-support help—experts are often hanging out there, and the groups are commonly watched by industry folks. DejaNews [see chapter 8] is the preeminent Usenet search tool.)

And browsing alphabetically or searching the database of company information brings up a lot more than just hot-linked URLs. Each listing provides the company's name and address, depart-

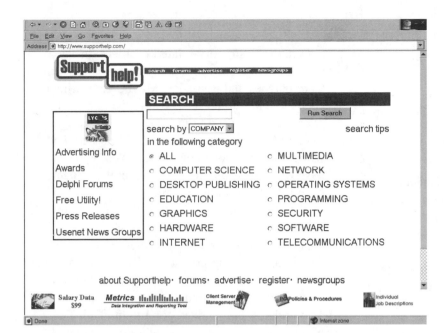

SupportHelp.com bills itself as "your one-stop-shop for locating Contact Information for Hardware and Software manufacturers."

mental contact names, phone numbers, e-mail addresses, the company's logo, how fast the Web site loads(!), and the date this information was last verified.

Kim Komando's Komputer Klinic (**http://www.komando.com/**), a spin-off from Komando's syndicated PC-oriented radio talk show, offers a large collection of computer help Q and A's (if you can handle the unconventional spelling). The search engine requires query operators such as AND and NEAR. Be sure to click on Search Tips

to read about all the features. Have you ever heard of Vector Space Queries? Find out about them here.

Frankly, the easiest thing to do is to go straight to the Get Help section and browse the list of Q and A's under the topic in which you're interested: Buying a Computer and Upgrading, DOS, Hardware, Internet, Macintosh, Memory, Networking, OS/2, Software, Shareware, Windows, Windows 95.

Compared to some of the other resources, the Tech Support Guy's site (**http://www.cermak.**

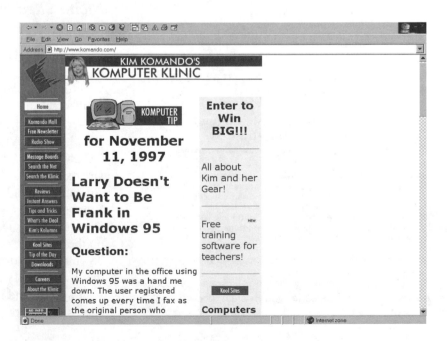

Lots of useful information here, but do you think her last name is really *Komando*?

com/techguy/) doesn't have a whole lot of information available; most of what's here appears to be Win 95 related. However, you can actually leave a question via an online form (or e-mail the Tech Guy directly), and he'll try to provide an answer. If he can't, it goes to the Unsolved Questions archive in the hope that another user can solve it.

PC Lube and Tune (**http://pclt.cis.yale.edu/pclt/**) "is a Service Station and convenience store . . . on the National Information Highway." You won't find tech support per se, but you will find a no-nonsense set of tutorials related to PC computing. Some of the stuff is quite geeky—Distributed Applications and the Web—but an Introduction to PC Hardware is a highly recommended read for anyone headed out to buy a PC who fears bedazzlement by a salesperson's jargon.

The purpose of the Healthy Computer home page (**http://edencen.ehhs.cmich.edu/~sfick/index.html**), according to its teacher-creators,

> is to encourage confidence in the average computer-user in how to manage one or more computers and prevent problems. Many of the suggestions are for computer use in an educational environment, but may be applied to a variety of settings. Most of the suggestions are from teachers who have had experience with computers, and a review has been done by professionals knowledgeable in computer care and use.

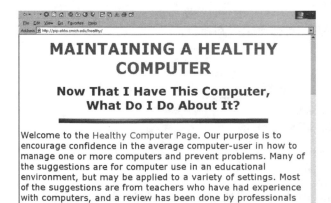

The Healthy Computer home page, created by teachers, lays out the basics for you in plain, uncomplicated English.

Keeping Track of Upgrades

Another tech support–related problem for the average computer user is keeping track of software patches and upgrades. Maybe your printer keeps locking up because you're using an outdated version of the printer driver. Or an upgrade to one of your programs has been released, and, while it's freely available on the Web, you first have to find out that it exists. Several companies have found opportunity here.

Oil Change, by CyberMedia, is a program that connects you via the Internet to Cybermedia's database, which contains information on more than a thousand software products. Oil Change compares the versions of the software on your PC to those on its own database and alerts you to those available updates and patches you might need. The program can then automatically download and install the patch for you. Although this is a commercial product, you can download a free, limited demo version from **http://www.cybermedia.com/products/oilchange/ochome.html**.

Variations on the same theme are TuneUp.com (**http://www.tuneup.com/**) and Versions.com (**http://www.versions.com/**), both online services rather than actual products. Both are subscription based; however, you can set up a limited free account at Versions.com and see how you like it.

Niche Sites for Windows Users

DriversHQ (**http://www.drivershq.com/**), according to its founders, "was formed for everyone who has searched the WWW for new and updated drivers for their hardware." Especially useful if you're seeking drivers for several devices, DriversHQ is nicely organized into categories: Bios Updates, Video Adapters and Monitors, CD-ROM and Disk Drives, Tape and Other Drives, Printers, Fax Modems and ISDN, Network Adapters, Sound and Multimedia Devices, Image Scanners, IDE controllers, SCSI Controllers, Input Devices, Other Devices. If you're a little bit fuzzy on the versions of your existing device drivers, download Driver Detective, a Win 95/NT program that will identify all of the hardware drivers on your system and make this information easily accessible to you.

Ever tried to start a Windows program only to receive an ominous error message complaining about a missing .dll file? Next time this happens to you, fire up your browser and head right for Dll World (**http://www.users.wineasy.se/martin/dll.htm**). This site offers a fairly complete collection of these mysterious Windows system files—not only those native to Windows itself, but also some support files for a variety of popular applications and games. Additionally, there are links to other sites where you might be able to locate system files not available here.

A friend who works in the information systems department of a large corporation refers to Windows 95 as "my job security." If you are fortunate enough to work in an organization that employs someone whose assigned mission is taming this particular beast, at least you've got a lap into which you can dump your PC problems. Alas, those of us who must serve as our own tech-support staff have to be extremely resourceful. If you're flying solo as a Win 95 user and are on the verge of yanking out your hair by the roots, take a look at Windows 95 Annoyances (**http://www.creativelement.com/win95ann/intro.html**). This site, according to its creators, "contains a list of annoying 'features' of Windows 95, and workarounds for most of them." At the top level, it's divided into eight main categories: Reducing Clutter (very valuable if you're getting maxed out on hard drive space); Coping with Windows 95 (fixing things that seem to annoy everyone); Networking, Shmetworking (including Internet-related problems); Third-Party Annoyances (grief caused by applications); Customize, Customize (if you want to make Win 95 look and work the way you prefer); Just Plain Annoying (seems to be a continuation of the Coping section); Getting It All to Work (keeping all parts of your system running); and, finally, Understanding Windows 95 (an overview of the operating system). Much of the information is provided by folks who appear to have a high level of knowledge and a "cut-to-the-chase" attitude. You'll also find a variety of features on topics like Getting to Know the Registry and User-Interface Problems and an outstanding collection of utility shareware and freeware that you can download. Can't find the answer you need? Think you can help someone else? Leave a message in the Reader Comments area. If you use Windows 95, this site belongs near the top of your bookmark list.

Finding Software on the Internet

Back in the Internet Dark Ages, before the advent of the World Wide Web—before gopher, even—there was already plenty of downloadable software available in FTP archives. In fact, besides e-mail and Usenet newsgroups, that was one of the main reasons people used the Internet.

Tons of software are still available on the Internet—and for every conceivable computing platform, including CP/M and Commodore and Amiga and umpteen flavors of Unix. To get some idea of the magnitude of what's available, take a look at the Software section in Yahoo! (**http://www.yahoo.com/Computers/Software/**). But thanks to various search tools and software mega-sites, it's easier than ever to find what you want or need.

It's now completely possible to buy a wide variety of commercial software programs over the Net—provide your credit-card number to a secure server, and download the program. Great for those who are into instant gratification, or who need something immediately. But most of the software available for downloading from the Net falls into one of three categories: shareware, freeware, and demonstration versions.

SHAREWARE

Commercial software that you can try out for free and then pay for if you wish to keep using it is called shareware. There are different types of shareware programs. Some are time limited—they'll work for a specified period and then expire. Some are feature limited ("crippleware"): certain features are disabled until you pay to "register" the program. And some have built-in guilt mechanisms, such as periodic "Please register" reminders that flash before your eyes. Still others are full-fledged, nonexpiring, no-nag applications whose authors rely on your honesty for compensation.

FREEWARE

This is just what it says—programs that you can download and use with no strings attached. While many are small utilities written by programmers for their own use and then released for public consumption, there are also full-blown freeware applications distributed by major software companies. A prime example is the Microsoft Internet Explorer Web browser. Check out Microsoft's Free Downloads page (**http://www.microsoft.com/msdownload/**) for this and other freeware programs.

If Mr. Gates is giving it away for nothing, you may want to take advantage.

DEMONSTRATION VERSIONS OF COMMERCIAL PRODUCTS

Many software companies don't want to release their applications as shareware, but they are eager to get their products before the eyes of the computer-owning, Web-surfing public. Demonstration versions of products have become widely available on the Internet. They are never full featured; typically, critical functions such as Save or Print are disabled. Nevertheless, this is not a bad way to test-drive a program you're interested in before laying out big bucks for the shrink-wrapped version. Check specific vendors' Web sites for downloadable demos, or try the ZDNet Software Library's Commercial Demos section (**http://www.hotfiles.com/demo.html**).

Internet Software

Okay, you probably already know that you can snag a copy of Netscape Navigator or Communicator directly from Netscape (**http://home.netscape.**

com/comprod/mirror/client_download.html). And Microsoft is just begging you to pay them a visit and download a free copy of Internet Explorer (**http://www.microsoft.com/ie/download/**).

The newest versions of Web browsers are, in fact, very flexible. Not only can you cruise the Web, but you can use them to read and send e-mail, read and post Usenet news messages, download files via FTP, and even travel around gopherspace. Alas, the built-in versions of these various non-browser utilities may not provide you with all the functions and features you want or need. Many, if not most, heavy e-mail users prefer a separate, full-featured e-mail application. And if you're doing a lot of file transfer—say, back and forth to a Web server to maintain pages—you may find it easier with a dedicated FTP client program.

While you can cruise around to various software sites looking for this stuff, you can save yourself a lot of time and aggro by taking advantage of Web sites that specialize in Internet-related software. You benefit not only from the convenience of one-stop shopping, but these mega-sites feature reviews and ratings of the various programs, plus live links to the different software-company Web sites and their download locations.

STROUD'S CWS APPS LIST

"Comprehensive file listings, ratings, and extensive reviews for the hottest Windows 3.X/95/NT applications" can be found at Stroud's CWS Apps List (**http://cws.iworld.com/**). You can browse through 16-bit apps (Win 3.X) or 32-bit apps (Win 95/NT), by application name or by category (from Active X Control Components to VRML Browsers). Or you can use the search engine to zero in on exactly what you want. Each and every application is tagged with a blue-star rating, explained thusly:

5 stars: Excellent application; an absolutely critical, must-have client

4 to 4.5 stars: Great app; definitely worth the download and price, if there is one

3 to 3.5 stars: Good application; but may not be the best in its class

2 to 2.5 stars: Fair application; may or may not be worth the download

1 to 1.5 stars: Who in their right mind created this abomination?

The ratings are done by Forrest Stroud, who started this project when he was a business major at the University of Texas and maintains this well-respected resource. He offers this caveat:

> I have graded the apps very subjectively—how can a grade based on one person's opinions not be subjective? I do not claim to be an expert on any one of these applications, no less all of them. I have, however, worked with and tested each of these apps and have found some to be better than others.

There's also a full review of each application, which includes a description of the features, pros and cons, and how the application compares to others in the same category. Reviews are dated, so you always know how fresh the information is. Besides an online user conference area, where folks can enter their own comments about particular applications, there are a variety of special pages that are well worth visiting on a regular basis:

- What's New (**new.html**) lists daily updates and recent changes.
- The Newest Apps (**newapps.html**) lists all Win 3.X apps released within the past two weeks.
- New for '95 Apps (**95newapp.html**) lists all Win 95 apps released within the past two weeks.
- Cool App of the Week (**coolapp.html**) features a new and exciting app each week.
- The Top 20 Apps (**top20.html**) lists the top-twenty (i.e., most popular) apps for the last two weeks.
- The CASPER Page (**casper.html**) is a "best of" recommended starting package for new users.
- Mirror Sites (**cwsapps.html**) lists CWSApps List mirror sites.

Note that this site is only for Windows applications; Stroud recommends that Macintosh users check out the Mac Internet collection at the University of Texas (**http://wwwhost.ots.utexas. edu/mac/internet.html**).

THE WELL CONNECTED MAC

The Well Connected Mac (**http://www.macfaq. com/**) is no longer being updated regularly, but it still has a good list of pointers to many other worthwhile Macintosh-related sites on the Inter-

net, including the Mac Orchard (**http://www. macorchard.com/**), "a carefully cultivated list of the most vital Internet applications and links for Macintosh Internet users, along with Internet software reviews contributed from The Mac Orchard's audience."

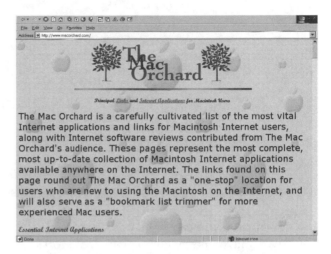

"There's nothing more vital to your Internet experience than the most powerful, most up-to-date Internet applications," according to the Mac Orchard, which endeavors to provide a selection of the best ones for Macintosh users.

TUCOWS

Regardless of which popular desktop computing platform you use, TUCOWS (the Ultimate Collection of Winsock Software), at **http://www.tucows. com/**, offers access to "the latest and greatest Windows 95, Windows 3.1, Macintosh, and even OS/2 and Unix Internet Software, performance rated and checked for viruses." This is a very popular site, with more than 140 mirrors in geographic locations all over the world. Users can select the closest mirror right from the main page, which the TUCOWS folks suggest will facilitate downloading.

After you choose a convenient mirror site, you can search for a particular application right from the main page or choose to browse under one of the platform headings. Any of these choices will take you to a page organized in table format, where you can click on categories of Internet applications and peruse the listings.

For each application, you'll find brief descriptive information, a rating (one to five cows), and a link for downloading the application. Everything

Mo-oo-ove to TUCOWS if you need Internet software for any major computing platform.

you download is directly from one or another TUCOWS mirror site, which is why these folks can keep their virus-checking promise.

VIRUS PROTECTION

Although, for heaven's sake, if you're going to be downloading software from the Net—or if you share your computer with anyone else—you really should obtain and install virus protection software. The name brands are Symantec's Norton AntiVirus (**http://www.symantec.com/avcenter/**) and McAfee Associates (**http://www.mcafee.com/**),

although many other good programs are available. As usual, you can find lots of information and pointers in Yahoo! (**http://www.yahoo.com/Computers_and_Internet/Security_and_Encryption/Viruses/**).

Another site with lots of information about computer viruses and antivirus software is Hitchhiker's Web Guide AntiVirus Resources page (**http://www.hitchhikers.net/av.shtml**). An extra-special feature here is a "reminder" service—you register to receive e-mail notification when updates to your favorite virus protection software

New viruses appear every day, and it's critical to keep your protection up-to-date, but very easy to forget to check for updates. Hitchhiker's Web Guide AntiVirus Resources page will remind you.

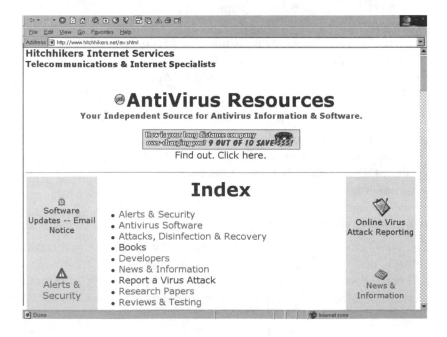

are available, and you can go right to the Hitchhiker's site to retrieve the update.

Those who want to keep up with what's going on in the browser world will definitely want to bookmark BrowserWatch (**http://browserwatch. internet.com/**). Check out Plug-In Plaza for the latest information about the ever-growing population of these add-ons and add-ins. And, conveniently, there are download links for everything.

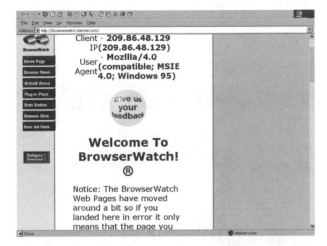

Which plug-ins are worth having? I certainly can't keep track of all the multimedia options available, but the folks here do a pretty good job.

Interested in rolling your own HTML? Choose your weapon from Carl Davis's HTML Editor Reviews (**http://www.webcommando.com/editrev/**). Don't miss the features comparison matrix that lets you assess HTML editors on a side-by-side basis. Each editor is given a rating (from five to one stars, in descending order of quality) by Davis, who claims to spend an average of eight hours working with each program in order to provide objective evaluations. Download links for each editor are available.

Software Mega-Sites

Whether you're looking for a utility program to fill a certain niche, an ultra-cool screen saver, an educational program for a small child, or the latest and hottest shareware games, several do-it-all sites can save you a lot of superfluous surfing.

ZDNET SOFTWARE LIBRARY

Browse ZDNet Software Library (**http://www. hotfiles.com/index.html**) by type of application

"Brought to you by the same people who publish *PC Magazine, PC/Computing, Mac User, Computer Shopper, Family PC* and more, our editors review, rate, and virus check thousands of programs to bring you only the cream of the crop."

or computing platform. (There's PC and Macintosh stuff here.) Check out the Editors' Picks, the Hot File of the Day, and the Top Downloads. Search for files by keyword. Get help on downloading and on how to handle a file once you've got it on your hard drive. Leave comments or questions in the discussion area. Note that the programs—mostly shareware, with some freeware and commercial demos—are reviewed and rated by ZDNet's own expert product-reviewing team.

DOWNLOAD.COM

ClNet makes its Download.com site available in two flavors: PC or Mac, both reachable via

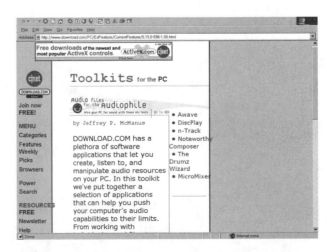

ClNet has pulled together a number of useful software "toolkits" to help you get the most out of your computer.

http://www.download.com/. Browse by category or choose from among several "toolkits"—groups of downloadable programs designed for a specific purpose, such as PC housekeeping, offline Web browsing, etc.

The search engine offers three levels of sophistication: Quick (type keyword or program title, choose a specific category or All); Simple (type two keywords, choose a specific category or All); and Power (use a variety of fields—title, author/publisher, description, full-text search, category, operating system, age of title, number of downloads). Full descriptions are available for all the programs in the Download.com database.

SHAREWARE.COM

Another C|Net service is Shareware.com (**http://www.shareware.com/**), which uses a "front door" called Virtual Software Library to search, simultaneously, a group of the largest software archives on the Internet. While this means little information is available for the individual titles it retrieves, Shareware.com's search engine covers a heck of a lot of ground—and many more computing platforms than just PC and Mac—via a drop-down box on the search form. A non-C/Net variation on this theme is FILEZ (**http://www.filez.com/**).

GAMECENTER.COM

Gamers will probably want to proceed first to C|Net's Gamecenter.com (**http://www.gamecenter.com/**). Not only can you search for computer games here, but you can collect hints and tips, read game-oriented news and feature articles, and browse through game reviews.

HAPPY PUPPY

The adolescent male in our household recommends this Web site (**http://www.happypuppy.com/**) as excellent for gamers.

For computer gamers, Happy Puppy is another one of those "just-slide-the-pizza-under-the-door-and-go-away" sites.

11

Not-So-Stupid Browser Tricks

. . . and Tips

Browser Wars

Once upon a time there was Lynx (**http://lynx. browser.org/**) and, prior to that, the venerable CERN line mode browser (**http://gita.lanl.gov/ misc/QuickGuide.html**). What was appearing on the Web in its earliest days was basically all text all the time, which sounds pretty boring. Then in 1993, an application called Mosaic (**http://www. ncsa.uiuc.edu/SDG/Software/Mosaic/**)—developed at the National Center for Supercomputing Applications (NCSA) at the University of Illinois in Urbana–Champaign—changed the face of the Web forever. Now, in the late nineties, after you've spent ten minutes waiting for some huge image map to load, or happened upon yet-another multimedia confection requiring its own special plug-in or "helper application," or been blinded by a particularly hellacious pastiche of background pattern and text color, or had your system crash due to someone's badly written Java "crapplet" (**http:// www.wired.com/wired/4.06/jargon.watch.html**) . . . you can begin to get just a little bit nostalgic for plain vanilla ASCII text.

In fact, nearly 40 percent of the more than fifteen thousand participants in Georgia Tech's Sixth Annual WWW Survey (**http://www.cc. gatech.edu/gvu/user_surveys/survey-10-1996/ graphs/use/Image_Loading.html**) in 1996 indicated that they surf at least some of the time with graphics turned off—i.e., they disable the automatic image-loading feature in their browsers. Thus, it's not surprising that Lynx is still a favorite tool of serious researchers who value speed and efficiency. Even now, many libraries and other institutions provide text-only access to the Internet (certainly cutting down on the hysteria over pornographic images).

Things have come a very long way in a relatively short time. Today's browsers can incorporate e-mail and Usenet news readings, Web page creation, news and entertainment "channels," live chats, and videoconferencing. The result of all this "improvement" may turn out to be what some are already calling browser backlash. Many, if not most, users do not want or need all of the features included with the newest versions, or they don't want to pay the price in performance. Thus, people may be slow to upgrade and, once they do, may think better of it and revert to an earlier ver-

sion of the browser they prefer. Being slow to upgrade is never a bad idea anyway, especially when it comes to Internet software in general and browsers in particular. Buggy products are the norm rather than the exception in just about every company's earlier releases. We've all become beta testers, whether we like it or not.

Text-based browsers aside, a viable alternative to the two dominant bloated RAM hogs, Netscape Navigator and Microsoft Internet Explorer, does indeed exist. Opera, a streamlined graphical browser developed in Norway, has been gaining fans on a global basis. First of all, it's less than 800K to download. Second, its developers claim Opera will run successfully on older, slower PCs—at minimum, a 386SX machine with 8M RAM. If this is true, libraries and other institutions that need additional Internet stations may be able to resurrect some of their old boat anchors and put them online.

Opera is available for Win 95/NT and Windows 3.1x in four different languages: English, Norwegian, Swedish, and Spanish. It supports a variety of multimedia file formats—MIDI and WAV, Video for Windows (AVI), MPEG Video, and four different graphic types: JPEG, GIF (including animated GIFs), XBM, and BMP. It can also handle most enhanced HTML features, such as tables, frames, forms, and client side image maps.

While Opera doesn't include fully functional e-mail and news programs like Explorer and Navigator, it does allow you to send (not receive) and read (not post) Usenet news, and it does link to your freestanding e-mail program. Special attention has been given to useful features for the physically challenged:

- A full keyboard interface, which facilitates browsing by using the keyboard
- A zoom function, which allows focusing in on page contents—graphics or text—to any level
- The ability to select the fonts a user wants or needs for the different HTML headers and text—in any color—and to render links in 3-D so that they stand out
- Audio feedback on clicking, page loading, error messages, etc.

Although the developers keep adding different features, version 3.0 of Opera does not support

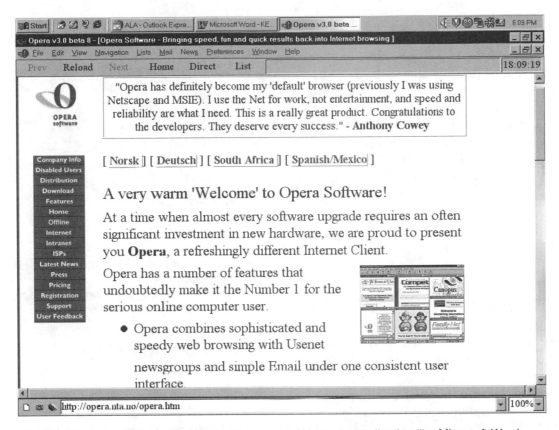

I find Opera works particularly well when I have a RAM-hungry application like Microsoft Word open and I need to browse the Web at the same time. Opera demands much less of the computer's resources than Navigator or Explorer.

Java applets, HTML editing, in-line VRML, ActiveX controls, and plug-in modules. Nonetheless, it's a good, solid product, once you get used to the interface, which is a bit quirky. (There is no Stop button on the toolbar, for example. You need to pull down the Navigation menu and click on Stop there.) Version 3.0 supports JavaScript and SSL, some Netscape plug-ins, and multimedia. Visit the Opera home page at **http://opera. nta.no/** to download an evaluation copy.

Mosaic is still around, too. While it's largely fallen behind the Netscape and Microsoft products, it's no slouch. According to a review at Stroud's Consummate Winsock Apps (**http:// cws.internet.com/**), "The newest releases contain many of Netscape's best features, including document caching, improved FTP support, internal support for gifs and jpegs, built-in news reader (with a recently added toolbar), new HTML tags (including centering, tables, and background images), and low cost (it's free!)." According to Stroud's review, Mosaic has also caught up to Netscape in terms of speed, "and some claim that it's even faster than Netscape now." Additionally, it offers a few unique features: AutoSurf, which automatically checks and tracks links; a spiffy new hot-list manager, much like Netscape's SmartMarks; and a Collaborate feature, which essentially allows you to surf the Web in concert with other people. It's available for Windows, Unix, and the Mac; the newest version, 3.0 for Windows 95/NT, may be downloaded from **ftp:// ftp.ncsa.uiuc.edu/Mosaic/Windows/v3.0/mos30. exe**. As far as NCSA is concerned, however, "active development of Mosaic is complete," so there will be no further upgrades.

The browser market is so dynamic that keeping up with the changes—new releases, new products, new trends—could consume more of your life than you are willing or able to devote to it. Fortunately, some folks are paid to do this for you. Two sites to bookmark if you want or need to keep up with what's happening on the bleeding edge: BrowserWatch, at **http://browserwatch. internet.com/,** affiliated with MecklerMedia, and Browsers.Com (**http://www.download.com/ Browsers/**), part of the huge C|Net site. The latter offers a free e-mail newsletter called Browser Alert, to which you may subscribe for either the PC or Macintosh platform.

Have It Your Way

You may have already heard that WWW actually stands for *World Wide Wait*. Sad to say, the individual end user has little control over the most significant factors affecting Web performance: bandwidth issues, Internet and Web provider hardware limitations, "dirty" phone lines, graphics-obsessed Web designers, and the staggering increase in the number of Net surfers.

However, there are lots of small things you can do to tweak your browser's performance, many of which will result in an observable increase in speed. Money helps: mainly, upgrading to a more powerful processor with a generous chunk of RAM. But there are several ways to try speeding up your browser that don't involve pulling out your wallet, and several changes you can make to its interface so that it works more efficiently or, if nothing else, makes surfing the Web a bit more aesthetically pleasing for you.

Turn Off Automatic Image Loading

Pictures on Web pages can add life to what would otherwise be a block of gray text, but graphics slow down Web browser performance substantially due to the time it takes these large files to be transmitted over the Internet and the time it takes your own machine to load and display them. Both Netscape and IE allow you to disable automatic image loading—in Netscape from the Options menu, and in IE from the View/Options/Advanced menu.

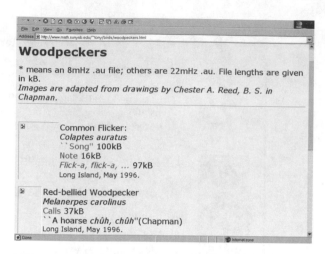

With image loading turned off, Web pages will display much more quickly, since text alone is not very bandwidth intensive. On each page, where an image would have been, a "placeholder" will be displayed.

Increase the Size of Your Browser's Cache

The cache, where the browser stores copies of recently viewed Web pages, is specifically designed to speed up performance. When you want to look at a page again, the browser simply whips the previously viewed copy out of its cache and displays it for you instead of going back out onto the Web to retrieve it. Browsers harbor two types of cache—memory and disk. Memory cache, which stores pages from your current surfing session, resides in your computer's RAM. Shut your browser down, and it's wiped out. Disk cache, typically larger, saves data from previous surfing sessions in a directory on your hard drive. RAM browser default cache settings are optimal for most computers in most circumstances. If you increase the default sizes, however, a performance improvement may result, since there's a greater likelihood of pages being loaded from your local cache rather than from a remote server on the Internet.

Initially, you might try doubling both default numbers and observing performance results. Keep in mind that, when you increase RAM cache, you're actually giving over a larger portion of your computer's total RAM to Navigator, which is likely to affect other applications you have running simultaneously—especially other RAM-intensive programs like high-end word processors. (I have not been able to find a way to adjust RAM cache in Internet Explorer. However, it's entirely possible that Microsoft has named this function something else in an attempt to be more user-friendly.) Increasing disk cache means giving up more hard drive space, and, since browsers perform "cache maintenance" upon shutdown, it will take longer for the program to quit.

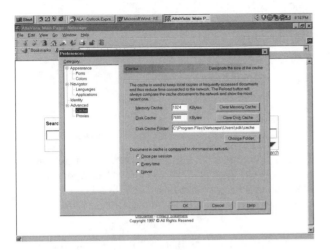

Actually ten to twenty megabytes of disk cache is enough for most people unless you spend a lot of time surfing graphics-intensive sites. So do the math and adjust the setting accordingly.

By the way, disk cache can be especially useful when you're not connected to the Internet. Say you've already logged off, but you suddenly realize you need to take another quick look at a page you've just visited. For Windows users, several utility programs can examine and display the contents of your cache. The Browser Add-Ons section of TUCOWS (see chapter 10) is a good place to find these; some suggested programs are MSIE Cache Explorer (for IE), Netscape Cache Explorer (for Navigator), and UnMozify (for Navigator). Macintosh equivalents are also available. But the quick way to examine Navigator's disk cache on any platform is to type *about:cache* in the location box (where URLs are displayed). To do the same thing with IE 3.x, choose Go from the menu bar and click on Open History Folder. In IE 4.x, go to View/Options/General, click the Settings button in the Temporary Internet Files section, and then click the View Files button. You'll be looking at the contents of the Temporary Internet Files subdirectory in your hard drive's Windows directory.

Incidentally, it's not a bad idea to clear out your browser's cache periodically; getting rid of old and corrupted files will improve performance. If your browser starts acting funky, you may want

to try this first. Both IE and Navigator offer convenient one-button cache-flushing options.

Hang Up; Dial Again

You've clicked on that link or typed in that URL. The browser's status line says Connect: Contacting Host and sometimes also Waiting for Reply, but nothing happens. This is the Web's version of a busy signal. Really good resources on the Internet often become victims of their own popularity. Many people want to access a server at the same time, but the server can only handle so many simultaneous connections.

Sausage Software, creators of the popular HotDog Web editor, offers a nifty little utility called Jackhammer that does the same thing for busy Web sites that an auto-redial phone does for perpetual busy signals. It will hammer away at the Web site of your choice until it gets in and then will spawn another browser window for you. You can get more information and download a trial copy from its Web site at **http://www.sausage.com/**.

Need for Speed? Use the Keyboard!

If you're a fast typist, going back and forth between the keyboard and the mouse to do your surfing can be a nuisance. Both Navigator and IE support a full complement of keyboard shortcuts, most of which work the same in both browsers. (Commands are case *insensitive*.)

- Alt + left arrow: Goes back to previous page
- Alt + right arrow: Goes forward to next page
- Up/Down arrow: Scrolls up/down (or Page Up/Down keys for larger jump)
- Home key: Goes to top of page
- End key: Goes to bottom of page
- Ctrl + B: Displays bookmark file in Navigator, Favorites folder in IE
- Ctrl + D: Adds current page to bookmark list or Favorites folder
- Ctrl + H: Opens History file (Navigator) or History folder (IE)
- Ctrl + L: Opens box for you to type in URL of a new Web page
- Ctrl + N: Opens new browser window
- Ctrl + R: Reloads current page
- Ctrl + W: Closes browser
- Ctrl + F: Brings up Find text search box

Change Your Default Home Page

I always assume that everyone knows this, but I keep running into people to whom it's news. You are *not* locked into traveling to the home pages of Netscape or Microsoft every time you start your browser, depending on whose product you're using. There is a reason that Netscape's home page is often reported to be the most popular site on the World Wide Web. It gets the most hits because Netscape currently owns the lion's share of the browser market. When you download and install one of Netscape's browsers—Navigator or Communicator—it comes configured with Netscape Central as its default home page. This is not, of course, true of Microsoft's Internet Explorer. Mr. Gates certainly doesn't want you automatically taken to Netscape's site. Guess what IE's default home page is.

You are not obliged to accept these defaults. You can and probably should change your default home page to a URL that you find more useful. In Netscape Navigator, make this change from Options/General Preferences/Appearance, in the Startup section of the page. I'd advise choosing Blank Page rather than Home Page Location for the Browser Starts With option, for the simple reason that you may not want to go to your default home page when you start your browser. If you're automatically taken there first, it will delay you in getting to the URL you actually want to visit. You can always get to your default home page fast by clicking on Home in the browser's button bar.

You may choose as a default home page any HTML file residing on your hard drive, including

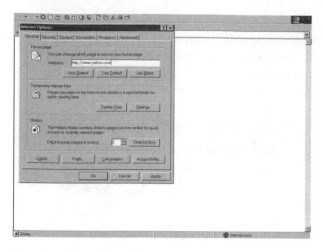

If you're using Internet Explorer, change your default home page in View/Options/General. Clicking the Use Blank button will start the browser with a blank page rather than a specified Web page.

Netscape's bookmark.htm, which lives in the Netscape directory. If you know a little HTML, you can make your own home page, save it to your hard drive, and have IE load that as the default.

Change Colors or Fonts

Some Web page creators use color combinations that are quite capable of inducing gastric distress. You don't have to suffer! In Navigator, go to Options/General Preferences and select the Colors tab. Check the box at the bottom of the dialog panel that says Always Use My Colors, Overriding Document. The default background "my color" is white, which is the best choice if you want to print out pages or make screen captures, as I did for this book. If you're using Communicator, do this at Edit/Preferences/Appearance/Colors. For Internet Explorer, make this adjustment under View/Options/General, and click on the Colors button.

Similarly, you can change the font in which text will appear in your browser's window. I don't have a problem with Times New Roman, which is the default in both the Netscape and the Microsoft products. If you spend a lot of time surfing the Web, however, you may want to bump up the font size. Default is twelve points, but when my eyes are tired, I sometimes change it to fourteen. Alternately, if you have sharp, young eyes, you may want to go down in point size to ten, which will increase the amount of text you are able to see at one time in your browser window.

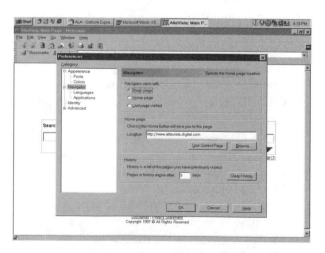

To change your default home page in Communicator, click on Edit/Preferences, and highlight Navigator in the Category panel of the resulting dialogue box.

Error Messages: Is It You or Is It Them?

If You See . . .	It Means . . .
Bad Request 400	Browser made incorrect request for remote document. Server confused; try again. If you see this repeatedly, e-mail site administrator.
Unauthorized 401	Usually server is expecting some sort of encryption ID, or you mistyped password and may have opportunity to retype. Otherwise, back out and try again.
Forbidden 403	Requested document forbidden to you. May be restricted to local users, or server may be configured improperly.
Not Found 404	Common message—requested document not at that location. It may have moved or been removed, or you may have typed wrong URL. Try "jumping back" in URL one level at a time—i.e., retype URL omitting last letter group and try to link from there. If not, go back another level or two.
Internal Error 500	Server couldn't send requested document due to server software error. E-mail request to fix it to site administrator.
Not Implemented 501	Server doesn't support requested feature.
Service Temporarily Overloaded 502	Just what it says. Try again later.
Gateway Timeout 503 or 503 Service Unavailable	Connection timed out due to server problems, Internet problems, or sometimes browser problem. Try again later.
Unable to Locate the Server or The Server Does Not Have a DNS Server	Browser can't find requested remote server. Could be due to incorrect URL, problems with Winsock software connecting to your Internet provider, or problems at provider's end involving DNS (Domain Name Service), which keeps track of Internet servers.
Network Connection Refused by Server	Remote server may not be accepting connections or may be too busy.
Too Many Connections— Try Again Later	Usually generated by overly busy FTP site, which can support only so many simultaneous users.
File Contains No Data	Usually indicates you've gotten to right server but no Web documents on it. You may have "arrived" when stuff was being shuffled around or updated. Try later.
Helper Application Not Found	Browser can't handle requested file type. File-handling capability of most browsers can be extended with helper applications or plug-ins, which display files browser can't read. Error dialogue box usually provides information about file type and offers choice of saving file to hard disk or obtaining necessary helper (or browser plug-in) usually by connecting directly to site where you can find it.
NNTP Server Error	You're trying to but can't access a Usenet newsgroup. Browser isn't set up to contact Internet provider's news server or provider may not carry that particular newsgroup—or may not carry a Usenet newsfeed at all.

We've all seen them. As a matter of fact, we're all too familiar with some of them. What's the story with all those error messages?

Plug-Ins

What are plug-ins? Basically, they're add-in component programs for your browser that enable you to access specialized multimedia content on Web sites. Granted, a lot of this stuff is bandwidth-intensive frivolity. But some applications out there are clever. And some are particularly essential or noteworthy.

For example, you hop into your car for the drive home after work, and, as is your habit, you crank up NPR's *All Things Considered*. Unfortunately, commentator Daniel Pinkwater is in the middle of his essay. But if you have Web access from home, you're in luck. You can surf right over to NPR's Web site (**http://www.npr.org/**) and listen to a file of the complete broadcast—if your computer has a sound card and speakers, of course, and if you've downloaded a free copy of Progressive Networks' RealAudio plug-in (**http://www.realaudio.com/**) for your browser. The program itself has an interface like a little tape recorder and supports something called streaming audio. This allows you to listen to a sound file as it downloads rather than waiting till the whole file has made it to your hard drive. Which means you can also listen to live radio programming from a number of stations that "broadcast" on the Net. The sound is surprisingly good over a 28.8 kbps modem connection, and it's downright amazing over an ISDN or other high-speed line. (A newer version of this plug-in, RealPlayer, not only supports streaming audio but also streaming video—interesting, but intermittently balky over a dial-up Internet connection.)

The technology is also being used for real-time "Webcasting." You can listen to a wide range of live programming—sports events, celebrity interviews, on-the-air radio shows, breaking news—and you can have it playing in the background as you use your computer for other things.

Adobe Acrobat, an authoring program that allows the sharing of elaborately formatted documents across a range of computing platforms, has been around longer than the World Wide Web. But the Web has certainly increased its penetration and reputation. Acrobat files end in *.pdf,* which stands for *portable document format*. In order to display and/or print a .pdf file, you need a (free) piece of

The premier programming guide is Timecast (**http://www.timecast.com/**), both for live audio and video and a wide range of other sites that offer RealAudio or RealVideo.

software called Adobe Acrobat Reader, available for all major computing platforms from Adobe's Web site (**http://www.adobe.com/prodindex/acrobat/readstep.html**). You can get a freestanding version, but you're probably going to want the plug-in version for the browser of your choice, since most of us are much more likely to encounter .pdf documents on the Web than anywhere else.

Why should you even care about .pdf files? First and foremost, from the researcher's perspec-

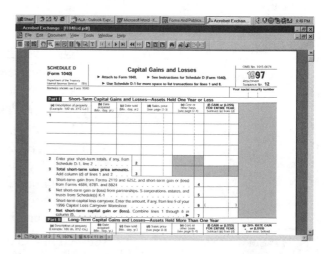

If you want to download a tax form from the Internal Revenue Service Web site (**http://www.irs.ustreas.gov/prod/cover.html**), you'll need Acrobat Reader in order to view it and print it out.

tive, Adobe Acrobat has become the standard format for disseminating U.S. government documents.

There's a logical reason that this format is used. Essentially, it preserves the original look of the document, which would be impossible to accomplish in HTML alone. The feds are not the only ones publishing on the Net in .pdf format. Many other folks find Adobe Acrobat an attractive option for making their documents available on the Web, especially organizations that put a lot of material on their Web sites but don't have the time to reformat everything in HTML. They buy a copy of Adobe Acrobat and crank existing document files through it to create .pdf files, which can then be uploaded to the appropriate Web server directory. Adobe maintains a directory of links to Web sites that use Acrobat at **http://www.adobe. com/prodindex/acrobat/pdfweb.html**. Most sites that offer documents in .pdf format provide a direct link for downloading the Acrobat Reader software.

More than 150 different plug-ins are available for download at Netscape's In-Line Plug-Ins page (**http://home.netscape.com/comprod/products/ navigator/version_2.0/plugins/index.html**). While I didn't bother to count the individual plug-ins available from BrowserWatch's Plug-In Plaza (**http://browserwatch.internet.com/plug-in. html**), the Web page listing all of them is a hefty 133K. These are the two spots to go if you're looking for something special—or if you've just *got* to experience all of these for yourself. If you'd like to experiment with a few of the more interesting ones, look for these:

- With Macromedia Shockwave, view sites designed with Macromedia's Director, a multimedia authoring program that features top-of-the-line audio, animation, and interactivity. Flash is its newer, lower-bandwidth alternative.
- Apple Quicktime VR is a must-have for movie buffs wanting to view Web-based video clips, or serious gamers looking to navigate 3-D sites.
- Some other interesting choices have been culled out by the folks at Ziff-Davis's 2D Internet Magazine (**http://www.2dnet.com/ zdimag/content/anchors/199705/12/toolvox. html**).

The Virtual Pack-Rat Phenomenon

The bookmark file, or, in Internet Explorer, the Favorites folder, can be a researcher's best friend—or worst nightmare. If you have even a small tendency toward being an information junkie, there's a large tendency to bookmark every other site you see. It's the cyberspace equivalent of being a pack rat. Before you know it, you've got more sites in your bookmark file than Yahoo! has in its entire database. Except yours aren't organized so nicely. They may not be organized at all. Which pretty much dumps you back at square one: How can you find your way back to that site you just *know* has exactly what you need? Do you scroll feverishly through your lengthy bookmark list, hoping for a memory jog? And when you finally locate the bookmark you want, you click on it and get a 404.

I'm not wild about either of the bookmark management tools built into the two major browsers. Lots of people must feel the same way; if you cruise through any Internet-related software site like TUCOWS or Stroud's CWS Apps (see chapter 10), you'll find an ever-growing selection of special utilities devoted to browser bookmark management. Almost always, trial versions are available for download.

I haven't found any third-party software application that does the job well enough to make me want to drag myself over the learning curve. I stick with the tools that are native to Navigator and Explorer, which have been improving over time. You can create topical folders and group bookmarks into them logically; for the vast majority of people, that's enough.

Cookies

On the Internet, nobody knows you're a dog. But don't bet the farm on that assumption. On the Internet these days, it's probably well known that you are, in fact, a dog, as well as what breed or breeds you are, what brand of kibble you prefer, and whether or not you've been neutered.

I can tell you firsthand, as a former Web server administrator for a nonprofit regional library network, that when you connected to our site, our server log told us what site you had connected from, what time of the day you connected, and which of our Web pages you accessed. And we were a small, relatively unsophisticated operation, not going out of its way to amass and analyze user statistics, inasmuch as we had no interest in selling products or services to the Net-surfing public, nor in seducing advertisers into purchasing space on our Web site.

By and large, however, you've got to face the fact that if you use the Web, you are highly desirable to advertisers and marketers. Although truly accurate statistics about who's online have been difficult to come by, certain assumptions are being made—mainly, that if you're savvy enough to have gotten yourself onto the Web, you're probably gainfully employed, with a higher-than-average education level and household income, which makes you a Desirable Demographic. Lots of people with the big bucks to develop sophisticated information-gathering tools are extremely interested in learning about you.

Want to see what kind of information is being gathered about you as you blithely surf your way around the Internet? A good place to start is the Privacy Demonstration at the Center for Democracy and Technology (CDT) site (**http://www.13x. com/cgi-bin/cdt/snoop.pl**). At the very least, these people can tell where you dialed in from, what kind of computer and browser you're using, and whether or not you've previously visited the site.

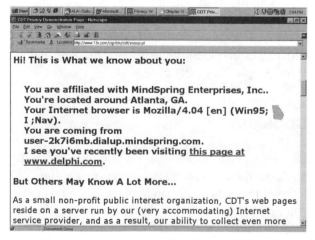

Close, but no cigar. MindSpring Enterprises is my Internet provider and it's "located around Atlanta, GA." But the rest of the information about my browser (Mozilla=Netscape), my operating system, and the page from which I came is accurate.

Plenty of good material is here about the data being gathered about you as you use the Internet, including how they are gathered and some of the ways in which they can be used—and why you should care. CDT offers an excellent hypothetical reason for worry: "If your repeated visits to Web sites containing information on cigarettes results in free samples, coupons, or even e-mail to you about a new tobacco product, you may not be concerned. However, if your visits to these Web sites result in escalating insurance premiums due to categorization as a smoker. . . ."

If the word *cookie* immediately makes you think of Pepperidge Farm, visit Andy's Netscape HTTP Cookie Notes at **http://www.illuminatus. com/cookie.fcgi**. According to Andy, "A cookie is a little nugget of information that is sent to your browser from a World Wide Web server. This block of data can be anything—a unique user ID generated by the server, the current date and time, the IP address of where the browser is logged onto the Net, or any other chunk of data." Cookies (or "client-side persistent information," according to the CDT) allow Web sites you've visited to store information about your visit on *your* hard drive. As a result, whenever you return to that site, its server can "read" the cookie to see when and if you've visited before and what you looked at while you were there.

If you want some idea of how often the Web sites you visit are leaving cookies on your computer, both the Netscape and Microsoft browsers have a feature that you can turn on to warn you before your computer accepts a cookie. In IE 4.x, find this in View/Options/Advanced. In Netscape 3.x, go to Options/Network Preferences/Protocols; in 4.x, Edit/Preferences/Advanced. Check off the appropriate Warn Before box, and surf on as usual. Turn it on, and you will shortly be driven completely nuts by all the remote sites that want to leave a little piece of themselves on your server.

After the point is made, you can disable the cookie warning or disable cookies altogether—i.e., set your browser not to accept any. Before you're too quick to do this, however, you need to know that not all cookies are bad. They are also used for efficient, convenient things—saving log-in information so you don't have to retype a user name and password every time you visit the *New York Times* site, for instance. Or keeping track of the books you wish to purchase in a virtual shopping basket at Amazon.com.

Ideally, what you want is control over which remote sites can and cannot leave cookies on your hard drive. Yes to Lands End. No to the numerous Internet advertising services that like to keep track of which of their ad banners you've seen. And so forth. Fortunately, there are now software solutions that don't involve putting up with the nuisance of the Warn Before feature in your browser. I like a little shareware program called Cookie Pal. Essentially, it permits you to decide which sites you will and won't accept cookies from by creating a series of filters, which you can view and edit whenever you like. PGPcookie.cutter, Cookie Monster, and Cookie Cutter 1.0 are similar programs you'll find at any of the large shareware sites (see Chapter 10).

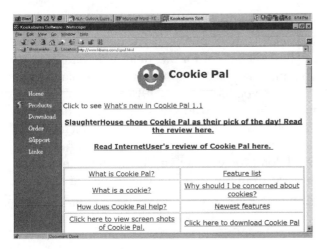

Download a trial copy of Cookie Pal from any of the big Internet shareware sites or directly from Kookaburra Software (**http://www.kburra.com/cpal.html**).

If you're really uncomfortable about the fact that you're leaving readily identifiable footprints around the Web, you might want to give the Anonymizer (**http://www.anonymizer.com/**) a try. This Web site acts, essentially, as a middleman between you and the remote resources you want to retrieve. By placing its own URL in front of the URL you want to visit, it hides the identity of your server, computer, and other personal details. If, for example, you wanted to use Digital's AltaVista search engine, the URL would look like **http://www.anonymizer.com:8080/http://www.**

altavista.digital.com/. Detailed information is available in an FAQ at the site, including instructions on how always to be anonymous by configuring your browser to use the Anonymizer as your default home page.

The Electronic Privacy Information Center (EPIC), at **http://www.epic.org/**, is the place to go if you want to keep up with cutting-edge online privacy issues. You'll also find advice about "safe surfing," tools like encryption software for those who are concerned about e-mail security, and lots of links to other privacy-related organizations, publications, Net sites, etc. Also worth a visit is the Privacy Rights Clearinghouse (**http://www. acusd.edu/~prc/**), a nonprofit consumer education and research center administered by San Diego's Center for Public Interest Law. Here you'll find fact sheets—in English and Spanish—about a wide range of privacy hot buttons, like cellular phone transmissions, credit cards and credit reports, medical information, and so forth.

Browser Tips and Tricks

This eclectic collection has been siphoned from experience, Internet mailing lists, knowledgeable people, lots of reading. I'm staying away from information related to browser e-mail or Usenet news-reading features and leaning more toward information that will help improve your browser's performance and increase your own searching efficiency.

NONANONYMOUS FTP

You may already know that you can log onto any anonymous FTP site with your browser, using the URL syntax *ftp://host.domain*. You can also log onto FTP sites that require a specific user name and password. Use this syntax in the browser location box: *ftp://yourusername:yourpassword@ host.domain*.

Make sure you use the colon to separate your user name from your password to the left of the @ sign. (Note that your password will be visible to anyone who can see your monitor, or if anyone cruises through your browser's cache after you're done with the computer, so be judicious in your use of this tip.)

WINDOWS 95 MEMORY LEAKS

If you're a Win 95 user who seems to be experiencing way too many freezes or crashes while surfing, you may want to download and install Microsoft's upgrade patch for the Win 95 Winsock stack. Winsock applications—e.g., browsers—that open and close Winsock connections all day long can eventually drain enough memory out of your system to the point where it stops functioning. The upgrade patch, available at **http://support. microsoft.com/support/kb/articles/Q148/3/36. asp**, will make sure Windows releases all of its memory resources to the general memory pool each time you close down a Winsock application.

MAILING WEB PAGES FROM YOUR BROWSER

Sometimes you're out surfing and you stumble across some jewel of a site that you must share with a friend, your significant other, a coworker. Choose Mail Document from the File menu; Navigator will open an e-mail window and automatically include the current Web page as a file attachment. You just type in the e-mail address of your intended recipient and click on Send. In IE, go to File/Send and make a choice: Page by EMail, Link by EMail, or Shortcut to Desktop.

DITHERING?

Some wildly creative Web graphic designers employ more colors in their images than the average computer video display can handle. Navigator offers a couple methods of coping with this: dithering, a process that "creates" a color that comes as close as possible to the intended hue, and color substitution, whereby Navigator substitutes colors it feels are appropriate for those that are unavailable in your video display. Dithering takes more time than color substitution but may produce more accurate rendering of images. The choice is yours. Go into Options/General Preferences, select the Images tab, and pick: Automatic (the default setting, lets Navigator determine the most appropriate type of color display); Dither (most closely match your computer's available colors); Substitute Colors (with the closest match). There is no similar control in IE, but you can

exercise limited control over how page colors are displayed from View/Internet Options.

JUST SAY NO!

Sick of scrolling marquees and bouncing heads? Go to Options/Network Preferences, select Languages, and uncheck the two boxes labeled Enable Java and Enable JavaScript. In IE, the check box can be found in View/Options on the Security tab. Be aware, however, that you may be crippling some useful or essential page features.

WHEN RELOAD WON'T

Sometimes, when you click the Reload or Refresh button, your browser doesn't respond. Try a Super Reload—hold down the Shift key while clicking on Reload again. (Mac users should use the Option key while clicking Reload.)

DROP THAT PENCIL!

Never write down a URL if you can avoid it. (You might get it wrong, for one thing.) For another, you might not be able to read your own handwriting when you look at it later. Use the Clipboard feature for all it's worth. It's much better than scribbling down the URL by hand and then typing it into an e-mail message to share with a friend. (And don't forget that you can highlight and copy any text from a Web page that's displayed in your browser's window.)

SWIPING IMAGES

See a .gif or a .jpeg image you like as you're cruising the Web? It can be yours! Position your mouse pointer over the image and right click, then choose Save Image As. Works for Navigator and IE. (Mac users should hold down the mouse button until the extended menu appears.) Do watch out for the copyright police.

CAN'T REMEMBER? AUTOSEARCH!

Can't remember the URL of a Web site you want to visit? IE users can take advantage of Autosearch. Just type *go* in the address bar, followed by a keyword that describes what you're looking for. IE automatically starts (via Yahoo!) a search for you.

12

Information Quality, Information Quantity

The Good, the Bad, and the Overwhelming!

Evaluating Internet Resources

Are They That Different from Print Resources?

When I took the core course Basic Information Sources and Services at the University of South Florida School of Library and Information Science (**http://www.cas.usf.edu/lis/welcome.html**) in the mideighties, I lucked out. My instructor was a man by the name of Kenneth F. Kister—author of *Kister's Best Encyclopedias: A Comparative Guide to General and Specialized Encyclopedias* (**http://www.oryxpress.com/authors/a00056. htm**), as well as purchasing guides for other standard reference materials like dictionaries and atlases. Not only was Ken a veritable fountain of knowledge about reference materials and the publishing industry, he was fascinating to listen to; it seemed as if each three-hour class were over before it had barely gotten started.

One of the things Ken required us to do was to keep a reference notebook. Each week, we would tackle a different category of reference materials— atlases, dictionaries, or maybe subject-specific resources, for business, science, etc. Each of us would go to the library, examine all the standard reference works in a particular category, and write an evaluation of each item. At the end of the course, we handed in our completed notebooks, upon which the bulk of the course grade was based.

Variations on this theme are standard operating procedure at all library schools. For an online example, take a look at Evaluation and Comparison of Various Information Sources (**http://www.emporia. edu/s/www/slim/students/leonlars/809N/Mainmenu. htm**), by Carrie Bonebreak and Lars Leon, students at Emporia (Kansas) State University's School of Library and Information Management. I'm using this particular Web site as an example because its two developers included a selection of Web sites along with the other, more traditional resources they evaluated as part of their project.

But is it reasonable to judge Internet resources by the same criteria we apply to more traditional media like books, periodicals, CD-ROM products, and commercial online databases? Well, yes and no. Information is information; its physical location is merely a characteristic rather than a blanket indicator of quality . . . or lack thereof. Right?

Well, Internet resources possess some unique characteristics that need to be taken into consideration. Most of these have to do with the fact that the barriers of entry for Internet publishing are so low as to be almost nonexistent. For example, Internet accounts are relatively inexpensive and often include a few megabytes of space for individual Web pages. Learning basic HTML coding is relatively easy and may not even be necessary, since most word-processing programs will now save a document in HTML format. Heck, you may not even need to spend a dime! There are public access Internet computers in many libraries, and a surprising number of services offer free Web page space (**http://www.yahoo.com/Business_and_ Economy/Companies/Internet_Services/Web_ Services/Free_Web_Pages/**).

So if you're wondering why there's so much garbage on the Internet, this is the reason. It's a classic example of "the tragedy of the commons," as described in a famous essay (**http://savers.org: 80/free/FP/TragedyCommons.html**) by Garrett Hardin, professor emeritus of human ecology at the University of California, Santa Barbara, originally published in the journal *Science* in 1968. Hardin postulated that all "common property resources" tend to be overexploited by individuals pursuing their own self-interest, which results in eventual degradation unless the intensive use is somehow restrained. To illustrate this principle, he used the example of the common pasturelands in medieval England, where each farmer increased the size of his own herd until the common pasture became overgrazed, to the collective detriment of the community.

Enough philosophizing. Let's start coping.

Some General Considerations

Because the Web has been so "overgrazed" by vanity publishers, quick-buck artists, and every individual or organization with an ax to grind, it requires more effort on the part of the individual researcher to locate and identify high-quality information. But the good stuff is out there. Make no mistake about that. Internet resources can and should be judged by the same stringent criteria by which you evaluate any other information.

ACCURACY

Is the information reliable and error free? Has it been through any sort of filtering process designed to catch errors in fact or judgment? This can be a tough call on the Internet and needs to be taken into consideration with other criteria. One big factor: Does the organization providing the information have a vested interest in maintaining its professional reputation—e.g., a scientific association that publishes "peered" journals, a large news organization, etc.?

AUTHORITY

Who created the resource? What are his or her credentials? Is the "publisher" reputable—i.e., what entity maintains the server on which the resource is located? Examine the URL. Does it identify an academic institution (.edu), a federal government agency (.gov), or a nonprofit organization (.org)? Is the organization providing the information an appropriate provider for the subject matter in question—i.e., a law school for legal information or a hospital for health information? Is there a tilde (~) in the URL? This often indicates a personal rather than an institutional Web page. Which doesn't mean the information isn't valuable. But you may need to take a closer look at the authorship. Is there an e-mail link for the person maintaining the resource? You can always write and ask about it.

OBJECTIVITY

Can you detect any bias in the content or the presentation of the information? Is it emanating from a source that is likely to have a particular point of view on the subject in question? This doesn't mean the information is useless. But you need to take care that you seek out the other side of the agenda. For example, if you're going to use information you found at the National Rifle Association's Web site, you should probably surf over to the Coalition to Stop Gun Violence and see what those folks have to say.

CURRENCY

Is the information static or is it frequently updated? How much does this matter for the type of information in question? If you see a date on the page, can you tell if it's the date the resource was created, the date it was placed on the Web, or the date it was last updated? Beware the Internet ghost town—a disheartening number of resources still "exist," but nobody "lives there" anymore (Ghost Sites of the Web—**http://www.disobey. com/ghostsites/**). Sometimes you can find out the age of a resource by choosing View/Document Info from your browser's toolbar.

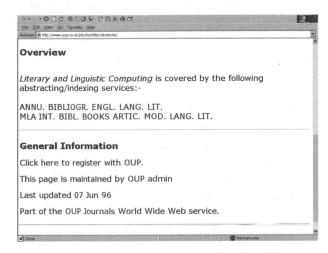

This page was last modified by its authors on June 7, 1996. Is this okay for your current research purposes, or should you look for something more current?

SCOPE

What are the limits of this resource in terms of breadth and depth? Who is the intended audience? Children or adults? Novices or experts? Laymen or scholars? What about geographic or chronological coverage? How does it compare to identical or similar print resources?

Specific Considerations for Different Types of Resources

Jan Alexander and Marsha Tate—reference librarians at Widener University, Chester, Pennsylvania—have created checklists of questions that need to be asked about five specific types of Web pages that they've identified—advocacy, business/marketing, informational, news, and personal. With their permission, I've included these in appendix B. (Their excellent presentation Teaching Critical Evaluation Skills for World Wide Web Resources is available at **http://www.science.widener.edu/ ~withers/webeval.htm**.)

Pointers to Bibliographies on Internet Information Quality Issues

Librarians all over the world have been confronting the task of evaluating Internet information. The sites below represent a sampling of these efforts.

- Critical Evaluation Surveys, maintained by Kathy Schrock, N. H. Wixon Middle School, Dennis, Massachusetts (**http://www.capecod. net/Wixon/eval.htm**)
- Information Quality WWW Virtual Library, maintained by Dr. T. Matthew Ciolek, Australian National University (**http://www. ciolek.com/WWWVL-InfoQuality.html**); included as a subdivision is a collection of pointers, Evaluation of Information Sources, maintained by Alastair Smith, Victoria University of Wellington, New Zealand (**http://www. vuw.ac.nz/~agsmith/evaln/evaln.htm**)
- Internet Source Validation Project: References, maintained by Memorial University Faculty of Education, Newfoundland, Canada (**http://www.stemnet.nf.ca/Curriculum/Validate/refers.html**)
- Resources: Other Sites about Evaluating Information on the Internet, maintained by Andrea Bartelstein and Anne Zald, University of Washington, Seattle (**http://weber.u.washington. edu/~libr560/NETEVAL/resources.html**)
- Web Evaluation Techniques: Bibliography, maintained by Jan Alexander and Marsha Tate, Wolfgram Memorial Library, Widener University, Chester, Pennsylvania (**http://www. science.widener.edu/~withers/wbstrbib.htm**)

Keeping Up with What's New

Is there an iota of doubt in your mind that keeping up with everything that's happening on the Internet is an impossible task? People like me try to do this for a living, and most of us are completely overwhelmed. Which means that those of you with "real" jobs are really behind the proverbial eight ball.

Except that you don't have to be, if you make some basic decisions about just what it is you want to keep track of, how much time you want to devote to it, and what's the most efficient way—for you—to acquire and manage information.

Professional librarians can certainly provide some guidance in this area. Internet aside, they are continually faced with the problem of keeping up with the torrent of new books, periodicals, and, in most cases, CD-ROM products and commercial databases. How do they cope? Certainly not by reading or trying all this stuff themselves.

They rely on respected third-party resources—publishers' announcements, professional review journals, established directories like *Books in Print* or *Magazines for Libraries*, and a variety of subject-specific publications and services.

This strategy is eminently suited to the Internet. There's no way in the world that you could possibly visit every new Web site, even if you had no interest at all in eating, sleeping, and having a "life." Besides, you don't really *want* to visit every new Web site—the boring, stupid ones; the crassly commercial ones; the patently offensive ones (definitely a matter of personal taste); the highly technical or scholarly ones in professionally irrelevant fields.

What most of us want is to learn about potentially useful and interesting new resources in those subjects areas that are important to us. Personally, I'm not particularly interested in sites containing information about professional football. My teenage son, however, would probably want to check these out. He, on the other hand, would not "waste" his time browsing food and cooking sites, but I have a colleague who "collects" these in her personal bookmark list. Right now, I'm working with a lot of engineers and scientists, and I'm very interested in learning about sites containing useful information for them. In the meantime, I have an attorney friend who just got "wired," and I've been forwarding him information about Internet resources of interest to the legal community.

Keeping Up Online

As a matter of fact, one of the best ways of learning about interesting stuff on the Internet is to develop a circle of wired friends who know what your personal and professional interests are. As you're all out there covering different hunks of cyberturf, everyone can be passing along the occasional item of interest to whoever would appreciate it. Forwarding messages from Internet mailing lists or using your browser's mail function to send a relevant site to a friend takes almost no time at all. (Just make sure the person on the other end is a willing recipient. Personally, I like it when friends or colleagues forward stuff to me, but other folks may feel bombarded or overwhelmed.)

Taking this to a more formal level, you may want to sign on to an Internet mailing list in your area of professional or personal interest. If you read chapter 7, you know there's a list for virtually every profession or avocation. Relevant new Internet resources get announced on these lists routinely. If there's a useful new government Web server out there, you better believe that the folks on GOVDOC-L—a mailing list for government documents librarians—will find out about it. New database of surnames? Get the nitty-gritty on ROOTS-L, the genealogy mailing list.

CARR-L, the Internet mailing list devoted to computer-assisted research and reporting, was originally conceived as a communications vehicle for working journalists and journalism educators. But Elliott Parker, the journalism prof at Central Michigan University who is CARR-L's list owner, does such a fine job of passing along useful Internet news and resources that the list has attracted a large following of researchers and just plain information junkies. Information about joining CARR-L can be found at **http://www.jmk.su.se/dig/guide/ listservs/carr-l.html**.

The mother of all Internet resource announcement services is Gleason Sackman's Net-Happenings mailing list, sponsored by InterNIC Information and Education Services. If you want an eye-opening look at the sheer diversity of resources available on the Internet, sign onto this

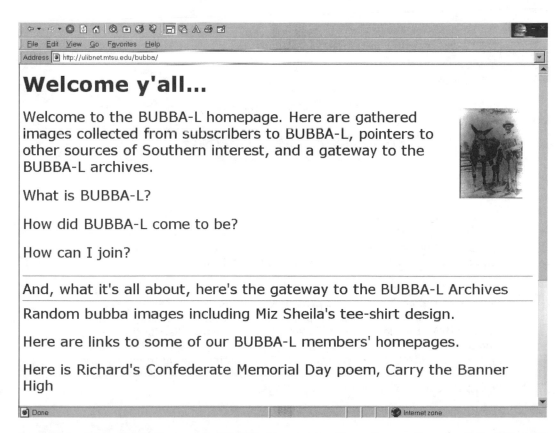

If something interesting debuts on the Web that has to do with southern culture, you'll hear about it on BUBBA-L (**http://ulibnet.mtsu.edu/bubba/**).

list for a while. Because the list is moderated by Sackman, a former educator, the signal-to-noise ratio is very high. Still, the list generates an endless torrent of e-mail messages, and the average person might find the volume overwhelming.

But there are other ways to take advantage of this resource. The *digest* format of the list, which is the default format for new subscribers, results in just one message a day containing all of that day's announcements. As you might expect, however, the size of each individual digest message is huge. For those who find the Usenet newsgroup format easier to manage, Net-Happenings is gatewayed as the newsgroup comp.internet.net-happenings.

Finally, all of the list messages are archived. You can browse or search the archive at **http://scout.cs.wisc.edu/scout/net-hap/**, where you'll also find instructions for subscribing to the mailing list as well as a resource submittal form, if you'd like to share information about some neat new thing on the Internet.

By the way, if you read Usenet newsgroups, comp.infosystems.www.announce consists of nothing but announcements of new Web sites in a variety of categories. An archive of these announcements—browsable by category or searchable by keyword—may be found at **http://sunsite. unc.edu/gerald/ciwa/**.

A variety of electronic newsletters that announce new Internet resources or provide news about the Internet itself are available by (free) e-mail subscription. Here are some of the more interesting ones, with the addresses of their Web sites where you can either sign up or obtain subscription information:

- EDUPAGE (thrice weekly summary of information technology news)—**http://www. educom.edu/web/edupage.html**

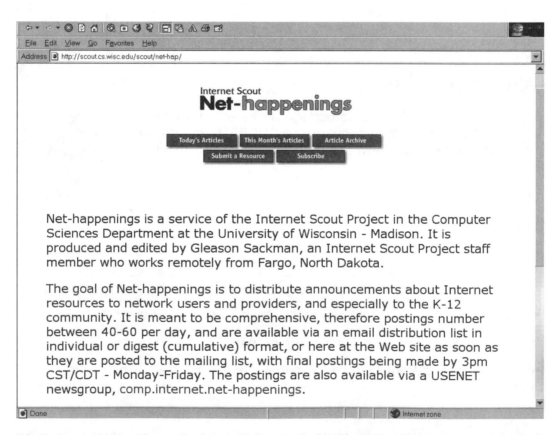

What's new and interesting on the Internet? Stop by the Net-Happenings home page and check recent announcements . . . or search the archives.

- IAT Infobits (educational technology-oriented pointers from the Institute for Academic Technology's Information Resources Group)—**http://www.iat.unc.edu/infobits/infobits.html**
- Internet Index (occasional missive containing quirky selection of Internet facts and statistics)—**http://www.openmarket.com/intindex/**
- Internet Resources Newsletter (edited by Heriot-Watt University Library staff, a monthly electronic journal about Internet resources of interest to "academics, students, engineers, scientists, and social scientists")—**http://www.hw.ac.uk/libWWW/irn/irn.html**
- The Internet TourBus ("Why surf when you can ride the bus?")—**http://www.worldvillage.com/tourbus.htm**
- Net Announce (twice-weekly newsletter with announcements of upcoming events, new Websites and other Internet resources, and updates about new content at existing resources)—**http://www.erspros.com/net-announce/**
- Netcetera (NorthWestNet's monthly update on new resources, applications, services)—**http://www.nwnet.net/netcetera/**
- Netsurfer Digest (available in text or HTML format; "your guide to interesting news, places, and resources online")—**http://www.netsurf.com:80/nsd/**
- The Scout Report (news and reviews from InterNIC Information and Education Services, subject-specific reports in science and engineering, business and economics, and social sciences)—**http://wwwscout.cs.wisc.edu/scout/report/**
- Seidman's Online Insider (covers commercial online services)—**http://www.onlineinsider.com/**
- TidBITS (especially good for things Macintosh)—**http://www.tidbits.com/**
- NetBITS (Internet-specific publication by TidBITS folks)—**http://www.netbits.net**
- Weekend Web Picks (reviews three top URLs in a different category every week)—**http://www.netogether.com/picks.html**
- The Weekly Bookmark (Net news and site reviews)—**http://www.weeklyb.com/**
- Yahoo!'s Picks of the Week (sites selected by Yahoo! staff; lighter fare)—**http://www.yahoo.com/picks/**

Suppose you don't want to wait for news of what's new on the Net to come to you. You can visit a whole bunch of What's New pages out there. Most of the major indexes and search engines offer something like this. You can even click right on Netscape's What's New button.

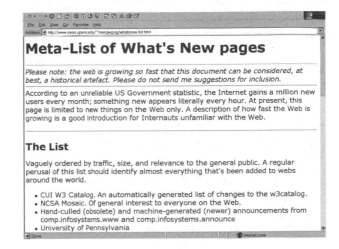

If you'd like to visit many What's New pages in one surfing session, take advantage of the Meta-List of What's New Pages (**http://www.seas.upenn.edu/~mengwong/whatsnew.list.html**). Last time I checked, about thirty-five What's New sites were listed. "Please note," says the disclaimer on this Meta-List, "the Web is growing so fast that this document can be considered, at best, a historical artefact [*sic*]."

Meanwhile, there are a number of variations on the current-awareness-by-e-mail theme. Keeping up with Usenet newsgroups, for example, is almost impossible these days due both to the number of groups as well as the sheer volume of messages posted to them, too much of which is irrelevant garbage. And yet, for the latest gossip, Usenet is the place to go. Say you work for a company that has released a new software product, and you want to see what the masses are saying about it. You could spend an inordinate amount of time trolling the appropriate newsgroups, of course. But there's a better way.

Several free services allow you to register topics in which you are interested. Then—daily, weekly, or whatever, depending on your preference—these "agents" make a sweep of Usenet newsgroup postings and cull out anything mentioning your subject of interest. The results are either e-mailed to you, or you receive a notice that the agent has found something, and you can surf directly to the service's Web site to peruse the new information. Interested? Try these:

REFERENCE.COM

Set up Active Queries that let you store topic searches on Reference.COM's (**http://www.reference.com/**) computer, and have them run automatically each day for some number of days. Register with your e-mail address and choose a password.

AT1—YOUR GATEWAY TO THE INVISIBLE WEB

There's a lot of nifty stuff here at **http://www.at1. com/**, including the ability to run free searches of proprietary databases (although you'll pay to receive full-text results). Set up agents to scan Usenet newsgroup postings by using natural language queries. Or register URLs you wish to track with URLy Warnings, and receive e-mail notification whenever something on that Web page changes. (Another site that provides this service is

NetMind's URL-Minder at **http://www.netmind. com/html/url-minder.html.**)

THE INFORMANT—YOUR PERSONAL SEARCH AGENT ON THE INTERNET

The Informant (**http://informant.dartmouth. edu/**) is a notification service that works in two ways:

1. You can enter up to three sets of keywords. a periodic interval of three, seven, fourteen, thirty, or sixty days (which you specify), the Informant uses the AltaVista, Lycos, or Excite search engines to find the ten Web pages that are most relevant to your keywords. If a new page appears in the top-ten, or if one of the previous top-ten pages has been updated, the Informant sends you an e-mail message.

2. You can enter up to five URLs that are of particular interest to you. At a periodic interval of

The Informant is not a search engine itself. It uses Lycos, AltaVista, Excite, and Infoseek.

three, seven, fourteen, thirty, or sixty days (which you specify), the Informant checks these Web pages and sends you e-mail if one or more of them have been updated. Once you receive the e-mail, you return to the Informant, where you will find a table of your new or updated Web page.

Keeping Up off the Grid

According to "Jargon Watch," in the October 1996 *Wired* (**http://www.wired.com/wired/4.10/ jargon_watch.html**):

> Off the Grid—Euphemism for being off the Net. "Sorry I didn't e-mail you last week; I was off the grid in Mexico." Also refers to someone who lives in a rural area without running water, electricity, or phone service.

Of course, there's *Wired* magazine (**http:// www.wired.com/**)—fat, colorful, and filled with attitude . . . as well as itself. Still worthwhile reading (if you can manage the "interesting" design and colorful typography) for the interviews with techno-interesting people and the in-depth articles on telecommunications issues.

Some other Internet magazines—all of which have Web sites, naturally—worth a look are:

Boardwatch (**http://www.boardwatch.com/**), originally a magazine for the bulletin board system (BBS) community, has expanded its scope and now covers the Internet and major online services as well. Less glitzy and hype-ridden than most Net pubs.

Inter@ctive Week (**http://www.zdnet.com/ intweek/**) is Ziff-Davis's weekly newspaper that covers all aspects of the Internet and interactive technology—alliances, events, issues, key players, products, services, and strategies. If you qualify, a subscription is free.

Web Week (**http://www.webweek.com/**) is Mecklermedia's weekly newspaper for Internet technology and e-commerce. This is another one that you can receive for free if you qualify.

Yahoo! Internet Life (**http://www.zdnet.com/ yil/welcome.html/**) is another Ziff-Davis effort, this one aimed at the mass-market/ mainstream Internet user.

ZD Internet Magazine (**http://www.zdnet.com/ zdimag/**), from guess who, is aimed more at Web developers and other tech-type folks.

Professional publications in library and information science now provide Internet coverage as a matter of routine—usually at least a regular column. Inasmuch as they are directed toward information professionals rather than the general public, you'll find serious and authoritative content. These aren't as easy to find on the newsstand, but your local library may carry any or all of them, depending on its size and professional periodicals budget. Most have some sort of Internet presence:

American Libraries, the official publication of the American Library Association, includes "The Internet Librarian" column by Karen G. Schneider (**http://www.ala.org/a/online/**)

The author of this book writes a column called "Internet Waves" for *Information Today*, "The Newspaper for Users and Producers of Electronic Information Services" (**http://www. infotoday.com/it/itnew.htm**).

Several other publications by the *Info Today* folks also include Internet coverage, such as *Computers in Libraries* (**http://www.infotoday. com/cilmag/ciltop.htm**) and *MultiMedia Schools* (**http://www.infotoday.com/ MMSchools/index.html**).

Library Journal (**http://www.bookwire.com/ ljdigital/**) now features a regular "WebWatch" column.

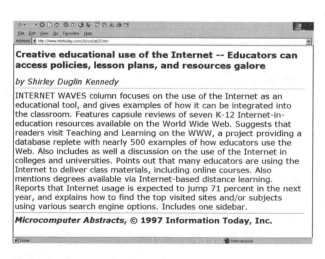

Blatant self-promotion by your author.

College and Research Libraries News (**http://www.ala.org/acrl/c&rlnew2.html**) offers an Internet resources review column also available online.

Online, Inc. (**http://www.onlineinc.com/**), publishes several "journals of record" for the information profession. *Database* (**http://www.onlineinc.com/database/index.html**) and *Online* (**http://www.onlineinc.com/onlinemag/index.html**) are targeted toward the hands-on information professional and include the columns "On the Nets," by Greg Notess, and "Net Sitings," by John Makulowich. You can usually find these columns' full text online.

Appendix A

Chapter-by-Chapter Sites and URLs

Preface

IguanaCam
http://iguana.images.com/dupree/

Chapter 1: Why Is It So Hard to Find Things on the Internet?

Amazon.com
http://www.amazon.com/

Tim Berners-Lee
http://www.w3.org/Peoplc/Berners-Lee-Bio.html

The Infamous Exploding Whale
http://www.xmission.com/~grue/whale/

Project Vote Smart
http://www.vote-smart.org/

Paul's (Extra) Refrigerator
http://hamjudo.com/cgi-bin/refrigerator/

CNN
http://www.cnn.com/

Library of Congress Subject Headings
gopher://marvel.loc.gov/11/services/cataloging/
weekly/

National Library of Medicine MeSH
http://www.nlm.nih.gov/databases/databases.html

Thesaurus of ERIC Descriptors
http://ericir.syr.edu/Eric/

Yahoo! Body Art
http://www.yahoo.com/Arts/Visual_Arts/Body_Art/

Web Pages That Suck
http://www.webpagesthatsuck.com/

Periodic Table of Elements
http://www.universe.digex.net/~kkhan/periodic.html

RiceInfo Information by Subject Area: Economics
gopher://riceinfo.rice.edu:70/00/Subject/
Economics/About/

"Squirrels" warning from Patrick Crispen's Internet
Roadmap Tutorial
http://rs.internic.net/nic-support/roadmap96/
map01.html

AltaVista
http://www.altavista.digital.com/

Yahoo!
http://www.yahoo.com/

O.J. "Not Guilty"
http://www.cnn.com/US/OJ/daily/9510/10-03/
index.html

Bob Metcalfe predicts the impending collapse of the
Internet
http://www.infoworld.com/cgi-bin/
displayArchives.pl?dt_iwe47-96_24.htm

Chapter 2: Starting Points

Argus Clearinghouse Mission Statement
http://www.clearinghouse.net/mission.html

Bryan Pfaffenberger's *Web Search Strategies*
http://watt.seas.virginia.edu/~bp/searchme/
welcome.htm

BUBL Information Service
http://bubl.ac.uk/

BUBL Link
http://bubl.ac.uk/link/

BUBL Link subject tree
http://bubl.ac.uk/link/subjects/

BUBL Link Dewey Decimal System arrangement
http://link.bubl.ac.uk/isc2/

BUBL Link random browsing
http://bubl.ac.uk/link/random/

BUBL's FAQ
http://bubl.ac.uk/admin/faq.htm

BUBL's Library and Information Science Collection
http://www.bubl.bath.ac.uk/BUBL/Library.html

BUBL's collection of library and information science journals
http://bubl.ac.uk/journals/lis/

BUBL lis-link e-mail list
http://www.mailbase.ac.uk/lists/lis-link/

CyberDewey
http://ivory.lm.com/~mundie/CyberDewey/CyberDewey.html

Dewey Decimal Classification Hundred Divisions
http://ivory.lm.com/~mundie/CyberDewey/DivisionSummary.html

Tradewave Galaxy
http://galaxy.einet.net/

About the Galaxy
http://galaxy.einet.net/about.html

Gopher Jewels
http://galaxy.einet.net/GJ/

Hytelnet (Galaxy)
http://galaxy.einet.net/hytelnet/START.TXT.html

Hytelnet (University of Saskatchewan)
http://library.usask.ca/hytelnet/

WebCATS
http://library.usask.ca/hywebcat/

Hytelnet (gopher based)
gopher://liberty.uc.wlu.edu/11/internet/hytelnet/

Galaxy's guest editors
http://galaxy.einet.net/editors.html

Yahoo!
http://www.yahoo.com/

Yahoo! history
http://www.yahoo.com/docs/pr/history.html

Yahooligans!
http://www.yahooligans.com/

My Yahoo!
http://my.yahoo.com/

Yahoo! Get Local
http://local.yahoo.com/local/

Yahoo! What's New (daily)
http://www.yahoo.com/new/

Yahoo! What's New (weekly)
http://www.yahoo.com/picks/

Yahoo! Maps
http://maps.yahoo.com/yahoo/

Beatrice's Web Guide
http://www.bguide.com/

Yahoo! FAQ
http://www.yahoo.com/docs/info/faq.html

Yahoo! Search Help
http://search.yahoo.com/search/help?

Yahoo! Search Options
http://search.yahoo.com/search/options/

Yahoo! dead link reporting
http://www.yahoo.com/docs/writeus/deadlink.html

Yahoo! live chat
http://chat.yahoo.com/

World Wide Web Virtual Library: Aviation
http://macwww.db.erau.edu/www_virtual_lib/aviation.html

Argus Clearinghouse Submission Guidelines
http://www.clearinghouse.net/submit.html

World Wide Web Virtual Library resource administration guidelines
http://www.w3.org/pub/DataSources/bySubject/Administration.html

Argus Associates
http://argus-inc.com/

Argus Clearinghouse
http://www.clearinghouse.net/

Argus Clearinghouse rating system
http://www.clearinghouse.net/ratings.html

Argus Clearinghouse FAQ
http://www.clearinghouse.net/faq.html/#staff

Argus Clearinghouse staff
http://www.clearinghouse.net/staff.html

Argus Clearinghouse Digital Librarian's Award
http://www.clearinghouse.net/dla.html

Argus Clearinghouse Internet Searching Center
http://www.clearinghouse.net/searching/find.html

World Wide Web Virtual Library LC classification scheme
http://vlib.stanford.edu/LibraryofCongress.html

About the World Wide Web Virtual Library
http://vlib.stanford.edu/AboutVL.html

Links to other virtual libraries from the World Wide Web Virtual Library
http://vlib.stanford.edu/Virtual_libraries.html

World Wide Web Virtual Library project overview
http://vlib.stanford.edu/Overview.html

World Wide Web Virtual Library: History (University of Kansas)
http://history.cc.ukans.edu/history/WWW_history_main.html

Palm Beach Community College library staff (Doug Cornwell)
http://www.pbcc.cc.fl.us/llrc/about.htm

Chapter 3: Selective Subject Trees and Resource Catalogs

Netscape's Search Page
http://home.netscape.com/home/internet-search.html

Excite
http://www.excite.com/

Infoseek
http://www.infoseek.com/

Lycos/Point Top 5% Sites
http://point.lycos.com/categories/

WebCrawler
http://www.webcrawler.com/

Whole Internet User's Guide and Catalog
http://www.ora.com/catalog/twi2/

LookSmart
http://www.looksmart.com/

Magellan
http://www.mckinley.com/

Magellan? Search Voyeur
http://voyeur.mckinley.com/cgi-bin/voyeur.cgi

Yanoff's Internet Services List
http://www.spectracom.com/islist/index.html

SpectraCom
http://www.spectracom.com/home.html

The Awesome Lists
http://www.clark.net/pub/journalism/awesome.html

Nerd World Media
http://www.nerdworld.com/

Nerd World Easy Access Category Tree
http://www.nerdworld.com/cattree.html

PC Magazine's Top 100 Web Sites
http://www.zdnet.com/pcmag/special/web100/_open.html

WebDictionary
http://pantheon.cis.yale.edu/~jharris/webdict/webdict.html

ASCII art owls
http://www.crg.cs.nott.ac.uk/~anb/Football/General/owls.html

NetPartners Company Site Locator
http://www.netpart.com/company/search.html

WhoWhere? EDGAR
http://edgar.whowhere.com/

The Syndicate
http://www.itlnet.com/moneypages/syndicate/

CNN Financial Network Reference Desk
http://www.cnnfn.com/resources/referencedesk/

Inc. 500
http://www.inc.com/500/about.html

Motley Fool
http://www.fool.com/

Financial Data Finder (Ohio State University Department of Finance)
http://www.cob.ohio-state.edu/dept/fin/osudata.htm

A Business Compass
http://www.abcompass.com/directory.html

Investment FAQ Home Page
http://www.invest-faq.com/

A Business Researcher's Interests
http://www.brint.com/interest.html

CNN Financial Network
http://www.cnnfn.com/

Madalyn: A Business Research Tool
http://www.udel.edu/alex/mba/main/netdir2.html

Federal Web Locator
http://www.law.vill.edu/Fed-Agency/fedwebloc.html

The United States Government Manual (National Archives and Records Administration)
http://www.access.gpo.gov/nara/nara001.html

Catalog of Federal Domestic Assistance
http://www.gsa.gov/fdac/

GPO Access System databases
http://www.access.gpo.gov/su_docs/aces/aaces003.html

Federal Depository Library Gateways
http://www.access.gpo.gov/su_docs/aces/aaces004.html

University of Michigan Libraries Documents Center
http://www.lib.umich.edu/libhome/Documents.center/stats.htm

GPO Access Sales Product Catalog (Publication Reference File)
http://www.access.gpo.gov/su_docs/sale/prf/prf.html

StateSearch (National Association of State Information Resource Executives)
http://www.nasire.org/

State and Local Government on the Net (Piper Resources)
http://www.piperinfo.com/state/states.html

Full-Text State Statutes and Legislation on the Internet
http://www.prairienet.org/~scruffy/f.htm

Municipal Code Corporation
http://www.municode.com/

Yahoo! Get Local
http://local.yahoo.com/local/

Chapter 4: Virtual Libraries and Newsrooms

Librarians' Index to the Internet
http://sunsite.berkeley.edu/InternetIndex/

Edinburgh Engineering Virtual Library
http://www.eevl.ac.uk/welcome.html

University of Virginia Science and Engineering Libraries
http://www.lib.virginia.edu/science/SELhome.html

Frank Potter's Science Gems
http://www-sci.lib.uci.edu/SEP/SEP.html

University of Iowa Center for Global and Regional Environmental Research
http://www.cgrer.uiowa.edu/servers/servers_references.html

INFOMINE
http://lib-www.ucr.edu/

Internet Public Library
http://www.ipl.org/

Associations on the Net
http://www.ipl.org/ref/AON/

POTUS (Presidents of the United States)
http://www.ipl.org/ref/POTUS/

Internet Public Library MOO
http://www.ipl.org/moo/

Science Fair Project Resource Guide (IPL Teen Division)
http://www.ipl.org/youth/projectguide/

IPL Reference Center
http://www.ipl.org/ref/

Ready Reference Using the Internet
http://k12.oit.umass.edu/rref.html

Researchpaper.com
http://www.researchpaper.com/

Start Your Research Here (Old Dominion University Library)
http://www.lib.odu.edu/start/index.html

The Idea Generator (ODU Library)
http://www.lib.odu.edu/idea/ideagenerator.html

Infonautics Corporation
http://www.infonautics.com/

Electric Library
http://www.elibrary.com/

RiceInfo
http://riceinfo.rice.edu/Internet/

Rice's Subject Guides to Internet Resources
http://www.rice.edu/Fondren/Netguides/netguides.html

School Librarian Links
http://www.yab.com/~cyberian/

Kathy Schrock's Guide for Educators
http://www.capecod.net/Wixon/wixon.htm

Grant Sources for Educators
http://www.capecod.net/Wixon/business/grants.htm

Where the Wild Things Are: A Librarian's Guide to the Best Information on the Net
http://www.sau.edu/CWIS/Internet/Wild/index.htm

Unaccustomed As I Am
http://speeches.com/index.shtml

WebGEMS: A Guide to Substantive Web Resources
http://www.fpsol.com/gems/webgems.html

Jenny's Cybrary to the Stars
http://sashimi.wwa.com/~jayhawk/index.html

Online Catalogs with Webbed Interfaces
http://www.lib.ncsu.edu/staff/morgan/alcuin/
wwwed-catalogs.html

WebCATS: Library Catalogs on the World Wide Web
http://library.usask.ca/hywebcat/

Hytelnet on the World Wide Web
http://library.usask.ca/hytelnet/

PEG: A Peripatetic Eclectic Gopher—Libraries
gopher://peg.cwis.uci.edu:7000/11/gopher.
welcome/peg/LIBRARIES/

Library of Congress WWW/Z39.50 Gateway
http://lcweb.loc.gov/z3950/gateway.html

CARL UnCover Web
http://uncweb.carl.org/

The Library Web Manager's Reference Center
http://sunsite.berkeley.edu/Web4Lib/faq.html

Professional Organizations in the Information Sciences
http://witlioof.sjsu.edu/organizations.html

St. Joseph County Public Library's List of Public
Libraries with Internet Services
http://sjcpl.lib.in.us/homepage/PublicLibraries/
PublicLibraryServers.html

Writing for the Web: A Primer for Librarians
http://bones.med.ohio-state.edu/eric/papers/primer/
webdocs.html

Library Job Postings on the Internet
http://www.sils.umich.edu/~nesbeitt/libraryjobs.html

Palm Beach Post
http://www.pbpost.com/

Barbara's News Researcher's Page
http://www.gate.net/~barbara/

Poynter Institute for Media Studies Library Research
Center
http://www.poynter.org/research/research.htm

Columbia University Journalism Library
http://www.columbia.edu/acis/documentation/journ/
journnew.html

University of North Carolina School of Journalism and
Mass Communications Library
http://sunsite.unc.edu/journalism/

Special Libraries Association News Division Home Page
http://sunsite.unc.edu/slanews/

Expert Sources (Kitty Bennett)
http://sunsite.unc.edu/slanews/internet/experts.html

St. Petersburg Times
http://www.sptimes.com/

Bibliography of essential reference books for news
libraries
http://sunsite.unc.edu/slanews/reference/books.html

Dallas Morning News
http://www.dallasnews.com/)

The Beat Page
http://www.reporter.org/beat/

Reporter's Internet Survival Guide
http://www.qns.com/~casey/

Scoop Cybersleuth's Internet Guide
http://scoop.evansville.net/

Evansville (Indiana) Courier
http://www.evansville.net/newsweb/

Scoop Cybersleuth Kids Room
http://www.evansville.net/kidsroom.html

Computer-Assisted Research and Reporting Links
(Ryerson)
http://www.ryerson.ca/~dtudor/carcarr.htm

Investigative Journalism on the Internet (JournalismNet)
http://www.journalismnet.com/

Finding Data on the Internet: A Journalist's Guide
http://nilesonline.com/data/links.shtml

Statistics Every Writer Should Know
http://nilesonline.com/stats/

David Milliron's Links to Searchable Databases
http://www.lib.msu.edu/corby/reference/milliron.
htm

Kennedy School of Government One-Stop Journalist
Shop
http://ksgwww.harvard.edu/~ksgpress/journpg.htm

MediaSource
http://www.mediasource.com/

MediaSource Journalists' Source List
http://www.mediasource.com/Links.html

Stockholm International Peace Research Institute
http://www.sipri.se/

New York Times Navigator
   http://www.nytimes.com/library/cyber/reference/
   cynavi.html

Wired Cybrarian
   http://www.wired.com/cybrarian/

Chapter 5: Major Web Search Engines

Northern Light
   http://www.nlsearch.com/

AltaVista
   http://www.altavista.digital.com/

AltaVista help
   http://www.altavista.digital.com/av/content/help.htm

AltaVista Personal Search
   http://www.altavista.digital.com/av/content/
   searchpx.htm

Excite
   http://www.excite.com/

AOL Netfind
   http://www.aol.com/netfind/home.html

Web periodicals searched by Excite Newstracker
   http://nt.excite.com/sources.html

HotBot
   http://www.hotbot.com/

Forum One Forum Finder
   http://www.forumone.com/

HotBot FAQ
   http://help.hotbot.com/faq/index.html

Infoseek
   http://www.infoseek.com/

InfoBeat
   http://www.infobeat.com/

Hoover's Online
   http://www.hoovers.com/

Lycos
   http://www.lycos.com/

Lycos Top 5%
   http://point.lycos.com/categories/

World City Guide
   http://cityguide.lycos.com/

Lycos PeopleFind
   http://www.lycos.com/peoplefind/

Lycos StockFind
   http://www.stockfind.newsalert.com/

CompaniesOnline
   http://www.companiesonline.com/

Lycos RoadMaps
   http://www.lycos.com/roadmap.html

Lycos TopNews
   http://lnews.lycos.com/headlines/TopNews/

Lycos Help Guide
   http://www.lycos.com/help/boolean-help.html

Open Text Index
   http://index.opentext.net/

WebCrawler
   http://www.webcrawler.com/

MapQuest
   http://www.mapquest.com/

Northern Light
   http://www.nlsearch.com/

Northern Light FAQ
   http://www.northernlight.com/docs/annafaq.htm

Chapter 6: When One Is Not Enough

All-in-One Search Page
   http://www.albany.net/allinone/

The Internet Sleuth
   http://www.isleuth.com/

Search.Com
   http://www.search.com/

All-in-One Search Pages
   http://www.yahoo.com/Computers_and Internet/
   Internet/World_Wide_Web/Searching_the_Web/
   All_in_One_Search_Pages/

Cyber 411
   http://cyber411.com/

MetaCrawler
   http://www.metacrawler.com/

SavvySearch
   http://guaraldi.cs.colostate.edu:2000/

Dogpile
   http://www.dogpile.com/

Highway 61
   http://highway61.com/

Inference Find
http://m5.inference.com/ifind/

ProFusion
http://www.designlab.ukans.edu/profusion/

EchoSearch
http://www.iconovex.com/

Internet FastFind
http://service.symantec.com/iff/faq_iff.html

WebCompass
http://www.quarterdeck.com/qdeck/products/
webcompass/

WebSeeker
http://www.bluesquirrel.com/seeker/

WebFerret
http://ferretsoft.com/netferret/webferret.htm

TUCOWS
http://www.tucows.com/

Chapter 7: Doing the Private Eye Thing

E-Mail Addresses of the Rich and Famous
http://www.nctweb.com/books/richfam.html

IBM Whois Server
http://whois.ibm.com/

Bigfoot
http://www.bigfoot.com/

Four11 Directory Service
http://www.four11.com/

Yahoo! People Search (incorporating Four11)
http://yahoo.four11.com/

InfoSpace
http://www.infospace.com/

Verisign (digital IDs)
http://digitalid.verisign.com/

Internet Address Finder
http://www.iaf.net/

Usenet Addresses Database
http://usenet-addresses.mit.edu/

WhoWhere?
http://www.whowhere.com/

100 Hot Web Sites
http://www.100hot.com/

Geocities
http://www.geocities.com/

WhoWhere? EDGAR
http://edgar.whowhere.com/EDGAR

AT&T's AnyWho Directory
http://www.anywho.com/

411 Locate
http://www.411locate.com/

Housernet
http://www.housernet.com/

Housernet's list of other home page directories
http://www.housernet.com/explore/docs/other.html

The People Page
http://www.peoplepage.com/

World E-Mail Directory
http://www.worldemail.com/

Global Meta-People Finder
http://trendy.net/sites/peoplefind/index.html

ESP (E-Mail Search Program)
http://www.esp.co.uk/

America Online member home pages
http://home.aol.com/

CompuServe/Sprynet member home pages
http://www.sprynet.com/ourworld/searchow/

Delphi member home pages
http://www.delphi.com/dir-html/simple_web_
search.html

Earthlink member home pages
http://www.earthlink.net/company/free_web_pages.
html

Mindspring member home pages
http://www.mindspring.com/dbase/

Switchboard
http://www.switchboard.com/

Database America
http://www.databaseamerica.com/html/index.htm

Canada 411
http://canada411.sympatico.ca/

Telephone Directories on the Web
http://www.contractjobs.com/tel/

Telephone Directories on the Net
http://www.procd.com/hl/direct.htm

Yahoo!'s phone directory links
http://www.yahoo.com/Reference/Phone_Numbers/

El Jefe's Pay Phone Directory
   http://www.televar.com/~eljefe/payfonedir.html

AMA Physician Select
   http://www.ama-assn.org/aps/amahg.htm

Martindale-Hubbell Law Directory
   http://lawyers.martindale.com/marhub/

West's Legal Directory
   http://www.wld.com/

College E-Mail Addresses FAQ
   http://www.qucis.queensu.ca/FAQs/email/college.
   html

Angry Grandma's Adoptee's Links Page
   http://www.ior.com/~laswi/bookmark.htm

How to Contact a Celebrity
   http://www.islandnet.com/~luree/howto.html

ProfNet Experts Database
   http://www.profnet.com/ped.html

Dead People Server
   http://www.city-net.com/~lmann/dps/

The Obituary Page
   http://catless.ncl.ac.uk/obituary/

Social Security Death Index
   http://www.ancestry.com/SSDI/Main.htm

American Marriage Records
   http://www.ancestry.com/marriage/

netAddress Book of Transportation Professionals
   http://dragon.princeton.edu/~dhb/TRANSPORT_
   NAB/

Horus's History Links
   http://www.ucr.edu/h-gig/horuslinks.html

The HistoryNet (National Historical Society)
   http://www.thehistorynet.com/home.htm

University of Kansas Index of Resources for Historians
   http://kuhttp.cc.ukans.edu/history/index.html

A Stalking We Go!
   http://www.glr.com/stalk.html

CULTURE-People-Lists (John December, Computer-
Mediated Communications)
   http://www.december.com/cmc/info/culture-
   people-lists.html

FAQ: How to Find People's E-Mail Addresses
   http://www.qucis.queensu.ca/FAQs/email/finding.
   html

Gopher-based directory of e-mail address servers at
universities and research institutions
   gopher://merlot.gdb.org:70/11/phonebooks

Web-based interface to the preceding resource
   http://home.cdsnet.net/~zachbo/others.html

INTERNET-Searching-People (John December,
Computer-Mediated Communications)
   http://www.december.com/cmc/info/internet-
   searching-people.html

InterNIC Internet Network Information Center White
Pages Directory Services
   http://ds.internic.net/ds/dspgwp.html

Magnum P.I. in Cyberspace (NetGuide Live)
   http://www.netguide.com:10101/knowhow/
   snapguides/friend/index.html

NAIS Private Investigator's Link List (Ralph D. Thomas,
National Association of Investigative Specialists)
   http://www.pimall.com/nais/links.html

Training: Finding E-Mail Addresses (U.S. Region 2
EPA NY Library)
   http://www.epa.gov/Region2/library/mailhelp.htm

Webgator: Investigative Resources on the Web
   http://www.inil.com/users/dguss/wgator.htm

Discussion Lists: Mailing List Manager Commands
   http://lawwww.cwru.edu/cwrulaw/faculty/milles/
   mailser.htm

Informus Corporation
   http://www.informus.com/ssnlkup.html

WWW to Finger Gateway
   http://www.cs.indiana.edu:800/finger/gateway/

Chapter 8: Mailing Lists and Usenet Newsgroups

Information Today
   http://www.infotoday.com/

Accessing the Internet by E-Mail FAQ
   ftp://rtfm.mit.edu/pub/usenet/news.answers/
   internet-services/access-via-email

Drew Smith's home page
   http://www.cas.usf.edu/lis/faculty/smithd.html

Library-Oriented Lists and Electronic Serials
   http://info.lib.uh.edu/liblists/liblists.htm

Discussion Lists: WWW Library Resources
   http://www.netstrider.com/library/listservs/

Listservs: Inter-Links
http://alabanza.com/kabacoff/Inter-Links/listserv/
subscribe.html

Listservers: What They Are and What They Can Do
for You
http://www.gslis.ucla.edu/LIS/lab/unote05.html

CataList
http://www.lsoft.com/lists/listref.html

Publicly Accessible Mailing Lists
http://www.neosoft.com/internet/paml/index.html

Southern Connecticut State University Buley Library:
Professional Resources for Librarians on the WWW
http://library.scsu.edu/libbib.html

CyberFiber's Newsgroups
http://www.cyberfiber.com/news/

Newsgroups: WWW Library Resources
http://www.netstrider.com/library/newsgroups

Internet Roadmap Tutorial
http://internic.net:80/nic-support/roadmap96/
syllabus.html

Usenet Info Center Launch Pad
http://sunsite.oit.unc.edu/usenet-i/home.html

Find newsgroups by keyword search
http://www.cen.uiuc.edu/cgi-bin/find-news

Usenet Newsgroups Information for Beginners
http://www.geocities.com/ResearchTriangle/8211/

SELF-DISCIPLINE: Towards Better News Discussions
http://www.eiffel.com/discipline/

Usenet: The Global Watering Hole
http://www.eff.org/papers/eegtti/eeg_68.html

A Primer on How to Work with the Usenet Community
ftp://rtfm.mit.edu/pub/usenet/news.announce.
newusers/A_Primer_on_How_to_Work_with_the_
Usenet_Community

Emily Postnews Answers Your Questions on Netiquette
ftp://rtfm.mit.edu/pub/usenet/news.announce.
newusers/Emily_Postnews_Answers_Your_
Questions_on_Netiquette

DejaNews
http://www.dejanews.com/

Tillman/Howe search tips presentation
http://www.tiac.net/users/hope/tips/sld001.htm

Reference.COM
http://www.reference.com/

FAQ archive at MIT
ftp://rtfm.mit.edu/pub/usenet-by-group/

Infinite Ink: Finding and Writing Periodic Postings
http://www.jazzie.com/ii/internet/faqs.html

Yahoo!'s FAQ links
http://www.yahoo.com/Reference/FAQs/

alt.folklore.urban FAQ
http://www.cis.ohio-state.edu/hypertext/faq/
usenet/folklore-faq/part1/faq.html

Chapter 9: Intelligent Life outside the Web

Whole Internet User's Guide and Catalog
http://www.ora.com/catalog/twi2/

Gopher Jewels
http://galaxy.einet.net/GJ/

Tradewave Galaxy
http://galaxy.einet.nct/galaxy.html

Gopher Jewels (forms-based search)
http://galaxy.einet.net/gopher/gopher.html

Gopher Jewels (gopher-bascd version)
gopher://cwis.usc.edu/11/Other_Gophers_and_
Information_Resources/Gopher-Jewels

PEG
gopher://peg.cwis.uci.edu:7000/11/gopher.
welcome/peg

Big Ugly Smiley
gopher://geneva.acs.uci.edu:1070/00/franklin/
gleanings/Big%20Ugly%20Smiley

Washington and Lee University's Netlink Server
gopher://liberty.uc.wlu.edu/11/internet/new_
internet%09%092B

Veronica FAQ
gopher://veronica.scs.unr.edu:70/00/veronica/
veronica-faq

Yahoo!'s list of Veronica servers
http://www.yahoo.com/Computers_and_Internet/
Internet/Gopher/Searching/Veronica/

Yahoo!'s list of Jughead servers
http://www.yahoo.com/Computers_and_Internet/
Internet/Gopher/Searching/Jughead/

Library of Congress Z39.50 gateway
http://lcweb.loc.gov/z3950/gateway.html

Hytelnet (University of Saskatchewan)
http://library.usask.ca/hytelnet/

MELVYL (University of California)
telnet://melvyl.ucop.edu/

CARL UnCover
http://uncweb.carl.org/

Kevin Savetz's Unofficial Internet Book List
http://www.northcoast.com/savetz/booklist/

Connecting to Internet-Accessible Online Catalogs
Using Telnet
http://www.gslis.ucla.edu/LIS/lab/unote15.html

WAIS at Sweden's Lund University
http://www.ub2.lu.se/auto_new/UDC.html

Yahoo!'s list of finger gateways
http://www.yahoo.com/computers_and_Internet/
Internet/World_Wide_Web/Gateways/Finger_
Gateways/

OAK Software Repository
http://oak.oakland.edu/

TUCOWS
http://www.tucows.com/

Shareware.com
http://www.shareware.com/

Image archive at Finnish University and Research
Network
ftp://ftp.funet.fi/pub/pics/

Yahoo!'s list of Archie servers
http://www.yahoo.com/Computers_and_Internet/
Internet/FTP_Sites/Searching/Archie/

Perry Rovers FTP-List
http://www.iaehv.nl/users/perry/ftp-list.html

FTP search
http://ftpsearch.ntnu.no/

Internet Now
http://www.internet-now.com/main3.htm

Chapter 10: Computers and Computing

Mindspring Internet Services
http://www.mindspring.com/

Microsoft
http://www.microsoft.com/

ZDNet's Company Finder
http://www.zdnet.com/cgi-bin/texis/cofinder/
cofinder/

Ziff-Davis magazines
http://www5.zdnet.com/findit/mags.html

ZDNet product reviews
http://www.zdnet.com/products/

ZDNet
http://www.zdnet.com/

SupportHelp.com
http://www.supporthelp.com/

Kim Kommando's Komputer Klinic
http://www.komando.com/

The Tech Support Guy
http://www.cermak.com/techguy/

PC Lube and Tune
http://pclt.cis.yale.edu/pclt/

Healthy Computer
http://edencen.ehhs.cmich.edu/~sfick/index.html

CyberMedia Oil Change
http://www.cybermedia.com/products/oilchange/
ochome.html

TuneUp.com
http://www.tuneup.com/

Versions.com
http://www.versions.com/

DriversHQ
http://www.drivershq.com/

Dll World
http://www.users.wineasy.se/martin/dll.htm

Windows 95 Annoyances
http://www.creativelement.com/win95ann/intro.html

Yahoo!'s software links
http://www.yahoo.com/Computers/Software/

Microsoft Free Downloads
http://www.microsoft.com/msdownload/

ZDNet Software Library commercial demo section
http://www.hotfiles.com/demo.html

Download Netscape
http://home.netscape.com/comprod/mirror/client_
download.html

Download Internet Explorer
http://www.microsoft.com/ie/download/

Stroud's CWS Apps List
http://cws.iworld.com/

Mac Internet Collection at the University of Texas
http://wwwhost.ots.utexas.edu/mac/internet.html

The Well Connected Mac
http://www.macfaq.com/

The Mac Orchard
http://www.macorchard.com/

TUCOWS
http://www.tucows.com/

Norton AntiVirus
http://www.symantec.com/avcenter/

McAfee Associates
http://www.mcafee.com/

Yahoo!'s virus links
http://www.yahoo.com/Computers_and_Internet/
Security_and_Encryption/Viruses/

Hitchhiker's Web Guide AntiVirus Resources
http://www.hitchhikers.net/av.shtml

BrowserWatch
http://browserwatch.internet.com/

Carl Davis's HTML Editor Reviews
http://www.webcommando.com/editrev/

ZDNet Software Library
http://www.hotfiles.com/index.html

Download.com
http://www.download.com/

Shareware.com
http://www.shareware.com/

FILEZ
http://www.filez.com/

Gamecenter.com
http://www.gamecenter.com/

Happy Puppy.com
http://www.happypuppy.com/

Chapter 11: Not-So-Stupid Browser Tricks

Lynx Browser
http://lynx.browser.org/

CERN Line Mode Browser
http://gita.lanl.gov/misc/QuickGuide.html

Mosaic Browser
http://www.ncsa.uiuc.edu/SDG/Software/Mosaic/

Java "crapplet"
http://www.wired.com/wired/4.06/jargon.watch.html

Georgia Tech's Sixth Annual WWW Survey
http://www.cc.gatech.edu/gvu/user_surveys/
survey-10-1996/graphs/use/Image_Loading.html

Opera Browser
http://opera.nta.no/

Stroud's Consummate Winsock Apps
http://cws.internet.com/

Download Mosaic
ftp://ftp.ncsa.uiuc.edu/Mosaic/Windows/v3.0/
mos30.exe

BrowserWatch
http://browserwatch.internet.com/

Browsers.Com
http://www.download.com/Browsers/

Sausage Software
http://www.sausage.com/

National Public Radio
http://www.npr.org/

RealAudio
http://www.rcaaudio.com/

Timecast
http://www.timecast.com/

Adobe Acrobat Reader
http://www.adobc.com/prodindex/acrobat/
readstep.html

IRS tax forms
http://www.irs.ustreas.gov/prod/cover.html

Adobe's list of links to sites that use Acrobat
http://www.adobe.com/prodindex/acrobat/
pdfweb.html

Netscape's In-Line Plug-Ins
http://home.netscape.com/comprod/products/
navigator/version_2.0/plugins/index.html

BrowserWatch's Plug-In Plaza
http://browserwatch.internet.com/plug-in.html

33 Best Plug-Ins: ZD Internet Magazine
http://www.zdnet.com/zdimag/content/anchors/
199705/12/toolvox.html

Privacy Demonstration at the Center for Democracy
and Technology
http://www.13x.com/cgi-bin/cdt/snoop.pl

Andy's Netscape HTTP Cookie Notes
http://www.illuminatus.com/cookie.fcgi

Kookaburra Software
http://www.kburra.com/cpal.html

The Anonymizer
http://www.anonymizer.com/

Digital's AltaVista
http://www.anonymizer.com:8080/http://www.
altavista.digital.com/

Electronic Privacy Information Center
http://www.epic.org/

Privacy Rights Clearinghouse
http://www.acusd.edu/~prc/

Kernel upgrade patch for Windows 95 Winsock
http://support.microsoft.com/support/kb/articles/
Q148/3/36.asp

Chapter 12: Information Quality, Information Quantity

University of South Florida School of Library and
Information Science
http://www.cas.usf.edu/lis/welcome.html

Kister's Best Encyclopedias blurb
http://www.oryxpress.com/authors/a00056.htm

Evaluation and Comparison of Various Information
Sources
http://www.emporia.edu/s/www/slim/students/
leonlars/809N/Mainmenu.htm

Yahoo!'s list of links to free Web page providers
http://www.yahoo.com/Business_and_Economy/
Companies/Internet_Services/Web_Services/Free_
Web_Pages/

Tragedy of the Commons
http://savers.org:80/free/FP/TragedyCommons.html

Ghost Sites of the Web
http://www.disobey.com/ghostsites/

Teaching Critical Evaluation Skills for World Wide
Web Resources
http://www.science.widener.edu/~withers/
webeval.htm

Critical Evaluation Surveys (Kathy Schrock)
http://www.capecod.net/Wixon/eval.htm

Information Quality WWW Virtual Library
http://www.ciolek.com/WWWVL-InfoQuality.html

Evaluation of Information Sources (WWW VL)
http://www.vuw.ac.nz/~agsmith/evaln/evaln.htm

Internet Source Validation Project
http://www.stemnet.nf.ca/Curriculum/Validate/
refers.html

Resources: Other Sites about Evaluating Information
on the Internet
http://weber.u.washington.edu/~libr560/
NETEVAL/resources.html

Web Evaluation Techniques: Bibliography
http://www.science.widener.edu/~withers/
wbstrbib.htm

CARR-L (Computer-Assisted Research and Reporting)
Mailing List
http://www.jmk.su.se/dig/guide/listservs/carr-l.html

BUBBA-L Mailing List
http://ulibnet.mtsu.edu/bubba/

Net-Happenings Mailing List
http://scout.cs.wisc.edu/scout/net-hap/

comp.infosystems.www.announce archive
http://sunsite.unc.edu/gerald/ciwa/

EDUPAGE
http://www.educom.edu/web/edupage.html

IAT Infobits
http://www.iat.unc.edu/infobits/infobits.html

Internet Index (Win Treese)
http://www.openmarket.com/intindex/

Internet Resources Newsletter
http://www.hw.ac.uk/libWWW/irn/irn.html

Internet Tourbus
http://www.worldvillage.com/tourbus.htm

Net Announce
http://www.erspros.com/net-announce/

Netcetera
http://www.nwnet.net/netcetera/

Netsurfer Digest
http://www.netsurf.com:80/nsd/

Scout Report
http://wwwscout.cs.wisc.edu/scout/report/

Seidman's Online Insider
http://www.onlineinsider.com/

TidBITS
http://www.tidbits.com/

NetBITS
http://www.netbits.net

Weekend Web Picks
http://www.netogether.com/picks.html

The Weekly Bookmark
http://www.weeklyb.com/

Yahoo!'s Picks of the Week
http://www.yahoo.com/picks/

Meta-List of What's New pages
http://www.seas.upenn.edu/~mengwong/
whatsnew.list.html

Reference.COM
http://www.reference.com/

AT1: Your Gateway to the Invisible Web
http://www.at1.com/

NetMind's URL-Minder
http://www.netmind.com/html/url-minder.html

The Informant: Your Personal Search Agent on the Internet
http://informant.dartmouth.edu/

"Off the Grid" (*Wired* "Jargon Watch")
http://www.wircd.com/wired/4.10/jargon_watch.
html

Wired
http://www.wired.com/

Boardwatch
http://www.boardwatch.com/

Inter@ctive Week
http://www.zdnet.com/intweek/

Web Week
http://www.webweek.com/

Yahoo! Internet Life
http://www.zdnet.com/yil/welcome.html

ZD Internet Magazine
http://www.zdnet.com/zdimag/

"The Internet Librarian" (*American Libraries*)
http://www.ala.org/a/online/

"Internet Waves" column (*Information Today*)
http://www.infotoday.com/it/itnew.htm

Computers in Libraries
http://www.infotoday.com/cilmag/ciltop.htm

MultiMedia Schools
http://www.infotoday.com/MMSchools/index.html

Library Journal Digital
http://www.bookwire.com/ljdigital/

College and Research Libraries News
http://www.ala.org/acrl/c&rlnew2.html

Online, Inc.
http://www.onlineinc.com/

Database magazine
http://www.onlineinc.com/database/index.html

Online magazine
http://www.onlineinc.com/onlinemag/index.html

APPENDIX B

Web Page Checklists

Checklist for an Advocacy Web Page
(http://www.science.widener.edu/~withers/advoc.htm)

How to Recognize an Advocacy Page

An Advocacy Web Page is one sponsored by an organization attempting to influence public opinion (that is, one trying to sell ideas). The URL address of the page frequently ends in *.org* (organization). Examples: National Abortion and Reproductive Rights Action League, the National Right to Life Committee, the Democratic Party, the Republican Party.

Questions to Ask about the Web Page

Note: The greater number of questions listed below answered yes, the more likely the source is of high quality. The questions in **bold type** must be answered yes for the source to be of value in your research.

Criterion 1
AUTHORITY

1. **Is it clear what organization is sponsoring the page?**

2. Is there a link to a page describing the goals of the organization?

3. **Is there a way of verifying the legitimacy of this organization? That is, is there a phone number or postal address to contact for more**

information? (Simply an e-mail address is not enough.)

4. Is there a statement that the content of the page has the official approval of the organization?

5. Is it clear whether this is a page from the national or local chapter of the organization?

6. Is there a statement giving the organization's name as copyright holder?

Criterion 2
ACCURACY

1. Are the sources for any factual information clearly listed so they can be verified in another source? (If not, the page may still be useful to you as an example of the ideas of the organization, but it is not useful as a source of factual information.)

2. Is the information free of grammatical, spelling, and other typographical errors? (These kinds of errors not only indicate a lack of quality control, but can actually produce inaccuracies in information.)

Criterion 3
OBJECTIVITY

1. Are the organization's biases clearly stated?

2. If there is advertising on the page, is it clearly differentiated from the informational content?

Criterion 4
CURRENCY

1. Are there dates on the page to indicate:
   a. when the page was written?
   b. when the page was first placed on the Web?
   c. when the page was last revised?

2. Are there any other indications that the material is kept current?

Criterion 5
COVERAGE

1. Is there an indication that the page has been completed and is not still under construction?

2. Is it clear what topics the page intends to address?

3. Does the page succeed in addressing these topics, or has something significant been left out?

4. Is the point of view of the organization presented in a clear manner with its arguments well supported?

Compiled by J. Alexander (Janet.E.Alexander@widener.edu) and M. Tate (Marsha.A.Tate@widener.edu), Wolfgram Memorial Library, Widener University, 1 University Place, Chester, PA 19013, July 1996
Date Mounted on Server: August 5, 1996
Last Revised: October 28, 1996

Copyright © Widener University 1996

Checklist for a Business/Marketing Web Page
(http://www.science.widener.edu/~withers/busmark.htm)

How to Recognize a Business/ Marketing Web Page

A Business/Marketing Web Page is one sponsored by a commercial enterprise (usually it is a page trying to promote or sell products). The URL address of the page frequently ends in *.com* (commercial). Examples: Adobe Systems, Inc., the Coca-Cola Company, and numerous other large and small companies using the Web for business purposes.

Questions to Ask about the Web Page

Note: The greater the number of questions listed below answered yes, the more likely the source is of high quality. The questions in **bold type** must be answered yes for the source to be of value in your research.

Criterion 1
AUTHORITY

1. **Is it clear what company is sponsoring the page?**

2. Is there a link to a page describing the nature of the company, who owns the company, and the types of products the company sells?

3. **Is there a way of verifying the legitimacy of this company? That is, is there a phone number or postal address to contact for more information? (Simply an e-mail address is not enough.)**

4. Is there a way of determining the stability of this company?

5. Is there a statement that the content of the page has the official approval of the company?

6. Is there a statement giving the company's name as copyright holder?

Criterion 2
ACCURACY

1. Has the company provided a link to outside sources, such as product reviews or reports filed with the SEC (Securities and Exchange Commission), which can be used to verify company claims?

2. Are the sources for any factual information clearly listed so they can be verified in another source?

3. Is the information free of grammatical, spelling, and other typographical errors? (These kinds of errors not only indicate a lack of quality control, but can actually produce inaccuracies in information.)

Criterion 3
OBJECTIVITY

1. For any given piece of information, is it clear what the company's motivation is for providing it?

2. If there is advertising on the page, is it clearly differentiated from the informational content?

Criterion 4
CURRENCY

1. Are there dates on the page to indicate:
   a. when the page was written?
   b. when the page was first placed on the Web?
   c. when the page was last revised?

2. Are there any other indications that the material is kept current?

3. For financial information, is there an indication it was filed with the SEC, and is the filing date listed?

4. For material from the company's annual report, is the date of the report listed?

Criterion 5
COVERAGE

1. Is there an indication that the page has been completed and is not still under construction?

2. If describing a product, does the page include an adequately detailed description of the product?

3. Are all of the company's products described with an adequate level of detail?

4. Is the same level of information provided for all sections or divisions of the company?

Compiled by J. Alexander (Janet.E.Alexander@widener.edu) and M. Tate (Marsha.A.Tate@widener.edu), Wolfgram Memorial Library, Widener University, 1 University Place, Chester, PA 19013, July 1996
Date Mounted on Server: August 5, 1996
Last Revised: October 28, 1996

Checklist for an Informational Web Page
(http://www.science.widener.edu/~withers/inform.htm)

How to Recognize an Informational Web Page

An Informational Web Page is one whose purpose is to present factual information. The URL address frequently ends in *.edu* or *.gov,* as many of these pages are sponsored by educational institutions or government agencies. Examples: dictionaries, thesauri, directories, transportation schedules, calendars of events, statistical data, and other factual information such as reports, presentations of research, or information about a topic.

Questions to Ask about the Web Page

Note: The greater the number of questions listed below answered yes, the more likely the source is of high quality. The questions in **bold type** must be answered yes for the source to be of value in your research.

Criterion 1
AUTHORITY

1. **Is it clear who is sponsoring the page?**

2. Is there a link to a page describing the purpose of the sponsoring organization?

3. **Is there a way of verifying the legitimacy of the page's sponsor? That is, is there a phone number or postal address to contact for more information? (Simply an e-mail address is not enough.)**

4. Is it clear who wrote the material, and are the author's qualifications for writing on this topic clearly stated?

5. If the material is protected by copyright, is the name of the copyright holder given?

Criterion 2
ACCURACY

1. Are the sources for any factual information clearly listed so they can be verified in another source?

2. Is the information free of grammatical, spelling, and other typographical errors? (These kinds of errors not only indicate a lack of quality control, but can actually produce inaccuracies in information.)

3. Is it clear who has the ultimate responsibility for the accuracy of the content of the material?

4. If statistical data are presented in graphs and/or charts, are they clearly labeled and easy to read?

Criterion 3
OBJECTIVITY

1. Is the information provided as a public service?

2. Is the information free of advertising?

3. If there is advertising on the page, is it clearly differentiated from the informational content?

Criterion 4
CURRENCY

1. Are there dates on the page to indicate:
   a. when the page was written?
   b. when the page was first placed on the Web?
   c. when the page was last revised?

2. Are there any other indications that the material is kept current?

3. If material is presented in graphs and/or charts, is it clearly stated when the data were gathered?

4. If the information is published in different editions, is it clearly labeled what edition the page is from?

Criterion 5
COVERAGE

1. Is there an indication that the page has been completed and is not still under construction?

2. If there is a print equivalent to the Web page, is there a clear indication of whether the entire work is available on the Web or only parts of it?

3. If the material is from a work which is out of copyright (as is often the case with a dictionary or thesaurus) has there been an effort to update the material to make it more current?

Compiled by J. Alexander (Janet.E.Alexander@widener.edu) and M. Tate (Marsha.A.Tate@widener.edu), Wolfgram Memorial Library, Widener University, 1 University Place, Chester, PA 19013, July 1996
Date Mounted on Server: August 5, 1996
Last Revised: October 28, 1996

Checklist for a News Web Page
(http://www.science.widener.edu/~withers/news.htm)

How to Recognize a News Web Page

A News Web Page is one whose primary purpose is to provide extremely current information. The URL address of the page usually ends in *.com* (commercial). Examples: *USA Today, Philadelphia Inquirer,* CNN.

Questions to Ask about the Web Page

Note: The greater the number of questions listed below answered yes, the more likely the source is of high quality. The questions in **bold type** must be answered yes for the source to be of value in your research.

Criterion 1
AUTHORITY

1. **Is it clear what company is sponsoring the page?**

2. Is there a link to a page describing the goals of the company?

3. **Is there a way of verifying the legitimacy of the company? That is, is there a phone number or postal address to contact for more information? (Simply an e-mail address is not enough.)**

4. Is there a non-Web equivalent version of this material that would provide a way of verifying its legitimacy?

5. If the page contains an individual article, do you know who wrote the article and his or her qualifications for writing on this topic?

6. Is it clear who is ultimately responsible for the content of the material?

7. Is there a statement giving the company's name as copyright holder?

Criterion 2
ACCURACY

1. Are sources for factual information clearly listed so they can be verified in another source?

2. Are there editors monitoring the accuracy of the information being published?

3. Is the information free of grammatical, spelling, and other typographical errors? (These kinds of errors not only indicate a lack of quality control, but can actually produce inaccuracies in information.)

Criterion 3
OBJECTIVITY

1. Is the informational content clearly separated from the advertising and opinion content?

2. Are the editorials and opinion pieces clearly labeled?

Criterion 4
CURRENCY

1. Is there a link to an informational page that describes how frequently the material is updated?

2. Is there an indication of when the page was last updated?

3. Is there a date on the page to indicate when the page was placed on the Web?

  a. If a newspaper, does it indicate what edition of the paper the page belongs to?

  b. If a broadcast, does it indicate the date and time the information on the page was originally broadcast?

Criterion 5
COVERAGE

1. Is there a link to an informational page that describes the coverage of the source?

2. If you are evaluating a newspaper page and there is a print equivalent, is there an indication of whether the Web coverage is more or less extensive than the print version?

Compiled by J. Alexander (Janet.E.Alexander@widener.edu) and M. Tate (Marsha.A.Tate@widener.edu), Wolfgram Memorial Library, Widener University, 1 University Place, Chester, PA 19013, July 1996
Date Mounted on Server: August 5, 1996
Last Revised: October 28, 1996

Checklist for a Personal Home Page
(http://www.science.widener.edu/~withers/perspg.htm)

How to Recognize a Personal Home Page

A Personal Home Page is one published by an individual who may or may not be affiliated with a larger institution. Although the URL address of the page may have a variety of endings (e.g., *.com*,*.edu,* etc.), a tilde (~) is frequently embedded somewhere in the URL.

Questions to Ask about the Page

Note: The greater the number of yes answers to these questions, the more likely the source is of high quality. The questions in **bold type** must be answered yes for the source to be of value in your research.

Criterion 1
AUTHORITY

1. Is it clear what individual is responsible for the page?

2. Does the individual responsible for the page indicate his or her qualifications for writing on this topic?

3. Is there a way of verifying the legitimacy of this individual? (The answer to this question is probably almost always no. Thus, personal home pages can rarely be used as a source for factual information, although they can be a useful source for personal opinions.)

Criterion 2
ACCURACY

1. Are the sources for any factual information clearly listed so they can be verified in another source? (If not, the page may still be useful to you as an example of the ideas of the individual, but it is not useful as a source of factual information.)

2. Is the information free of grammatical, spelling, and other typographical errors? (These kinds of errors not only indicate a lack of quality control, but can actually produce inaccuracies in information.)

Criterion 3
OBJECTIVITY

Are the person's biases clearly stated?

Criterion 4
CURRENCY

1. Are there dates on the page to indicate:
   a. when the page was written?
   b. when the page was first placed on the Web?
   c. when the page was last revised?

2. Are there any other indications that the material is kept current?

Criterion 5
COVERAGE

Is there an indication that the page has been completed and is not still under construction?

Compiled by J. Alexander (Janet.E.Alexander@widener.edu) and M. Tate (Marsha.A.Tate@widener.edu), Wolfgram Memorial Library, Widener University, 1 University Place, Chester, PA 19013, July 1996
Date Mounted on Server: August 5, 1996
Last Revised: October 28, 1996

APPENDIX C

Citing Electronic Resources

MLA (Modern Language Association) Citations of Electronic Sources
http://www.cas.usf.edu/english/walker/mla.html

The basic component of the reference citation I have compiled is simple:

Author's Lastname, Author's Firstname. "Title of Document." Title of Complete Work (if applicable). Version or File Number, if applicable. Document date or date of last revision (if different from access date). Protocol and address, access path or directories (date of access).

The pages that follow give specific examples, following this format. Please bear in mind, however, that, like the Internet itself, the information sources are in a constant state of flux and, therefore, this work will also need to change as the sites themselves proliferate and adapt to the new era of electronic print.

Style Sheet

Endorsed by the Alliance for Computers and Writing

FTP (File Transfer Protocol) Sites
To cite files available for downloading via FTP, give the author's name (if known), the full title of the paper in quotation marks, the document date if known and if different from the date accessed, and the address of the FTP site along with the full path to follow to find the paper, and the date of access.

Bruckman, Amy. "Approaches to Managing Deviant Behavior in Virtual Communities." Apr. 1994, ftp://ftp.media.mit.edu/pub/asb/papers/deviance-chi94.txt (4 Dec. 1994).

WWW (World Wide Web) Sites: *Available via Lynx, Netscape, Other Web Browsers*

To cite files available for viewing/downloading via the World Wide Web, give the author's name (if known), the full title of the work in quotation marks, the title of the complete work if applicable in italics, the document date if known and if different from the date accessed, the full *http* address, and the date of visit.

Burka, Lauren P. "A Hypertext History of Multi-User Dimensions." *The MUDdex*. 1993. http://www.apocalypse.org/pub/u/lpb/muddex/essay/ (5 Dec. 1994).

Telnet Sites: *Sites and Files Available via the Telnet Protocol*

List the author's name or alias (if known), the title of the work (if shown) in quotation marks, the title of the full work if applicable in italics, the document date if known and if different from the date accessed, and the complete telnet address,

---

Margins and line breaks on examples have been forced to simulate hanging indents in print, while trying to preserve margins for various-sized browser windows. For a more complete discussion of citation formats for both humanities styles and author-date styles, including in-text citations and specific examples, see the *Columbia Guide to Online Style,* by Janice R. Walker and Todd Taylor (in press).

along with directions to access the publication, along with the date of visit.

traci (#377). "DaedalusMOO Purpose Statement." *DaedalusMOO.* telnet://daedalus.com:7777, help purpose (30 Apr. 1996).

Synchronous Communications (MOOs, MUDs, IRC, etc.)

Give the name of the speaker(s) and type of communication (i.e., Personal Interview), the address if applicable, and the date in parentheses.

Pine_Guest. Personal interview. telnet://world.sensemedia.net 1234 (12 Dec. 1994).

WorldMOO Christmas Party. telnet world.sensemedia.net 1234 (24 Dec. 1994).

Gopher Sites: *Information Available via Gopher Search Protocols*

For information found using gopher search protocols, list the author's name (if known), the title of the paper in quotation marks, the date of publication if known and if different from the date accessed, any print publication information, and the gopher search path followed to access the information, including the date that the file was accessed.

"The Netoric Project." gopher://kairos.daedalus.com:70/00ftp%3APub%3AACW%3ANETORIC%3A-Welcome-(13 Jan.1996).

E-Mail, Listserv, and Newsgroup Citations

Give the author's name or alias (if known), the subject line from the posting in quotation marks, the date of the message if different from the date accessed, and the address of the listserv or newslist, along with the date of access in parentheses. For personal e-mail listings, omit the e-mail address.

Bruckman, Amy S. "MOOSE Crossing Proposal." mediamoo@media.mit.edu (20 Dec. 1994).

Seabrook, Richard H. C. "Community and Progress." cybermind@jefferson.village.virginia.edu (22 Jan. 1994).

Thomson, Barry. "Virtual Reality." Personal e-mail (25 Jan.1995).

Versions of this style sheet have also been included by permission in the following texts:

Anderson, Daniel, Bret Benjamin, Christopher Busiel, and Bill Parades-Holt. *Teaching Online.* New York: HarperCollins, 1996.

Crispen, Patrick. *Atlas for the Information Superhighway.* New York: SouthWestern, 1996.

Crump, Eric, and Nick Carbone. *The English Student's Guide to the Internet.* New York: Houghton-Mifflin, 1996.

Epiphany Project. *Field Guide to 21st Century Writing.* [N.p., 1996].

Fowler, H. Ramsey. *The Little, Brown Handbook.* New York: Addison Wesley Longman (in press).

Hacker, Diana. *A Pocket Style Guide.* New York: Bedford, 1997.

———. *A Writer's Reference.* New York: Bedford, 1997.

Hairston, Maxine, John J. Ruszkiewicz, and Dan Seward. *Coretext.* New York: Addison Wesley Longman, 1997.

———. *Coretext Online.* New York: Addison Wesley Longman, 1997.

Hairston, Maxine, and John J. Ruszkiewicz. *The Scott, Foresman Handbook.* New York: HarperCollins, 1996.

Hall, Donald, and Sven Birkerts. *Writing Well.* 9th ed. New York: Addison Wesley Longman (in press).

Lannon, John M. *Technical Writing.* 7th ed. New York: Addison Wesley Longman, 1997.

Trimbur, John. *A Call to Write.* New York: Addison Wesley Longman (in press).

Walker, Janice R., and Todd Taylor. *The Columbia Guide to Online Style.* New York: Columbia UP (in press).

Janice R. Walker (jwalker@chuma.cas.usf.edu), Department of English, University of South Florida, 4202 East Fowler Avenue, CPR 107, Tampa, FL 33620-5550

Date Mounted on Server: June 1996
Last Revised: December 1996
Version 1.0

APA (American Psychological Association) Citations of Electronic Sources
http://www.cas.usf.edu/english/walker/apa.html

Internet sources are not yet included in the *Publication Manual* of the American Psychological Association. Several people have addressed this need, but no one style has yet gained universal acceptance. The following citation guidelines, based on APA format, have been developed by Janice R. Walker of the University of South Florida, whose MLA-style format for citation of Internet resources has been endorsed by the Alliance for Computers and Writing and has gained wide acceptance among scholars and academics. The basic component of the reference citation is simple:

Author's Last Name, Initial(s). (Date of Work, if known). Title of work. Title of complete work. [protocol and address] [path] (date of message or visit).

Style Sheet

FTP (File Transfer Protocol) Sites

To cite files available for downloading via FTP, give the author's name (if known), the publication date (if available and if different from the date accessed), the full title of the paper (capitalizing only the first word and proper nouns), the address of the FTP site along with the full path necessary to access the file, and the date of access.

Johnson-Eilola, J. (1994). Little machines: Rearticulating hypertext users. ftp://daedalus.com/Pub/CCCC95/johnson-eilola (10 Feb. 1996).

WWW (World Wide Web) Sites

To cite files available for viewing or downloading via the World Wide Web, give the author's name (if known), the year of publication (if known and if different from the date accessed), the full title of the article, and the title of the complete work (if applicable) in italics. Include any additional information (such as versions, editions, or revisions), in parentheses immediately following the title. Include the full URL (the *http* address) and the date of visit.

Burka, Lauren P. (1993). A hypertext history of multi-user dungeons. *MUDdex.* http://www.utopia.com/talent/lpb/muddex/essay/ (13 Jan. 1997).

Tilton, J. (1995). Composing good HTML (Vers. 2.0.6). http://www.cs.cmu.edu/~tilt/cgh/ (1 Dec. 1996).

Telnet Sites

List the author's name or alias (if known), the date of publication (if available and if different from the date accessed), the title of the article, the title of the full work (if applicable) or the name of the telnet site in italics, and the complete telnet address, followed by a comma and directions to access the publication (if applicable). Last, give the date of visit in parentheses.

Dava (#472). (1995, 3 November). A deadline. *General (#554). *Internet Public Library.* telnet://ipl.sils.umich.edu:8888, @peek 25 on #554 (9 Aug. 1996).

Help. *Internet public library.* telnet://ipl.org.8888/, help (1 Dec. 1996).

Synchronous Communications (MOOs, MUDs, IRC, Etc.)

Give the name of the speaker(s), the complete date of the conversation being referenced in parentheses (if different from the date accessed), and the title of the session (if applicable). Next, list the title of the site in italics, the protocol and address (if applicable), and any directions necessary to access the work. If there is additional information such as archive addresses or file numbers (if

---

Margins and line breaks on examples have been forced to simulate hanging indents in print, while trying to preserve margins for various-sized browser windows. For a more complete discussion of citation formats for both humanities styles and author-date styles, including in-text citations and specific examples, see the *Columbia Guide to Online Style,* by Janice R. Walker and Todd Taylor (in press).

applicable), list the word "Available," a colon, and the archival information. Last, list the date of access, enclosed in parentheses. Personal interviews do not need to be listed in the references, but do need to be included in parenthetic references in the text (see the APA *Publication Manual*).

Basic IRC commands. irc undernet.org, /help (13 Jan.1996).

Cross, J. (1996, February 27). Netoric's Tuesday cafe: Why use MUDs in the writing classroom? MediaMOO. telnet://purple-crayon. media.mit.edu:8888, @go Tuesday. Available: ftp://daedalus.com/pub/ACW/NETORIC/ catalog.96a (tc 022796.log). (1 Mar. 1996).

Gopher Sites

List the author's name (if applicable), the year of publication (if known and if different from the date accessed), the title of the file or paper, and the title of the complete work (if applicable). Include any print publication information (if available) followed by the protocol (i.e., *gopher://*) and the path necessary to access the file. List the date that the file was accessed in parentheses immediately following the path.

Boyer, C. (1996). *About the virtual reference desk.* gopher://peg.cwis.uci.edu:7000/00/gopher. welcome/peg/VIRTUAL%20REFERENCE% 20DESK/about (31 Dec. 1996).

Cicero. (1896). "Pro Archia." In J. B. Greenbough (Ed.), *Select orations of Cicero.* Boston: Ginn. Project Libellus (Vers. 0.01). (1994). gopher:// gopher.etext.org, Libellus/texts/cicero/archia. text (11 Aug. 1996).

E-mail, Listservs, and Newsgroups

Give the author's name (if known), the date of the correspondence in parentheses (if known and if different from the date accessed), the subject line from the posting, and the name of the list (if known) in italics. Next, list the address of the listserv or newsgroup. Include any archival information after the address, listing the word "Available" and a colon and the protocol and address of the archive. Last, give the date accessed enclosed in parentheses. Do not include personal e-mail in the list of references. See the APA *Publication Manual* for information on in-text citations.

Bruckman, A. S. *MOOSE crossing proposal.* mediamoo@media.mit.edu (20 Dec. 1994).

Heilke, J. (1996, May 3). *Re: Webfolios.* acw-l @ttacs.ttu.edu. Available: http://www.ttu.edu/ lists/acw-1/9605 (31 Dec. 1996).

Laws, R. *UMI thesis publication.* alt.education. distance (3 Jan. 1996).

Date Mounted on Server: June 1996
Last Revised: December 1996
Version 1.0

Janice R. Walker (jwalker@chuma.cas.usf.edu), Department of English, University of South Florida, 4202 East Fowler Avenue, CPR 107, Tampa, FL 33620-5550

Glossary of Terms: Internet Searching

Adjacency (or proximity)—Search qualifier that allows you to look for words that are next to or near each other in a document. Most of the major search engines support adjacency, but some incorporate a default value instead of letting you choose how far apart your keywords should be. (See **Boolean searching,** below.)

Bookmark—Stored shortcut that allows you to quickly get back to the places you find useful on the Internet without having to remember and retype a **URL.** Your personal collection of bookmarks is called a *bookmark list* or a *hot list.*

Boolean searching—Use of the word ("operator") AND, OR, NOT, or NEAR to fine-tune your search request. For example, if you want information about the Jurassic period without pulling up results about the popular film *Jurassic Park,* you can type *jurassic not park.* All of the major Web search engines support Boolean searching in one form or another.

Browser—A software program you install on your computer to retrieve and display documents on a remote **Web server** while you're connected to the Internet. Netscape Navigator and Microsoft Internet Explorer are the two most popular Web browsers at this point. Lynx is a text-based Web browser that can be used with a "shell" Internet account (i.e., without graphical capabilities).

Client—A software application that's loaded onto your own computer and interacts with a remote **server** to get you the information you want. A Web **browser** is an example of a client.

Concept search—A search for documents related conceptually to a keyword, rather than those containing the actual keyword itself. Some, but not all, search engines support this.

Controlled vocabulary—A standardized set of keywords that identify the documents in a database. This improves a user's chances of finding every relevant document, because he or she doesn't have to consider every synonym when choosing search keywords.

Dead link—A **URL** that leads nowhere, typified by the infamous 404 Not Found error message. Internet resources can be somewhat ephemeral in nature. Computer names and Net addresses change; documents move or disappear. From the user's standpoint, the result is a dead link.

Document—Generic term for anything that appears in the main window of a Web **client.** Physically, it's a text file marked up with **HTML** tags.

False drops—Search results that, in theory, match the criteria input by a user but, in reality, don't contain the information actually desired.

FAQ—Frequently asked questions—a collection of commonly asked questions, with answers, about a specific subject, assembled in a conveniently organized list for easy reading.

FTP (or download)—File transfer protocol. The transfer of a file from a remote computer to yours.

Hit—Search result.

Home page—The first or top page of an individual's or organization's World Wide Web "home." Home pages typically contain some general information about the site and link to pages deeper down. The entire collection of Web pages is called a Web site.

HTML—HyperText Markup Language. The coding in a document that describes to a **browser** how to display the text, images, and other elements included in that document. Basically, it's a set of tags added to plain text files.

HTTP—HyperText Transfer Protocol. The "rule" that allows **Web servers** on computers all over the Internet to access and transfer documents.

Hypertext (or hypermedia)—"Hot spots" in a Web document that contain links to other documents or multimedia objects. They are usually differentiated by color on a Web page, indicating where a user can "click" to jump to another object.

Index (or catalog)—Searchable database of documents collected and organized by the underlying search engine software (e.g., the **spider,** or robot). When you enter keywords into an online search form, what you are actually searching is the individual search engine's index.

Internet Service Provider (ISP)—The company or organization that provides you with access to the Internet, either via a dial-up or direct (hard-wired) connection. The latter is more typical in an organizational setting.

Keyword—A word (or phrase) that a user believes is relevant to the information he or she is seeking. The user enters keywords into an online search form. The search engine then examines each record in its database to find those documents that match the keywords. A keyword search (as opposed to a **concept search**) is a search for documents containing one or more words specified by the user.

Link—A **hypertext** reference to another Web document (or another section of the same document). Links typically appear as highlighted or colored text on a document in a Web **browser** window.

Metasearch engine—A Web search tool that permits you to run your query through many different individual search engines simultaneously via a single interface.

Natural Language Query—A query in which you use normal conversational syntax, as if you were asking a question—*How can I get a red-wine stain out of upholstery?* Some search engines encourage you to type in a natural language query and then use "artificial intelligence" to process your request.

Phrase searching—A search for words found together in a specific phrase—e.g., *"America the Beautiful."* Some search engines want you to indicate phrases by enclosing the words in quotation marks. Others permit you to search keywords as a phrase via a choice on the query interface.

Query by example—A search in which the user tells the search engine to find more documents like a particularly relevant one that appeared in the results listing. This feature is typically available as a Find Similar link on those search engines that support it.

Relevancy—The degree to which a given document provides the information a user is looking for—as determined by the user.

Relevancy ranking—A search engine's arrangement of your results so that those most likely to be relevant to your query are displayed at the top of the list. Relevancy may be determined by any of a number of factors—such as multiple occurrences of keywords or how high up in a particular document they appear.

Search engine—Software running on a Web server that takes criteria input by a user and compares these criteria with the documents in its database to find a set of matching items. Search engines may vary tremendously in terms of the size of their databases as well as the complexity of the underlying software programs.

Server—A computer connected to a network—e.g., the Internet—which allows other computers to retrieve data, e.g., Web pages, from it.

Spamdexing (or index spamming)—The nefarious practice of some Web page creators (typically at commercial sites) of loading their home pages with irrelevant keywords in order to score more or better (up-top) hits on search engines. Knowing many people use search engines to look for sexually oriented material, the pages will be full of multiple instances of words like *sex, naked, nude, girls,* etc. By enclosing these terms in HTML comment tags, they are invisible to you when you see the page in your **browser** (although you'll see them if you View/Document Source from your **browser's** menu bar—a good thing to know next time you sit there scratching your head over the appearance of a seemingly unrelated Web page at the top of your search results list). Alternately, a Web page creator with less devious intentions who wants to improve the **relevancy ranking** of that page may include multiple instances of relevant keywords. Meanwhile, the search engine creators have been adjusting their algorithms to disregard apparent attempts at index spamming.

Spider (or robot or wanderer)—A software program that crawls around the Web from server to server, gathering information about documents to add to a search engine's database. Each search engine's spider is a little bit different in the type and the amount of information it collects—i.e., one may index just the **URL** and the first several words of a document, while another may index every word in a document.

Subject tree—A hierarchically arranged directory database in which you can browse by subject to find the information you want. At the top of the subject tree—the first page—are the most general subject categories. You choose one of these and then "drill down" through the directory to reach more specific subject headings.

Surfing—A slang term for serendipitous Web browsing—cruising from site to site and document to document in order to find items that are valuable and/or interesting to the user.

Truncation—The use of a wild-card character—typically an asterisk (*)—to substitute for actual letters in a keyword. Some search engines permit truncation only at the ends of keywords—i.e., *child** will retrieve hits containing the words *child, children, childless,* etc. Other search engines may allow this sort of substitution in the middle of a word—handy if you're not sure how to spell something.

URL—Uniform Resource Locator. The address where a resource "lives" on the Internet. Web URLs start with *http://*; gopher URLs with *gopher://*; **FTP** URLs with *ftp://*; and Usenet newsgroup URLs with *news://*.

Web server—A computer connected to the Internet that stores and distributes Web pages upon request. The "server" is actually a software program running on the computer.

Bibliography

URLs below may have changed or disappeared since reviewed as background material for this book. Although URLs in the body of the book have been updated just prior to publication, these citations were left unchanged to reflect the documents as used by the author for research.

Web-Based Resources

Abilock, Debbie. "Choose the Best Search Engine for Your Information Needs." August 8, 1996. http://www.nueva.pvt.k12.ca/us/~debbie/library/research/adviceengine.html.

Alexander, Janet E., and Marsha A. Tate. "Teaching Critical Evaluation Skills for World Wide Web Resources." October 30, 1996. http://www.science.widener. edu/~withers/webeval.htm.

Arment, Donna, Emily Grantham, and Andy Neustadter. "Evaluating Search Engines for the WWW." December 1996. http://httpsrv.ocs.drexel.edu/grad/sg95ycmf/index.html.

Babb, Chris. "Babb's Bookmarks: Internet Search Engines." April 1996. http://www.boardwatch.com/mag/6/apr/bwm8.htm.

Barlow, Linda. "The Spider's Apprentice: How to Use Web Search Engines." December 5, 1996. http://www.monash.com/spidap.html.

Barry, Tony, and Joanna Richardson. "Indexing the Net—A Review of Indexing Tools." July 11, 1996. http://bond.edu.au/Bond/Library/People/jpr/ausweb96/.

Berkeley Digital Library SunSITE. "Internet Search Tool Details." September 17, 1996. http://sunsite.berkeley.edu/Help/searchdetails.html.

Berlind, David. "Net Search Redux: Real Experts Speak." September 23, 1996. http://www.pcweek.com/archive/1330/pcwk0047.html.

Birmingham, Judy. "Selected Internet Search Engines." November 23, 1996. http://www.stark.k12.oh.us/Docs/search/.

Boucher, Bob. "A Higher Signal-to-Noise Ratio: Effective Use of Search Engines." October 16, 1996. http://www.state/wi/us/agencies/dpi/www/search.html.

Brownlee, Rowan. "Search Engine Reference List." April 1996. http://www.lib.berkeley.edu/Web4Lib/archive/9604/0103.html.

Churilla, Kenneth R. "Secrets of Searching the Web and Promoting Your Web Site." January 8, 1997. http://www.best.com/~mentorms/eureka_i.htm.

Ciolek, Matthew T., ed. "Information Quality WWW Virtual Library." February 6, 1997. http://coombs.anu.edu.au/WWWVL-InfoQuality.html.

Conte, Ron, Jr. "Searching on the Net: Guiding Lights." May 1996. http://www.internetworld.com/1996/05/guiding.html.

Crowe, Elizabeth P. "Search the Net in Style: Seek and Ye Shall Find." http://www.cnet.com/Resources/Tech/Advisers/Search/index.html.

December, John. "Top Keyword Resources of the Web." November 1996. http://www.december. com/web/top/keyword.html.

Digital Tools and Designs, Inc. "Finder's Digest: Special Report—Search Utility Shoot-Out." 1996. http:www.findspot.com/fdigsuso.html.

Eagan, Anne, and Laura Bender. "Untangling the Web: Spiders and Worms and Crawlers, Oh My: Searching on the World Wide Web." 1996. http://www.library/ucsb.edu/untangle/eagan. html.

Felt, Elizabeth, and Jane Scales. "A Selection of Internet Search Tools." August 27, 1996. http://www.kuleuven.ac.bc/Services/search. html.

Fondren Library, Rice University. "Search Tool Reviews." January 15, 1997. http://www.rice. edu/Fondren/Netguides/reviews.html.

Grassian, Esther. "Thinking Critically about WWW Resources." December 3, 1996. http://www. library.ucla.edu/libraries/college/instruct/ critical.htm.

Gray, Terry A. "How to Search the Web—A Guide to Search Tools." July 29, 1996. http:// issfw.palomar.edu/Library/TGSEARCH.HTM.

Grossan, Bruce. "Search Engines: What They Are, How They Work, and Practical Suggestions for Getting the Most Out of Them." September 2, 1996. http://webreference.com/content/ search/.

Hausauer, Jacob. "Jacob Hausauer's Page for Search Engines." March 1996. http://bingen. cs.csbsju.edu/~jwhausau/.

Hukins, Celia. "Internet Search Engines." January 1996. http://www.hop.man.ac.uk/staff/ chukins/SEARCHEN.html.

Intermediacy, Inc. "The Internet Consulting Detective's Tip of the Fortnight: AltaVista Advanced Search." July 7, 1996. http://www. intermediacy.com/sherlock/alta_vista_tip.html.

———. "The Internet Consulting Detective's Tip of the Fortnight: HotBot and Infoseek Ultra." September 29, 1996. http://www.intermediacy. com/sherlock/new_search_engines.html.

———. "The Internet Consulting Detective's Tip of the Fortnight: Search Engine Comparisons." November 24, 1996. http://www.intermediacy. com/sherlock/search_engine_compare.html.

———. "The Internet Consulting Detective's Tip of the Fortnight: Multi-Engine Searches." February 2, 1997. http://www.intermediacy.com/ sherlock/forttip.html.

Koch, Traugott. "Literature about Search Services." January 7, 1977. http://www.ub2.lu.se//desire/ radar/lit-about-search-services.html.

———. "Searching the Web: Systematic Overview over Indexes." January 21, 1997. http:// www.ub2.lu.se/tk/websearch_systemat.html.

Lager, Mark. "Untangling the Web: Spinning a Web Search." 1996. http://www.library.ucsb. edu/untangle/lager.html.

Lebedev, Alexander. "The Best Search Engines for Finding Scientific Information on the Web." September 29, 1996. http://www.chem.msu. su/eng/comparison.html.

Leighton, H. Vernon. "Performance of Four World Wide Web (WWW) Index Services: Infoseek, Lycos, Webcrawler and WWWWorm." June 25, 1996. http://www.winona.msus.edu/is-f/ library-f/libhome.htm/webind.htm.

Leonard, Andrew J. "Search Engines: Where to Find Anything on the Net." 1996. http://www. cnet.com/Content/Reviews/Compare/Search/.

LeRoy, Michael E. "How to Improve Your Search Results." 1995. http://www.browsefast.com/ searchex.htm#sectDevil.

Liu, Jian. "Understanding WWW Search Tools." September 1995; updated February 1996. http://www.indiana.edu/~librcsd/search/.

Matthew (meta@pobox.com). "The Open Text Boycott Is Over." November 22, 1996. http://freethought.tamu.edu/~meta/rs/ot/.

Mengel, Laura. "Finding Information Tutorial." February 16, 1996. http://www-ed.fnal.gov/ linc/spring96/find/find_tutorial.html.

Minnick, Bob (Northern Webs). "Search Engine Tutorial for Web Designers." 1996. http:// digital-café.com/~webmaster/set_old.html.

Mitchell, Steve. "General Internet Resource Finding Tools: A Review and List of Those Used to Build INFOMINE." March 1996. http://lib-www.ucr.edu/pubs/navigato.html.

Murphy, Kathleen. "Cheaters Never Win: Marketers Reveal Sneaky Ways to Grab Top Search Results." May 20, 1996. http://www.webweek.com/96May20/undercon/cheaters.html.

Murray, Janet, Patty Sorensen, and Sheryl Steinke. "Searching the 'Net: An Online Internet Institute Project." January 2, 1997. http://arlo.wilsonhs.pps.k12.or.us/search/html.

Netskills/Electronic Libraries Programme. "Netskills Searching Resource Pages." January 7, 1997. http://www.netskills.ac.uk/resources/searching/.

Nicholson, Scott. "Scott Nicholson's WWW Search Engine Selection Tool." July 3, 1996. http://users.why.net/redbear/scott/.

Northwestern University Library. "Evaluation of Selected Internet Search Tools." January 31, 1997. http://www.library.nwu.edu/resources/internet/search/evaluate.html.

Notess, Greg R. "On the Nets: Searching the World Wide Web—Lycos, WebCrawler and More." July 1995. http://www.onlineinc.com/onlinemag/OL1995/JulOL95/notess.html.

———. "On the Nets: The Infoseek Databases." August 1995. http://www.onlineinc.com/database/DB1995/AugDB95/notess.html.

———. "On the Nets: Searching the Web with AltaVista." June 1996. http://www.onlineinc.com/database/JuneDB/nets6.html.

———. "On the Nets: Internet 'Onesearch' with the Mega Search Engines." November 1996. http://www.onlineinc.com/online/online/onlinemag/NovOL/nets11.html.

Ormondroyd, Joan, Michael Engle, and Tony Cosgrave. "How to Critically Analyze Information Sources. October 20, 1996. http://www.library.cornell.edu/okuref/research/skill26.htm.

Overton, Richard. "Search Engines Get Faster and Faster, but Not Always Better." September 1996. http://www.pcworld.com/workstyles/online/articles/sep96/1409_engine.html.

Page, Adam. "The Search Is Over: The Search Engine Secrets of the Pros." October 1996. http://www.zdnet.com/pccomp/features/fea1096/sub2.html.

Pearce, Frederick. "Some Internet Search Engines . . . and an Explanation of How They Work." December 13, 1996. http://home.earthlink.net/%7Efpearce/engines.html.

Pederson, Rechs Ann. "Santa Cruz Public Libraries: Internet Search Tips." April 14, 1996. http://www.cruzio.com/~sclibs/internet/tips.html.

Pfaffenberger, Bryan. "Search Me! (Web Search Strategies)." November 5, 1995. http://watt.seas.virginia.edu/~bp/searchme/welcome.htm.

Randall, Neil. "The Search Engine That Could." June 5, 1996. http://www.zdnet.com/pccomp/features/internet/search/index.html.

Region 2 U.S. EPA (NY) Library. "Top Ten Advanced Internet Search Tips." 1996. http://www.epa.gov/Region2/library/powertip.htm.

———. "Top Ten Basic Internet Search Tips." 1996. http://www.epa.gov/Region2/library/tentips.htm.

Rhodes, Jim. "The Art of Business Web Site Promotion." February 5, 1997. http://wworks.com/%7Edeadlock/promote/.

Schlichting, Carsten, and Erik Nilsen. "Signal Detection Analysis of WWW Search Engines." 1996. http://www.microsoft.com/usability/webconf/schlichting/schlichting.htm.

Scoville, Richard. "Find It on the Net." January 1996. http://www.pcworld.com/reprints/lycos.htm.

Slot, Matt. "The Matrix of Internet Catalogs and Search Engines." December 5, 1996. http://www.ambrosiasw.com/~fprefect/matrix/.

Stanley, Tracey. "Searching the World Wide Web with Lycos and Infoseek." August 15, 1995. http://www.leeds.ac.uk/ucs/docs/fur14/fur14.html.

———. "AltaVista vs. Lycos." March 22, 1996. http://ukoln.bath.ac.uk/ariadne/issue2/engines/.

Steinberg, Steve. "Seek and Ye Shall Find . . . Maybe." May 20, 1996. http://www.hotwired.com/wired/4.05/indexing/index.html.

Sullivan, Danny. "A Webmaster's Guide to Search Engines." January 31, 1997. http://calafia.com/webmasters/.

Tillman, Hope N. "Evaluating Quality on the Net." November 30, 1996. http://www.tiac.net/users/hope/findqual.html.

Tillman, Hope N., and Walt Howe. "Tips and Tricks for Searching the Net." June 23, 1996. http://www.tiac.net/users/hope/tips/.

Tomaiuolo, Nicholas G., and Joan G. Packer. "Quantitative Analysis of Five WWW Search Engines." June 1996. http://neal.ctstateu.edu:2001/htdocs/websearch.html.

Tyner, Ross. "Sink or Swim: Internet Search Tools and Techniques." October 27, 1996. http://www.sci.ouc.bc.ca/libr/connect96/search.htm.

University of Pennsylvania Library. "Internet Search Tools." November 7, 1996. http://www.library.upenn.edu/resources/internet/searcht.html.

Venditto, Gus. "Search Engine Showdown." May 1996. http://www.internetworld.com/1996/05/showdown.html.

Walker, Janice R. "MLA-Style Citations of Electronic Sources." August 1996. http://www.cas.usf.edu/english/walker/mla.html.

Webster, Kathleen and Kathryn Paul. "Beyond Surfing: Tools and Techniques for Searching the Web." January 1996. http://magi.com/~mmelick/it96jan.htm.

Westera, Gillian. "Robert-Driven Search Engine Evaluation Overview." October 1996. http://aaa.curtin.edu.au/curtin/library/staffpages/gwpersonal/senginestudy/.

Wingfield, Nick. "Engine Sells Results, Draws Fire." June 21, 1996. http://www.news.com/News/Item/0,4,1635,00.html.

Winship, Ian R. "World Wide Web Searching Tools, an Evaluation." 1995. http://www.bubl.bath.ac.uk/BUBL/IWinship.html.

Yao, Aixiang. "Searching and Databases on the Web." November 20, 1996. http://ei.cs.vt.edu/%7Ewwwbtb/book/chap15/index.html.

Ziegler, J. Marcus. "Reviews of Search Engines from the Search Page." February 2, 1997. http://www.accesscom.com/~ziegler/search.html#search_reviews.

Zorn, Peggy, Mary Emanoil, and Lucy Marshall. "Advanced Searching: Tricks of the Trade." May 1996. http://www.onlineinc.com/onlinemag/MayOL/zorn5.html.

Print Magazine and Journal Articles

Courtois, Martin P. "Cool Tools for Web Searching: An Update." *Online* (May/June 1996): 29–36.

Morgan, Cynthia. "The Search Is On: Finding the Right Tools and Using Them Properly Can Shed Light on Your Web Search Efforts." *Windows Magazine* (Nov. 1996): 212–30.

Panepinto, Joe. "Family-Tested Web Sites: Searching the Web." *Family PC* (Sept. 1996): 47–50.

Singh, Amarendra, and David Lidsky. "All-Out Search." *PC Magazine* (Dec. 3, 1996): 213–49.

Tweney, Dylan. "Searching Is My Business: A Gumshoe's Guide to the Web." *PC World* (Dec. 1996): 182–96.

Ziegler, Bart. "Why Search Engines Don't Turn Up Many Web Sites." *Wall Street Journal* (Dec. 10, 1996): B1, B6.

Zilber, Jon, and John Papageorge. "Simple Search Secrets." *The Net* (February 1997): 37–41.

Books

Basch, Reva. *Secrets of the Super Net Searchers.* Pemberton Pr., 1996.

Berinstein, Paula. *Finding Images Online.* Pemberton Pr., 1996.

Calishain, Tara. *Official Netscape Guide to Internet Research.* Ventana, 1997.

Garvin, Andrew P. *The Art of Being Well Informed: What You Need to Know to Gain the Winning Edge in Business.* FIND/SVP, 1996.

Gilster, Paul. *Finding It on the Internet.* 2nd ed. New York: Wiley, 1996.

Harmon, Charles, ed. *Using the Internet, Online Services and CD-ROMs for Writing Research and Term Papers.* New York: Neal-Schuman, 1996.

Hill, Brad. *World Wide Web Searching for Dummies.* Indianapolis: IDG, 1996.

James-Catalano, Cynthia N. *Researching on the World Wide Web: Spend More Time Learning, Not Searching.* Prima, 1996.

Keeler, Elissa, and Robert Miller. *Netscape Virtuoso.* MIS Pr., 1996.

Krol, Ed. Adapted by Bruce Klopfenstein. *The Whole Internet User's Guide and Catalog.* Academic Ed. O'Reilly, 1996.

Lescher, John F. *Online Market Research: Cost-Effective Searching of the Internet and Online Databases.* Reading, Mass.: Addison-Wesley, 1995.

Olsen, J. W. and David D. Busch. *60 Minute Guide to Internet Explorer 3.* Indianapolis: IDG, 1996.

Pfaffenberger, Bryan. *Web Search Strategies.* MIS Pr., 1996.

Rowland, Robin, and Dave Kinnaman. *Researching on the Internet: The Complete Guide to Finding, Evaluating, and Organizing Information Effectively.* Prima, 1995.

Thomsen, Elizabeth. *Reference and Collection Development on the Internet: A How-to-Do-It Manual.* New York: Neal-Schuman, 1996.

Index